Journal for the Evangelical Study of the Old Testament

JESOT is published bi-annually online at www.jesot.org and in print
by Wipf and Stock Publishers.
199 West 8th Avenue, Suite 3, Eugene, OR 97401, USA

ISSN 2169-0685
ISBN 978-1-6667-3208-5

JESOT is an international, peer-reviewed journal devoted to the
academic and evangelical study of the Old Testament. The journal seeks
to publish current academic research in the areas of ancient Near Eastern
backgrounds, Dead Sea Scrolls, Rabbinics, Linguistics, Septuagint,
Research Methodology, Literary Analysis, Exegesis, Text Criticism, and
Theology as they pertain only to the Old Testament. The journal seeks to
provide a venue for high-level scholarship on the Old Testament from an
evangelical standpoint. The journal is not affiliated with any particular
academic institution, and with an international editorial board, online
format, and multi-language submissions, *JESOT* seeks to cultivate Old
Testament scholarship in the evangelical global community.

JESOT is indexed in *Old Testament Abstracts*, *Christian Periodical
Index*, The Ancient World Online (AWOL), and *EBSCO* databases

Journal for the Evangelical Study of the Old Testament

Executive Editor
STEPHEN J. ANDREWS
(Midwestern Baptist Theological
Seminary, USA)

Editor
RUSSELL L. MEEK
(Ohio Theological Institute, USA)

Book Review Editor
ANDREW M. KING
(Midwestern Baptist Theological
Seminary, USA)

RON HAYDON
(Wheaton College, USA)

Journal correspondence and manuscript
submissions should be directed to
rmeek@ohiotheological.org. Instructions for
authors can be found at https://wipfandstock.
com/catalog/journal/view/id/7/.

Books for review and review correspondence
should be directed to Andrew King at
aking@mbts.edu.

All ordering and subscription inquiries
should be sent to Orders@wipfandstock.com.

Editorial Board

[*JESOT* 7.2 (2021): 1–15]

Life Worth Living: A Case for Rhetorical Coherence in Deut 4:1–8[1]

BY STEPHEN D. CAMPBELL[2]

Aquila Initiative
stephenc@aquila-initiative.org

ABSTRACT: Deut 4:1–40 is generally regarded as a coherent text. In practice, however, the "canon formula" in 4:2 is for various reasons often treated by commentators in near isolation from its context. This essay argues that this interpretive decision results in the flattening of a key conceptual parallel within the introduction to Deut 4. It argues that Deut 4:2 is a crucial element in a parallel that this text establishes between the way Israel treats the words of God through Moses and the way Israel treats God. Without v. 2 this parallelism loses much of its sophistication: the object lesson of Baal-Peor (vv. 3–4) lacks context and what it means to keep the commandments and judgments of YHWH (vv. 2, 6) lacks definition.

KEY WORDS: Deut 4, Canon, Torah, Obedience, Baal Peor

---

1. An early draft of this paper was presented at the summer 2018 meeting of the British Society of Old Testament Study at St. John's College, Durham University. I am grateful for the many individuals who have assisted me along the way, especially Walter Moberly. Further implications of my conclusions in this essay can be found in Stephen D. Campbell, *Remembering the Unexperienced: Cultural Memory, Canon Consciousness, and the Book of Deuteronomy*, BBB (Göttingen: V&R, forthcoming).

2. Stephen D. Campbell (PhD, Durham University) is Academic Director and Professor of Bible and Theology at Aquila Initiative. He lives with his family in Bonn, Germany where he also serves as pastor of the International Baptist Church.

INTRODUCTION

The main pericope of Deut 4 (rightly called by many a paraenesis[3]) has been in recent decades read as a coherent text most easily divided into the following three portions: an introduction (vv. 1–8), a core (vv. 9–31), and a conclusion (vv. 32–40).[4] The introduction itself has been the subject of much discussion, not least because of the well-known "canon formula" at 4:2. With few exceptions, this particular verse has been understood in isolation from its context within the introduction. This interpretive decision is usually undertaken for at least one of two reasons. First, verse 2 is often read as a disturbance in the otherwise flowing language of Deut 4:1, 3–8. Secondly, the scholarly interests are often elsewhere: either the question of the ancients' self-understanding of canon, or else Deuteronomy's place within a growing biblical canon. In this paper, however, I hope to offer a fresh reading of the introduction, and I will argue for internal coherence and rhetorical progression within this important chapter's introduction that goes beyond what has been recognized by past treatments. In particular, emphasis is given to how verses 1–8 can be read coherently as they now stand in the received form. Particular attention is given to rhetorical concerns including repetition and logical parallelism. It is argued that Deut 4:2 should be read within the context of the introduction as a key element

---

3. Whether or not Deut 4:1–40 can rightly be called a "sermon" has been the subject of much discussion in recent years. This view is rightly associated with von Rad, who argued that the entire derteronomic framework exhibits paraenetic qualities indicative of a late monarchical, Levitical, oral preaching tradition. Gerhard von Rad, *The Problem of the Hexateuch and Other Essays* (London: SCM, 1984), 267–80; and Gerhard von Rad, "Ancient Word and Living Word," *Int* 15 (1961): 4. By 1964, however, von Rad was only willing to speak of Deut 4's "hortatory quality," in *Deuteronomy*, 21, 49. Although this view is widespread, it does, however, have its opponents. For an excellent overview of the issues and the strongest counter-argument to date see, Marc Zvi Brettler, "A 'Literary Sermon' in Deuteronomy 4," in *"A Wise and Discerning Mind": Essays in Honor of Burke O. Long*, BJS 325, ed. by Saul M. Olyan and Robert C. Culley (Providence: Brown Judaic Studies, 2000), 33–50. Although the real or only imagined oral tradition behind the written form of Deut 4 is a valid discussion, this particular issue is only marginal to the central concern of understanding this passage on a textual level. For this reason, the term "paraenesis" rather than "sermon" is more appropriate as this term includes exhortation in written form.

4. Eckart Otto, "Deuteronomium 1 ,1–4, 43," in *Deuteronomium 1–11*, vol. 1, HThKAT (Freiburg: Herder, 2012), 527. See also, Knut Holter, *Deuteronomy 4 and the Second Commandment*, StBL 60 (New York: Peter Lang, 2003), 13, 102.

in a parallel between how one treats the "words" of God given through Moses and how one treats God himself.

Like the chapter as a whole, Deut 4's introduction has likewise been variously divided by scholars, but for the present discussion it is helpful to consider a threefold division governed by rhetorical concerns. In the first two verses a group of commands is given: to listen to the statues and judgments that Moses is teaching Israel and to preserve these statues and judgments from alteration. The second two verses present a warning that I will argue is an illustration, or object lesson, presenting a conceptual parallel between how one treats the "words" of God given to Israel through Moses and how one treats God himself. Finally, verses 5–8 function as a promise to Israel; God presents to Israel what the nation can rightly expect from God if it proves faithful in keeping (i.e., preserving) and doing the words of YHWH. This structure is reflected below.

THE COMMAND: DEUT 4:1–2

On the heels of the recapitulation of the wilderness wanderings in chapters 1–3, Deuteronomy 4 turns to an entirely new theme,[5] namely, what is expected of Israel in the present and the future.[6] This transition is signalled by ועתה ("and now") and functions to separate the retrospective monologue of Moses (1:9–3:29) from his prospective monologue (4:1–40). An identical usage of ועתה ("and now") comes in 10:12 and likewise serves as a transition from an historical retrospect (9:6–10:11) to the command for Israel to circumcise its heart.

וְעַתָּה יִשְׂרָאֵל מָה יְהוָה אֱלֹהֶיךָ שֹׁאֵל מֵעִמָּךְ כִּי אִם־לְיִרְאָה אֶת־יְהוָה אֱלֹהֶיךָ לָלֶכֶת בְּכָל־דְּרָכָיו וּלְאַהֲבָה אֹתוֹ וְלַעֲבֹד אֶת־יְהוָה אֱלֹהֶיךָ בְּכָל־לְבָבְךָ וּבְכָל־נַפְשֶׁךָ: לִשְׁמֹר אֶת־מִצְוֹת יְהוָה וְאֶת־חֻקֹּתָיו אֲשֶׁר אָנֹכִי מְצַוְּךָ הַיּוֹם לְטוֹב לָךְ:

5. Lothar Perlitt, *Deuteronomium (2,24–4,40)*, BKAT 5/4 (Neukirchen-Vluyn: Neukirchener Verlag, 2006), 305. Dietrich Knapp, *Deuteronomium 4: Literarische Analyse und theologische Interpretation*, GTA 35 (Göttingen: Vandenhoeck & Ruprecht, 1985), 27–29.

6. Jack R. Lundbom, *Deuteronomy: A Commentary* (Grand Rapids: Eerdmans, 2013), 231 and 234.

> So now, Israel, what does the LORD your God require of you? Only to fear the LORD your God, to walk in all his ways, to love him, to serve the LORD your God with all your heart and with all your soul, and to keep the commandments of the LORD your God and his decrees that I am commanding you today, for your good.[7]

This transition consists of a phrase that is easily seen to function similarly to that of 4:1. In fact, I will argue that all of 4:1–8 communicates the same exhortation to covenant fidelity that is seen here in 12:12–13. Though the language of Deut 10:12–13 is more specific regarding God's expectation of faithfulness, 4:1–8 communicates the same expectations with the addition of a warning for failing to remain faithful and a promise of relational blessing for those who do remain faithful. It is to this opening command that we now turn.

The first command itself contains many characteristically deuteronomic features that help to bind verses 5–8 together. The first characteristic feature is the call for Israel to hear (שמע).[8] The objects of Israel's listening are the חקים ("statutes") and the משפטים ("judgments"). Interestingly, within the world of the text, the audience is depicted with all seriousness as a listening audience, one which can both hear the statues and judgments being taught by Moses and obey them. This characteristic feature of Deut 4 continues through the remainder of the paraenesis, and is an important aspect of Deuteronomy's ongoing significance. The second feature we find here is a focus on the חקים ("statutes") and the משפטים ("judgments") rather than the תורה ("instruction"), which is characteristically a non-deuteronomic term never occurring in the plural within the core of Deuteronomy, and only rarely elsewhere.[9] Within the introduction to Deut 4's paraenesis these two nouns occur together three times (vv. 1, 5 and 8). Several commentators have noted the frequent usage of these terms in conjunction in Deuteronomy,[10] and most scholars have tended to see the

---

7. Unless otherwise indicated, all translations are my own.

8. See also 5:1; 6:4; 9:1; 20:3; and 27:9. Weinfeld, however, notes two distinct vocative uses of שמע ("hear") in Deut: those uses with an object (as here and 5:1) and those uses without an object such as the well-known *Shema* of 6:4. Moshe Weinfeld, *Deuteronomy 1–11*, AB 5 (New York: Doubleday, 1991), 199.

9. Lundbom, *Deuteronomy*, 235.

10. See esp. Lundbom, *Deuteronomy*, 234–35, who catalogues well the various combinations of the dt. terms.

חֻקִּים ("statutes") and the מִשְׁפָּטִים ("judgments")—along with similar formulae—as signals of rhetorical structuring[11] or else a special exilic term for all of the legal instruction of Moses in Deut 5–26.[12] This being the case, on the level of rhetoric the threefold occurrence here in the introduction to Deut 4, with the first occurrence opening the chapter and the final two occurrences bracketing the final third of the introduction, establishes the חֻקִּים ("statutes") and the מִשְׁפָּטִים ("judgments") as a major thematic element within the chapter that also serves to tie the first eight verses together as a unit on its own terms.

A third characteristically deuteronomic theme is the depiction of Moses in verse 1, not as one commanding but foremost as one who is teaching the statutes and judgments of YHWH. This is not only the first usage of לָמַד ("teach") in Deuteronomy, but also the first usage in the Pentateuch.[13] The concept of Israel learning from their teacher Moses and then replicating this teaching by instructing future generations is widely recognized as an important deuteronomic theme.[14] In this case, the aim of the teaching is obedience to the statues and judgments. This concept of teaching, introduced here in verse 1, is

---

11. Perlitt, *Deuteronomium (2,24–4,40)*, 303. Accordingly, "Moses' speeches in Deuteronomy, in particular, develop their line of argument according to a rhetorical progression, with characteristic stages and turning points." Jean-Pierre Sonnet SJ, *The Book within the Book: Writing in Deuteronomy* (Leiden: Brill, 1997), 15.

12. Georg Braulik, "Die Ausdrücke für 'Gesetz' im Buch Deuteronomium," *Bib* 51 (1970): 53.

13. Moshe Weinfeld, *Deuteronomy and the Deuteronomistic School* (Oxford: Oxford, 1972), 203. The thematic importance of לָמַד ("teach") to Deuteronomy has been often asserted but has been recently documented in the excellent study by Wendy L. Widder, *"To Teach" in Ancient Israel: A Cognitive Linguistic Study of a Biblical Hebrew Lexical Set*, BZAW 456 (Berlin: de Gruyter, 2014), esp. 72–123.

14. See 4:5, 10 (2x), 14; 5:1, 31; 6:1; 11:19; 31:12, 19, 22. Georg Braulik, "Deuteronomy and the Commemorative Culture of Israel: Redactio-Historical Observations of the Use of לָמַד," in *The Theology of Deuteronomy: Collected Essays of Georg Braulik, O.S.B.*, trans. by Ulrika Lindblad (N. Richmond Hills: BIBAL, 1994), 183–98. Braulik notes that Deut uses לָמַד ("teach") more than any other book in the Pentateuch (Braulik, "Deuteronomy and the Commemorative Culture of Israel," 184). Interestingly, Braulik begins his article by citing Jan Assmann, *Das kulturelle Gedächtnis: Schrift, Erinnerung und politische Identität in frühen Hochkulturen* (München: C. H. Beck, 1997), and the important work that Assmann has done to understand the role of Deut in the memory culture of ancient Israel; he then proceeds to re-frame Assmann's work into a diachronic study with redaction-historical conclusions. In this sense, Assmann's re-framed discussion is re-re-framed.

essential throughout Deuteronomy, not least of all in the opening
verse of the chapter's core (v. 9):

רַ֣ק הִשָּׁ֣מֶר לְךָ֩ וּשְׁמֹ֨ר נַפְשְׁךָ֜ מְאֹ֗ד פֶּן־תִּשְׁכַּ֣ח אֶת־הַדְּבָרִ֣ים אֲשֶׁר־רָא֣וּ עֵינֶ֗יךָ
וּפֶן־יָס֙וּרוּ֙ מִלְּבָ֣בְךָ֔ כֹּ֖ל יְמֵ֣י חַיֶּ֑יךָ וְהוֹדַעְתָּ֥ם לְבָנֶ֖יךָ וְלִבְנֵ֥י בָנֶֽיךָ

> But guard yourself and watch yourself closely, lest you forget the
> things that your eyes have seen and lest they depart from your
> mind all the days of your life; <u>make them known to your children
> and your children's children.</u>

Fourthly, verse 1 exhibits the characteristic deuteronomic preoc-
cupation with the land into which Israel is destined to enter and possess.[15] However, the possession of the land is not a foregone
conclusion, as disobedience has prevented entry in the past (Deut
1:26–35). In this case, the indication is that if Israel desires to live,
enter, and possess the land that YHWH is giving to the nation, then
the nation must listen to its authoritative instructor and obey his
words. The particular deuteronomic association between the land and
the content of Moses's message can readily be seen by their frequent
use with the complex preposition למען ("so that").[16] In the case of
verse 1, the result of listening to the חקים ("statues") and the משפטים
("judgments") is that Israel will be allowed to live (למען תחיו).[17] This
claim that life comes as a result of obedience in turn establishes a

15. Many important studies have been conducted on the development of the land
theology within the Pentateuch as well as from a synchronic vantage point. For a helpful
overview and discussion of the issues involved, see Jerry Hwang, *The Rhetoric of Remembrance: An Investigation of the "Fathers" in Deuteronomy*, SIPHRUT 8 (Winona
Lake, IN: Eisenbrauns, 2012), 15–30. Perhaps the most concise and erudite distillation
of the dt. land formulation is provided by Jeffrey Tigay, *Deuteronomy (Devarim)* (Philadelphia: JPS, 1996), xvi.

16. For this dt. connection between "so that" (למען) and the land, see also 4:40; 5:16,
33; 6:18, 23; 8:1; 11:8, 9; 11:21; 16:20; 17:20; 23:21; 25:15; and 27:3.

17. Duane L. Christensen, *Deuteronomy 1–11*, WBC 6A (Dallas: Word, 1991), 72
diagrams, as is his pattern, Deut 4:1–40 as a chiasm. According to his proposal (see also
the comments of Weinfeld, *Deuteronomy 1–11*, 199), vv. 1–4 and 39–40 are corresponding elements both with the summary statement, "Keep YHWH's commandments that
you may live in the land." Although this formulation may be true in a very broad sense,
on the level of the text, only v. 1 promises life, entrance, and inheritance of the land.
Verse 40 promises that things will go well (ייטב) and that their days would be prolonged
(תאריך ימים). While it is true that vv. 1 and 40 are the only occurrences of למען in Deut 4,
contrary to Christensen the distinctive focus on the correspondence between obedience
and living seems to be a particular feature of v. 1 and its rhetorical relationship to v. 2.

strong connection between verses 1 and 3, as well as verses 5–8, as I will argue in due course. This "life" freely offered to the nation if it obeys the words of Moses consists of both physical existence and blessing from the God who speaks to the nation through Moses and who makes himself known through those words.

Verse 2 follows this rich collection of deuteronomic themes in verse 1 with a statement that does not appear *prima facie* to be relevant to the issues at hand or the rhetoric of the chapter's introduction. In fact, this verse has often been treated by scholars as nothing more than a principle of canonization intended to secure these words from alteration. In other words, commentators often treat this verse in near isolation from both verse 1 and verses 3–8. Characteristic of this approach is Timo Veijola. He addresses Deut 4 according to its redactional layers; he places verse 4 in the fourth such editorial layer and considers this verse to be a small addition that is different from its surrounding context.[18] Veijola continues, as most other commentators do, with a discussion of contemporary canon formulas such as those found in Ptah-Hotep,[19] Hammurabi,[20] Polybius,[21] and Maccabees.[22] All of this evidences a broad interest in this verse, and the similar text in 13:1 (Heb), as Nelson's "canon formula"[23] or Perlitt's "Wortlautschutzformel"[24] or Otto's "Wortsicherungsformel."[25]

---

18. Timo Veijola, *Das fünfte Buch Mose Deuteronomium (Kapitel 1,1–16,17)*, ATD 8.1 (Göttingen: Vandenhoeck & Ruprecht, 2004), 113.

19. Ptah-Hotep 18:7. For more on this topic and other related Egyptian texts, see Andreas Vonach, "Die sogenannte 'Kanon- oder Ptahotepformel:' Anmerkungen zu Tradition und Kontext einer markanten Wendung," *PzB* 6 (1997): 73–80.

20. ANET3, 178; rev. xxv 60–70; rev. xxvi 1–10.

21. Polybius, *Hist* vii 9:9.

22. 1 Macc 8:29–30.

23. Richard D. Nelson, *Deuteronomy: A Commentary*, OTL (Louisville: Westminster John Knox, 2002), 64. See also the discussions of Jan Assmann, *Cultural Memory and Early Civilization: Writing Remembrance, and Political Imagination* (Cambridge: Cambridge, 2011), 199. Also Weinfeld, *Deuteronomy and the Deuteronomistic School*, 260–65; and Weinfeld, *Deuteronomy 1–11*, 200.

24. Perlitt, *Deuteronomium (2,24–4,40)*, 308.

25. Otto, *Deuteronomium 1,1–4,43*, 542–43.

By contrast to these frequent concerns for the theme of canon, Jeffrey Tigay has argued that verse 2 is concerned less with forming canonical boundaries and more with establishing the best practices for relating to YHWH, that is, with singular devotion.[26] He notes that in both deuteronomic uses of the "canon formula"[27]—4:2 and 13:1 (Heb.)—the immediate context prohibits idolatry.[28] Furthermore, although דבר ("word") in this verse can readily be taken to indicate the entirety of Moses's instructions to Israel,[29] Tigay notes that Deuteronomy was never intended to be a complete and comprehensive law code.[30] On one hand, Tigay shows an acute awareness of the textual context, but on the other hand, I do not believe he goes far enough; I do not think that it is strictly necessary to interpret this text as having a singular perlocution, either to stymie the textual development of Moses's דברם ("words") or to prevent idolatry. As I will argue, the issues are more complex and require a more nuanced interpretation.

THE WARNING: DEUT 4:3–4

We now turn to verse 3, where the rhetoric becomes highly emphatic: not a simple Qal Perf. (ראיתם "you saw") but instead an emphatic construction consisting of the unnecessary subject עיניכם ("your eyes") plus the Qal Pred. Part. הראת ("are the ones that saw"). This precise grammatical construction also occurs in 3:21 and 11:7,[31] but this evidence is only a small portion of the overall picture of an

---

26. Tigay, *Deuteronomy*, 44.

27. The German term *Wortsicherungsformel* ("word preservation formula"), seems to better capture the language of the verse itself (דבר). Otto, *Deuteronomium 1,1–4,43*, 540. Alternatively, Perlitt, *Deuteronomium (2,24–4,40)*, 306 uses *Veränderungsverbot* ("prohibition on alteration"), which better captures the essence of the command.

28. Lundbom, *Deuteronomy*, 236 disagrees and believes that the repeated *Wortsicherungsformel* throughout the Christian canon gives credit to viewing this statement in Deut 4:2 as comprehensive warning against altering the words of Moses. Such a practice is well documented elsewhere as Lundbom notes.

29. Lundbom, *Deuteronomy*, 236; Christensen, *Deuteronomy 1–11*, 79; and Perlitt, *Deuteronomium (2,24–4,40)*, 306.

30. Tigay, *Deuteronomy*, 44.

31. Otto, *Deuteronomium 1,1–4,43*, 544; Perlitt, *Deuteronomium (2,24–4,40)*, 310; and Lundbom, *Deuteronomy*, 223.

emphatic deuteronomic rhetoric of sensory perception. The point to understand here, however, is that the text of Deuteronomy 4 envisages an audience that has had a personal visual experience of the events being described. Just as verse 1 depicts an audience that can hear the words of Moses, verse 3 depicts an audience that can recall to mind these events and make theological conclusions from them. But what is the event that the nation saw and can interpret?

We may now turn to the precise object of Israel's vision according to verse 3, that is, what God did in Baal-Peor (a place, see Hos 9:10) to those who followed after Baal-Peor (a deity, see Num 25:1–5). The audience within the world of the text is evidently able to recall to mind an event in which God's wrath was poured out on all the who followed after Baal-Peor when he destroyed them from "your midst." Although the contrast between the plural suffix (עיניכם "your [pl.] eyes") at the beginning of verse 3 and the singular suffix (מקרבך "from your [sg.] midst") at its end have understandably interested many scholars,[32] the essential aspect for our purposes is the contrast between the behaviors of two distinct groups of Israelites and God's distinct responses to these two behaviors. Verses 3–4 claim that two distinct actions were undertaken by Israelites at Baal-Peor: some followed after (הלך אחרי) Baal-Peor while others held fast (דבק) to YHWH. The relationship between verses 3–4 to what comes before in verse 1 has readily been seen by commentators, namely, the connection between the promise of "life" and the situation of Baal-Peor that can aptly be described as a life or death decision to follow after Baal or to hold fast to YHWH.[33] But much less recognized is these verses' conceptual relationship to verse 2. A look at the Hebrew text will perhaps help draw out this relationship.

וְעַתָּה יִשְׂרָאֵל שְׁמַע אֶל־הַחֻקִּים וְאֶל־הַמִּשְׁפָּטִים אֲשֶׁר אָנֹכִי מְלַמֵּד אֶתְכֶם ¹
לַעֲשׂוֹת לְמַעַן תִּחְיוּ וּבָאתֶם וִירִשְׁתֶּם אֶת־הָאָרֶץ אֲשֶׁר יְהוָה אֱלֹהֵי אֲבֹתֵיכֶם
נֹתֵן לָכֶם:

---

32. Knapp, *Deuteronomium 4*, 46.

33. Siegfried Mittmann, *Deuteronomium 1,1–6,3: literarkritisch und traditionsgeschichtlich untersucht*, BZAW 139 (Berlin: de Gruyter, 1975), 116; Patrick D. Miller, *Deuteronomy*, Interpretation (Louisville: John Knox, 1990), 54–55; Tigay, *Deuteronomy*, 44; Veijola, *Das fünfte Buch Mose Deuteronomium (Kapitel 1,1–16,17)*, 103; and S. R. Driver, *Deuteronomy*, 3rd ed. (Edinburgh: T. & T. Clark, 1902), 63.

לֹא תֹסִפוּ עַל־הַדָּבָר֙ אֲשֶׁר אָנֹכִי֙ מְצַוֶּה אֶתְכֶ֔ם וְלֹא תִגְרְע֖וּ מִמֶּ֑נּוּ לִשְׁמֹ֕ר 2
אֶת־מִצְוֺת֙ יְהוָ֣ה אֱלֹֽהֵיכֶ֔ם אֲשֶׁ֥ר אָנֹכִ֖י מְצַוֶּ֥ה אֶתְכֶֽם׃
עֵֽינֵיכֶם֙ הָרֹאֹ֔ת אֵ֛ת אֲשֶׁר־עָשָׂ֥ה יְהוָ֖ה בְּבַ֣עַל פְּע֑וֹר כִּ֣י כָל־הָאִ֗ישׁ אֲשֶׁ֤ר הָלַךְ֙ 3
אַחֲרֵ֣י בַֽעַל־פְּע֔וֹר הִשְׁמִיד֛וֹ יְהוָ֥ה אֱלֹהֶ֖יךָ מִקִּרְבֶּֽךָ׃
וְאַתֶּם֙ הַדְּבֵקִ֔ים בַּיהוָ֖ה אֱלֹהֵיכֶ֑ם חַיִּ֥ים כֻּלְּכֶ֖ם הַיּֽוֹם׃ 4

[1] So now, Israel, <u>listen</u> to the statutes and the judgments that I am teaching you to do, so that you may live and enter and occupy the land that the LORD, the God of your fathers, is about to give you.

[2] Do not add to the words I command you nor take away from it, <u>but keep</u> the commandments of the LORD your God as to which I am commanding you.

[3] Yours are the eyes that saw what the LORD did at Baal Peor—how LORD your God destroyed from among you all the men who followed after the Baal of Peor,

[4] while those of you who held fast to the LORD your God are all alive today.

Some interpreters such as Knapp have noted that it is clear that verses 3 and 4 offer an example from Israel's history, which has the purpose of explaining verses 1 and 2 and emphasizing their importance. Those who do not listen to the law (שמע v. 1) or pay close attention (שמר v. 2), but rather follow after other gods (הלך אחרי בעל־פעור v. 3), can expect to be annihilated (השמידו יהוה אלהיך מקרבד v. 3). But those who listen to the law and respect and cling to YHWH remain alive. Knapp writes,

> In vv. 3 and 4 something new arises, an example from Israel's history, which has the purpose of explaining the paraenetic vv. 1 and 2 and thus emphasizing their importance. Those who do not listen to the law (שמע v. 1) and pay close attention (שמר v. 2) and follow after other gods (Baal Peor), can expect to be annihilated by Yahweh. But he who listens to the law and respects and clings to Yahweh, remains, as the example makes clear, alive.[34]

The advantage of this interpretation is that it does not allow verse 2 to exist in isolation from its context. The life that is promised in verse 1 for listening to the statutes and the judgments cannot be obtained merely by listening but must be accompanied by a careful regard for Moses's words and a loyalty to YHWH—characterized by preservation (שמר). In this sense, loyalty to YHWH is likened to preserving

---

34. Knapp, *Deuteronomium 4*, 46 (author's translation).

the words of Moses from alteration while following after other deities is likened to altering the words of Moses. At first such an illustration from history seems purely emphatic in nature. However, as the text progresses, there appears to be a genuine choice between life and destruction.[35] Deut 4:1–4 establish a genuine choice to be made. In the case of Deut 4's rhetoric, as Knapp emphasizes, the contrast between life and death is established on the basis of a parallel structure. On the one hand, life consists of keeping the commandments of YHWH and is likened to holding fast to YHWH;[36] on the other hand death consists of adding to or taking away from the commandments of YHWH and is likened to following after Baal-Peor and receiving death as a just punishment. Thus, there exists a *double entendre* in the use of these concepts of "life" and "death." On the one hand, there is, as the example of Baal-Peor shows, a choice to be made between physical life and physical death.[37] On the other hand, there is the claim of the text that true life is only that which is in accordance with the words of YHWH through Moses, and that all other life is life not worth living.[38] However, there is no reason that the ambiguity of the text in this regard cannot allow both of these interpretations to stand simultaneously. In the first case, the example of Baal-Peor is an especially strong indication that obedience results in life while disobedience results in death. In the second case, a look at verses 5–8 envisages a life for Israel that is both full and blessed precisely because it is devoted to the obedience of YHWH statutes and judgments.

35. For an excellent article on this theme in Deut, see Heath A. Thomas, "Life and Death in Deuteronomy," in *Interpreting Deuteronomy: Issues and Approaches* (ed. by David G. Firth and Philip S. Johnson; Nottingham: Apollos, 2012), 177–93. See also Timothy A. Lenchak, *"Choose Life!" A Rhetorical-Critical Investigation of Deuteronomy 28, 69–30,20* (AnBib 129; Rome: Pontificio Istituto Biblico, 1993).

36. Weinfeld, *Deuteronomy 1–11*, 201 notes the close relationship between the contrast between following after Baal-Peor and holding fast to YHWH and what is expected of Israel in 13:5 (Heb.):

אַחֲרֵי יְהוָה אֱלֹהֵיכֶם תֵּלֵכוּ וְאֹתוֹ תִירָאוּ וְאֶת־מִצְוֹתָיו תִּשְׁמֹרוּ וּבְקֹלוֹ תִשְׁמָעוּ וְאֹתוֹ תַעֲבֹדוּ וּבוֹ תִדְבָּקוּן:

Here Israel is told to follow after YHWH (אחרי יהוה אלהיכם תלכו) and to hold fast to him (ובו תדבקון).

37. See Ibn Ezra, *ad loc.*

38. See Rabbi Kook as quoted in Nehama Leibowitz, *Studies in Devarim (Deuteronomy)*, trans. Aryeh Newman (Jerusalem: Eliner Library, 2010), 47.

THE PROMISE: DEUT 4:5–8

Regarding verses 5–8, the first feature worth noting is its beginning ראה-imp. ("see"), which is an obvious parallel to verse 1's שמע ("hear").[39] In terms of the world of Deuteronomy, this imperative is operating as an attention-grabbing device similar to the particle הנה ("behold"). However, Deut 1–4 demonstrates a definite preference for ראה-impv. ("see") acting as an attention-getter (1:8, 21; 2:24, 31; 3:27; and 4:5) over and against הנה ("behold," 1:10; 3:11). Here Israel is told to see that Moses *has* taught (למדתי-Perf) the חקים ("statutes") and משפטים ("judgments"), which—as I said above—functions in symmetry with verse 1 and establishes an *inclusio* between verses 5 and 8, thus justifying a treatment of these verses as a single rhetorical unit.

Verse 6 continues with two commands with these חקים ("statutes") and משפטים ("judgments") as their implied object, namely, to keep (ושמרתם) and to do (ועשיתם) them. According to Braulik, these terms "constitute a set expression."[40] Braulik continues by stating that,

> In the context of the deuteronomic linguistic world, as well as because of the exceptional brevity of the speeches within a wide rhetorical context, the two injunctives receive a clear stylistic profile: this is the formal pledging of the people to observe the statutes.[41]

Lohfink, accordingly, concludes that ושמרתם does not oblige the Israelites to learn the law as a prerequisite to obeying it.[42] But this assertion seems to my mind to be a step too far, since learning the חקים ("statutes") and משפטים ("judgments") in verse 1 establishes the context in which Israel is to keep and do them (vv. 5 and 14). Indeed, in verse 5, Moses is explicit that he has taught Israel to do that which he has instructed them. Thus, keeping and doing (v. 6) the

39. Weinfeld, *Deuteronomy 1–11*, 201.

40. Georg Braulik, "Wisdom, Divine Presence and Law: Reflections on the Kerygma of Deut 4:5–8," in *The Theology of Deuteronomy: Collected Essays of Georg Braulik, O.S.B.*, trans. Ulrika Lindblad (N. Richland Hills: BIBAL, 1994), 7.

41. Braulik, "Wisdom, Divine Presence and Law," 7.

42. Norbert Lohfink, *Das Hauptgebot: Eine Untersuchung literarischer Einleitungsfragen zu Dtn 5–11,* AnBib 20 (Rome: Pontificio Istituto Biblico, 1963), 68–70.

חקים ("statutes") and משפטים ("judgments") presupposes that Israel has learned (למד) what Moses has taught (למד, v. 5).

These commands are then followed by thee coordinate clauses, the first two beginning with כי ("for," vv. 6 and 7) and the third (ומי) beginning with the conjunction ו (in this case best translated "for") and the interrogative pronoun מי (in this case best translated "what," v. 8). These coordinate clauses serve as promises to Israel for fulfilling their role as a people called to obey God. These promises, moreover, should be understood as descriptions of what "life" is. The promise from Moses is that Israel will be known as a wise and understanding nation in the eyes of the people. In other words, Israel's greatness in the eyes of the nations is on the basis of its reputation.[43] Verses 7–8 continue with a contrast between Israel as a potentially great nation and other great nations. In the first case, Israel is a distinctly great nation because of the nearness of her god, who responds whenever Israel calls on him. In the second case, Israel is a distinctly great nation because of the wisdom of her laws. Implicit in these promises to Israel is a demand, for Israel must both call on YHWH and obey his laws in order for the nations to observe the evidences of their greatness. In other words, their greatness in the eyes of the nations is only a potential greatness that is actualized through responsiveness to YHWH. As Holter has noted,

> There is a mutual relationship between Israel's and Yahweh's respective ways of being incomparable. Israel's incomparability lies in her relationship to Yahweh, demonstarted [*sic*] by her observance of his decrees and judgments. And likewise, Yahweh's incomparability lies in his relationship to Israel, demonstrated by his speaking to and salvation of his people.[44]

In other words, YHWH's incomparability stems here from his character and the character of his laws. Accordingly, as Israel responds

---

43. Weinfeld, *Deuteronomy 1–11*, 202, and Lundbom, *Deuteronomy*, 238.

44. Holter, *Deuteronomy 4 and the Second Commandment*, 104. Although he never uses the phrase, MacDonald's theology of dt. monotheism can likewise be described in terms of mutuality, namely, a mutual election: YHWH has chosen Israel from among all the nations of the earth to be the special object of his love, and Israel is expected to choose YHWH from among all the gods of the earth to be the special object of its love. Nathan MacDonald, *Deuteronomy and the Meaning of "Monotheism,"* FAT II/1 (Tübingen: Mohr Siebeck, 2003).

obediently to YHWH, Israel becomes a great people among the nations of the world. As Nelson notes, it is the "nearness" of YHWH to Israel that makes them distinct.[45] This mutual distinctiveness becomes visibly apparent to the nations, therefore, through the laws of YHWH by the responsive obedience of Israel that is initiated by nearness and wisdom of YHWH himself.

Conclusion

As noted in the introduction Deut 4:2 has been understood, with few exceptions, in isolation from its context within the introduction (vv. 1–8) to the paraenesis of Deut 4:1–40. Many interpreters have determined that verse 2 evidences a disturbance in the otherwise flowing language of the chapter's introduction and therefore have determined to study this verse as a late addition. Closely associated with this line of thinking is the non-mutually exclusive view that verse 2 is important for understanding Israel's growing self-understanding of canon or else for developing contemporary theories and theologies of canon.

This paper, however, has argued that the decision to interpret verse 2 apart from its rhetorical context within Deut 4's introduction may be at the expense of understanding this important verse on its own terms as it presently stands in the received form. Furthermore, when attention is given to rhetorical concerns including repetition and logical parallelism, it is possible—and perhaps necessary—to read verse 2 as a key element in an established parallel between how Israel treats the "words" of God, whatever these might be, given through Moses and how Israel treats God himself. Without verse 2 this parallelism loses much of its sophistication: the object lesson of Baal-Peor (vv. 3–4) lacks context and what it means to keep (שמר, vv. 2, 6) the commandments and judgments of YHWH lacks definition.

If there is any rhetorical cohesion within Deut 4's introduction, it is to be found in the frequent repetition of its key terms and themes. Among these are the important structuring use of "statutes and judgments." Additionally, the parallel uses of command and historical retrospect establishes an essential contrast between life and death on one hand and faithfulness and unfaithfulness on the other hand. The promise of physical life, mentioned in the opening verse, is further developed

---

45. Nelson, *Deuteronomy*, 65.

in the closing verses into an expansive conceptual term that speaks of life as it can and YHWH be in contradistinction from the other nations through obedience to YHWH. All of these themes and terms establish Deut 4:1–8 as an intricate piece of text, to say nothing of its relationship to the wider context.

[*JESOT* 7.2 (2021): 16–36]

Achan Typology in the Former Prophets

DAVID G. FIRTH

Trinity College, Bristol

ABSTRACT: *The figure of Achan is marked as one of particular
importance in the book of Joshua where he is introduced as a
clear contrast to Rahab. Despite this, he is mentioned only once
more in Joshua and not again in the former prophets. However,
the narratological importance given to him was recognised in
the subsequent books of the Former Prophets, each of which
takes up the presentation of him and integrates it into their own
narrative. The goal of this paper is to trace this process and in so
doing outline a typological pattern that can be traced through the
Former Prophets.*

THE ACHAN STORY AS A NARRATIVE EVENT

First-time readers of Joshua encounter something of a surprise when
they meet the figure of Achan in the account of Israel's failure to
capture Ai (Josh 7). Nothing in the book to this point has led us to
anticipate a character like him, not least because his introduction
marks a largely unexpected change in Israel's fortunes. The victory at
Jericho could be reported without reference to any response by the local
population (even though Joshua 24:11 is well aware that there had been
resistance) because of the need to stress that it was Yahweh who had
won the battle. Israel, indeed, did little more than march around the
city the requisite number of times in a procession that is rather like a
liturgical march with horn section. Jericho had been closed up against
Israel (Josh 6:1), and although Israel's entry into the land had left the
hearts of the Amorite kings melted (Josh 5:1), there is no indication
that Israel knew anything about siege warfare. Jericho's decision to
close up tight would therefore have posed a major challenge, but this
challenge was overcome because Yahweh did what he had announced

in advance that he would do, giving the city over to the Israelites. In the process, the question of Rahab's status—something left unresolved in Joshua 2 when the scouts had come to her—is also addressed.[1] Rahab, a prostitute who would at first seem to have been precisely the sort of Canaanite we would expect to be placed under the ban, instead became an enduring part of Israel (Josh 6:25).

But just as Josh 6:1 had announced in advance the outcome of the events at Jericho, so also Josh 7:1 provides readers with guidance that is hidden from Israel as they moved to Ai. From the outset, readers know that Achan had taken from the things placed under the ban at Jericho (Josh 6:18–20, 24). This opening statement forces us to re-read the earlier statement of Josh 6:24 as we now discover that what might have appeared to be a statement suggesting complete obedience by Israel was in fact only a statement of what was generally true. Since Israel had successfully completed the capture of Jericho by the time Achan had taken from the banned items, his actions did not impact the events there. But they would have a devastating effect on the events at Ai, not least because Israel was unaware of them. So, although the scouts Joshua sent out and who came to Ai offer information that is militarily more helpful than those he had earlier sent to Jericho, they were ignorant of the fact that Ai was not a town that could be captured simply by the application of appropriate military strategy. There may be a degree of hubris in their report, since when Yahweh provides Joshua with instructions for the town's capture after the issue of Achan had been resolved it involved a much larger group (compare Josh 7:2–3 with Josh 8:1–8), though we might also read this as further evidence of the fact that Israel was not endowed with any significant military awareness. But before Ai could be captured, Israel had first to resolve the problem posed by Achan. Although Joshua's prayer after the initial failure to capture the town misunderstands the events, Yahweh nevertheless seems to have accepted the concern for his honor as the central element and therefore responded by highlighting what had gone wrong and how Israel could resolve it.[2] In the end, after Achan had been taken

---

1. See D. G. Firth, "Disorienting Readers in Joshua 1:1–5:12," *JSOT* 41 (2017): 413–30.

2. I explored this further in D. G. Firth, "Getting It Right while Getting It Wrong: Joshua's Prayer in Joshua 7," unpublished paper presented to the Old Testament Theology of Prayer group of IBR, Denver, 2018. I hope to publish this paper soon.

through a process which gradually identified him through a pattern that reversed his exemplary Israelite genealogy in Josh 7:1, he was brought before Joshua. There, Achan confessed to his crime, after which he and his immediate family were executed by stoning, a great cairn being raised over them as one of several cairns that mark important locations in Joshua's opening chapters.[3] Only after this could Israel capture Ai, though this time they needed directions from Yahweh. Although the approach taken was militarily more normal, Israel was still reminded that the land could only be taken when Yahweh fought for Israel and Israel participated on Yahweh's terms.

That Israel was able to resolve the problem caused by Achan does not change the fact that his story is introduced in a way that is unexpected. The import of this can be observed when we draw on the concept of event and eventfulness that Schmid develops as a general characteristic of narratology.[4] Although he here discusses elements of fiction, in that the narrative material of the Old Testament employs the self-same narrative techniques for describing historical events as fictional ones,[5] it is not inappropriate to draw on his work. For Schmid, an event is a change of state, though not all changes of state are an event. An event occurs when a change of state fulfills two criteria. First, the change must be real (at least within the narrative world) and, second, there must be a resultant change within the narrative world.[6] In that the Achan story represents a real change of state for Israel where they move from a state of continuing victory to defeat and finally back to victory, it is clear that these conditions are fulfilled. But even within this model, Schmid recognizes that not all events are equally eventful, and one of

3. See R. L. Hubbard Jr., "'What Do These Stones Mean?': Biblical Theology and a Motif in Joshua," *BBR* 11 (2001): 1–26.

4. W. Schmid, *Narratology: An Introduction* (Berlin: de Gruyter, 2010), 8–12. Greger Andersson, *Untamable Texts: Literary Studies and Narrative Theory in the Books of Samuel* (London: T. & T. Clark, 2009), offers numerous examples of how readings informed by narratology can lead to unconvincing interpretations of Old Testament narratives, especially when their historiographic nature is taken into account. Nevertheless, misuse of narratological material does not of itself discredit it as a tool that can, with critical awareness, be applied to the narratives of the Old Testament.

5. For example, fictional narration is often embedded within historical material, as for example in 2 Sam 14:1–20, where there is no change in narrative mode apart from an explicit naming of the narrator.

6. Schmid, *Narratology*, 9.

the most important mechanisms for highlighting those that have more significance is through the introduction of something unpredictable.[7] In that the change Israel experiences within this story can be reported only by holding back key information until it happens, this element is also clearly present. Without laboring the point, it soon becomes clear that the authors of Joshua have worked hard to surprise readers when they first encounter the Achan story. Schmid also points to noniterativity as a means for stressing eventfulness in that events which are not repeated have more impact than those which can occur multiple times. In that the Achan story is clearly self-contained and concluded, it is also noniterative. These factors indicate that the story is composed so that readers see it as an important event, one that represents a significant change of state for Israel.

THE SIGNIFICANCE OF THE EVENT

We might ask, though, why this would be done given that, apart from a genealogy in Chronicles, Achan himself is not mentioned anywhere outside of Joshua. Even within Joshua, apart from Josh 7, he is mentioned only in the story of the altar on the Jordan (Josh 22:20).[8] It is entirely possible to answer this from within the book of Joshua alone, and observe that Achan's story represents the first significant setback within the land, something noted in the narrator's opening observation that Israel had acted treacherously, introducing the verb מעל into the narrative. It is notable that the only other place where this verb occurs in the book is in Josh 22 (vv. 16, 20, 31), and indeed that both the verb and Achan's name occur together in Josh 22:20. Moreover, Achan stands in a clear contrast to Rahab. She is a Canaanite who is (in some way) integrated into the life of Israel, whereas Achan is an Israelite

---

7. Schmid, *Narratology*, 10.

8. He is called Achar in 1 Chronicles 2:7. Given that this makes more sense of the apparent play on his name in Joshua 7:24–25, it is likely that this is the correct form of his name. Given that the name Achan uses the same consonants as 'Canaan' it is not impossible that the name in Joshua represents a deliberate corruption of the name (cf. L. D. Hawk, *Joshua in 3-D. A Commentary on Biblical Conquest and Manifest Destiny* [Eugene, OR: Cascade, 2010], 87), following a similar pattern with *-baal* compound names in Samuel where this element is commonly changed to *-bosheth*.

who, in spite of his clear and impressive genealogy, is excluded.[9] That is, it is entirely possible to posit reasons why the book of Joshua introduces the figure of Achan, and to see his role as complete within it. Such a conclusion could be reached if we believe that Joshua was, in the first instance, composed as a work complete in itself.[10]

More commonly, Joshua is treated as part of a deuteronomistic history, in which case it is understood as having reached its final form at a date sometime after the events it describes, most commonly the exile, though a much wider range of dates than this is suggested. This is not the place to go into the various models for understanding this way of reading the Former Prophets as a whole, especially given the diverse ways in which the label "Deuteronomistic History" is often applied. However, the key element that holds these approaches together is that Joshua is always understood within the larger block Joshua—Kings. If we follow this model, then it is also possible that the figure of Achan is introduced and made so eventful precisely because the composers of this larger work saw his story as eventful for later generations, including perhaps those of the exile. On this approach, Achan is introduced into the account at this point because he is going to be significant for later parts of this collection, though if so, it is striking that comparatively few have noted any significance for this outside of some connections with Saul.[11]

We can modify this approach if we assume that the Former Prophets were an emerging collection of works, and in this way we might come back to understanding Joshua as a work complete in itself, and yet one that is taken up at various points by those who were responsible for bringing together later sections of the story.[12] Such an approach

---

9. See further D. G. Firth, "Models of Inclusion and Exclusion in Joshua," in *Interreligious Relations*, ed. H. Hagellia and M. Zehnder (London: T. & T. Clark, 2017), 70–88.

10. This would, for the most part, be the position developed by H. J. Koorevaar, *De Opbouw van het Boek Jozua* (Heverlee: Centrum voor Bijbelse Vorming-Belgie, 1990).

11. See M. Michael, "The Achan / Achor Traditions: The Parody of Saul as 'Achan' in 1 Samuel 14:24–15:35,'" *OTE* 26 (2013): 730–60.

12. For this approach, see especially H. J. Koorevaar, "The Book of Joshua and the Hypothesis of the Deuteronomistic History: Indications for an Open Serial Model," in *The Book of Joshua*, ed. E. Noort (Leuven: Peeters,2012), 219–32, and B. N. Peterson, *The Authors of the Deuteronomistic History: Locating a Tradition in Ancient Israel* (Minneapolis: Fortress, 2014).

would explain the particular significance given to the Achan story by those who wrote Joshua, while also allowing that later writers who, having observed the significance given to the account within Joshua, might then develop this in distinctive ways. This approach would mean that we do not expect each writer to use this material in the same way, though it is not unreasonable to think that there would be shared features present. The shared features, which draw on the Achan story to explore the significance of later events can rightly be called a typology in that the similarities between Achan and subsequent figures are used in meaningful ways to explore events, with the Achan story providing a grid assisting the interpretation of these later stories.[13]

This is the approach that is taken up here, exploring how an event which is given a high level of eventfulness by the authors of Joshua itself provides a typology that is taken up later in the Former Prophets. Indeed, since the first occurrence of the typology is found in Joshua itself, it is not unreasonable to propose that these later writers are following the pattern that Joshua has established. Although we can trace two principal strands of this typology—either focusing on Achan himself and his sin or the capture of Ai, for reasons of space consideration will only be given to those texts which develop a typology based on Achan himself.[14] In particular, we will note that the typologies are typically marked by the presence of one or more of keywords from the original story (typically one of מעל, לכד,עכר or נבלה),[15] the taking of things that do not properly belong to Israel-

---

13. Much fuller models of typology are, of course, possible, such as one where type and antitype are seen as being in a prophetic relationship. Discussion of the hermeneutics of such typology are beyond the scope of this paper for which this much simpler model suffices. For a recent overview, though with a strong preference for seeing types as foreshadowing what is later rather than the more basic option developed here, see A. Caneday, "Biblical Types: Revelation Concealed in Plain Sight to be Disclosed—'These Things Occurred Typologically to Them and Were Written Down for Our Admonition,'" in *Glory Revealed in Christ: Essays on Biblical Theology in Honor of Thomas R. Schreiner*, ed. D. Burk et al. (Nashville: B&H Academic, 2019), 135–55.

14. Nevertheless, it is important to see that the whole of Joshua 7:1—8:29 represents a coherent narrative unit that is complete in its own right. See N. Winther-Nielsen, *A Functional Discourse Grammar of Joshua* (Stockholm: Almqvist & Wiksell, 1995), 216, 227–28. However, a writer developing a typology is not bound to take the whole of the narrative, but only that part which is relevant to the theme being developed.

15. Each of these words is relatively rare but placed at a key point in Joshua 7:1—8:29. Although rarity is not necessarily a defining feature for identifying links more

ites, selection by lot or dealings with foreigners. The greater the level of these features, the stronger the typology, though only one can be enough to signify at least a typological echo across these texts. As I am not aware of a study which explores this typology, the goal of this paper is to trace out its general contours.

JOSHUA

Although the Achan story is initially recounted in Joshua, we also find the first instance of a typological use of it in Josh 22. Several features of the story show that a typology concerned with Achan is being developed, though there are two unique elements here. First, the verb מעל, which is given particular prominence in introducing the original story at Josh 7:1, occurs three times in this chapter (Josh 22:16, 20, 31). This rare verb, which seems to indicate a significant trespass, occurs nowhere else in the Former Prophets. This immediately generates links to the Achan story, but there is also the more obvious element that Achan himself is named within the story (Josh 22:20).[16] One curiosity here is that the typological elements are presented within the reported speech of the west-Jordan delegation sent to the eastern tribes, a speech which also creates a typology based on the sin at Peor reported in Num 25:1–13 along with a probable reference to the rebellion of the tribes in their initial refusal to enter the land (Num 14:9).[17] This constellation of intertextual references makes clear that the western tribes' speech intends to link the building of the altar on the Jordan with a number of points of previous sin within Israel. The Achan typology which is developed is thus contextualized within these earlier points in Israel's history where the sin of an individual or representative group within Israel has negatively impacted the nation as a whole. Although the various sins to which reference is made are

---

generally, the combination of rarity and narrative emphasis does point to connections being made.

16. In spite of redactional approaches which seek to divide the chapter into various layers (e.g., V. Fritz, *Das Buch Josua* [Tübingen: Mohr Siebeck, 1994], 220–21), it is better to read this chapter as a unified narrative—see T. Butler, *Joshua 13–24* (Grand Rapids: Zondervan, 2014), 246.

17. Note the presence of the verb מרד to describe the rebellion.

distinct from each other, they are linked by the fact that in each case the impact of the sin affects the nation as a whole.

Although there are thus several typologies running through this account, the Achan typology is particularly important, most notably because even before Achan's name is introduced the initial accusation made by the western tribes is of a breach of faith (מעל). The verb is here placed in a prominent position which (allowing for its phrasing here in a question) is similar to its use in 7:1. Within Joshua, therefore, the link with Achan is clear from the outset of their speech. Along with this, when Phinehas finishes his meeting with the eastern tribes after being satisfied that they have not in fact acted inappropriately in the building of the altar, he can declare that he knows they have not broken faith (מעל) and therefore delivered the people from Yahweh. Reference to the Achan story thus provides boundaries to the encounter between the tribes, with the naming of Achan (Josh 22:20) coming at its turning point. The clear implication is that the construction of the altar could have been as damaging for Israel as Achan's taking from the items placed under the ban (חרם) at Jericho.

In this case, the resolution of the story shows that the sin had not been committed. However, when creating a context for understanding a sin which may have placed Israel as a whole at risk, the narrative draws on Achan's sin as having established this possibility for Israel. Achan had in fact placed himself under the ban by taking from the devoted things at Jericho (Josh 6:18).[18] The suggestion is that, had the altar been an act of rebellion against Yahweh (Josh 22:16), then such an act would have meant that the eastern tribes were behaving like Canaanites, and thus liable to destruction. That the whole narrative shows that this was not the case, merely the perception of the western tribes, does not remove the typology. Rather, it establishes the Achan story as an important typological model that will be picked up and developed in different ways by later books in the Former Prophets. In particular, even though there is no evidence in this account of even a perception of taking items from under the ban, the Achan story still provides a dominant typology

---

18. Use of the word "trouble" here (using עכר) clearly anticipates the Achan story as a form of narrative foreshadowing or prolepsis. Since the book's compilers clearly know of the importance of the word for Achan's story this is not accidental and represents another example in Joshua of using *Leitworte* that create links across various narratives (note, e.g., the creative use of the verb עבר throughout Joshua 1–6), and thus contributes to the typology even though the story is only narrated subsequently.

for exploring a sin which could be understood as situating Israel in a place where Yahweh's anger can burn against them.

JUDGES

Josh 22 has enabled the Achan story to provide a pattern for sin which places Israel as a whole at risk through the sin of an individual or representative group. Although the particular sin the community feared was not committed in that case, the clear example of the typology in Judges does recount a sin that was committed. In this case, Achan typology runs through the whole of Judg 19–21, the second example of everyone doing as they wanted in Israel in the book's close.[19] Much of this typology is more evident in Judg 20, where the capture of Gibeah shows numerous links to the account of Ai's eventual capture in Josh 8:1–29, and to a lesser degree in Judg 21:8–12 where the Israelites determined they would place their own city of Jabesh-Gilead under the ban, echoing the important place of the ban in Achan's story. Indeed, the presence of an Achan typology may be an important factor in the otherwise curious note about bringing the women who were captured to Shiloh as being 'in the land of Canaan' (Judg 21:12).[20] In that Achan's story explores the impact of an Israel that becomes indistinguishable from the Canaanite population, the implication may well be that Israel's actions here show that they have, in effect, become Canaanite. In addition to these factors, we may note that Phinehas is also mentioned in Judges 20:28, allowing the possibility that the typology in Judges draws on both the original Achan story from Josh 7 and the first typological presentation in Josh 22.

However, because of the narrower focus taken within this paper, we will consider only the links established between events in Judges 19 and Achan. These wider links, however, function to confirm the

---

19. For this mode of reading Judges 17–21 rather than, as more commonly, seeing it as an appendix, see D. J. H. Beldman, *The Completion of Judges: Strategies of Ending in Judges 17–21* (Winona Lake, IN: Eisenbrauns, 2017), and I. M. Hamley, *Unspeakable Things Unspoken: An Irigarayan Reading of Otherness and Victimization in Judges 19–21* (Eugene, OR: Pickwick, 2019), 96–101.

20. This phrase matches Joshua 21:2, but there is a clear contrast in that the context in Joshua shows Israel seeking Yahweh's purposes whereas here they are seeking to subvert an oath they had made to Yahweh.

importance of the Achan typology in Judg 19 since these are not as pronounced as those in Josh 22. As is well known, the main typological relationship for Judg 19 is with the Sodom story from Gen 19.[21] Although the effectiveness of this relationship has been disputed, there is good reason to believe that the authors of Judges knew what they were doing with this material.[22] However, as was shown in Josh 22, narratives can make use of multiple typologies because they are not obliged to draw on the whole of the original example, and so can make particular use of elements that contribute to the message communicated in the new story.

The main point of connection between Judg 19 and the Achan story is centered on use of the word נבלה. This relatively rare word occurs only thirteen times in the Old Testament, and it is notable for the prominent place it receives in the original story. In response to Joshua's prayer after the initial failure to capture Ai, Joshua is told that the one who has taken the devoted things had both transgressed covenant and committed נבלה. Although often glossed as "folly" or something similar, it is notable in all cases where Achan typology is involved that it refers to a deliberate act which is contrary to what is meant to be done in Israel. Such an act would indeed be folly, but something like "outrage" or "sacrilege" is certainly defensible.[23] By placing the word at the conclusion of Yahweh's response it is thus given a particular prominence within the original Achan story.

In Joshua's own Achan typology, the word נבלה does not occur. However, it occurs four times within Judg 19–21. It is not necessary for my argument that each occurrence only evoke the Achan typology since the rape of Dinah has also provided an earlier account where the word is given particular prominence (Gen 34:7), and given that the first two occurrences (Judg 19:23–24) are expressly within the context of serious sexual abuse, it is possible that the Dinah story is initially slightly more prominent. Nevertheless, given that the Achan story has shown an Israelite behaving like a Canaanite, and of course

21. For the purposes of this paper, I assume that the typological flow is from Genesis to Judges, though the opposite direction is possible. However, because Judges 19 can be seen to draw together several different typologies, it does seem more likely that it is drawing on the Genesis account.

22. Hamley, *Unspeakable Things Unspoken*, 103.

23. Cf. *DCH*.

Dinah was raped by a Canaanite,[24] there is no reason why the Achan story itself might not include this as a minor typological element in its own presentation even though the nature of his sin was not sexual. But the account in Judges is clear that the behavior of the men of Gibeah was, like that of Achan, capable of being described as נבלה. In both occurrences in Judg 19, the word comes in the speech of the man who had taken the Levite and his attendant in from the square as he argues with the town's men that they should not expect to have sexual relations with the Levite since he was his guest. Indeed, in the twisted morality of the story, the man offered the town's men the opportunity to rape his virgin daughter along with the Levite's concubine, apparently deeming that better than them committing the נבלה of having sex with the Levite.

Taken on its own, the presence of the word נבלה may not be regarded as a significant marker of Achan typology. However, given that the reason the Levite had given for staying in Gibeah rather than Jebus was because the city was not at that time Israelite,[25] there is another minor connector to the Achan story. In Joshua, Achan is presented as the antitype to Rahab—he is the Israelite who becomes a Canaanite, whereas Rahab is the Canaanite who becomes a part of Israel. Here too, we encounter the expectation that Israelites should act in ways distinctive from Canaanites, but once again it is Israelites who follow the Canaanite pattern, exactly as happened in Achan's story.

None of these points is intended to suggest that the Achan story provides a major typology for the events of Judg 19. However, in that nothing in Gen 19 (the major background text) is described as נבלה then these elements contribute to us seeing the Achan story as one

---

24. As Susanne Scholz, *Rape Plots: A Feminist Cultural Study of Genesis 34* (New York: Peter Lang, 2000), 176–77, has noted, there is no one agreed definition of rape in the literature on this narrative. Indeed, L. M. Bechtel, "What if Dinah is Not Raped? (Genesis 34)," *JSOT* 62 (1994): 19–36, has argued that this is not a rape account, a conclusion that is developed to suggest that the main issue was the prohibition of free movement of peoples by E. van Wolde, "The Dinah Story: Rape of Worse?," *OTE* 15 (2002): 225–39. But as Y. Shemesh, 'Rape Is Rape Is Rape: The Story of Dinah and Shechem," *ZAW* 119 (2007): 2–21, has argued, this is an account of non-consensual sex, and although the Hebrew Bible might lack an explicit term designating "rape" that is still what is recounted. This would not mean that the issues van Wolde notes are not significant elements within the story, but a rape is still recounted.

25. Cf. Josh 15:63.

element that contributes to the presentation of these events. As the story progresses, these elements become more pronounced, though most are more closely associated with the capture of Ai. However, in the events which lead up to the battle for Gibeah in Judges 20, it is notable that the word נבלה comes to prominence in the Levite's speech to the assembly at Mizpah (Judg 20:4–10). Although the Levite is hardly the most reliable of narrators,[26] he accuses the men of Gibeah as having committed נבלה בישראל (Judg 20:6), matching exactly the phrasing from Josh 7:15, and it is this language which is taken up by the rest of the Israelites in their decision to repay Gibeah for what had happened. The Levite has (at least in part) associated the death of his concubine with the Achan story, perhaps missing the irony of his own association with it in the previous chapter. Nevertheless, all of this provides a bridge, so that a minor typological element in the first half of the story becomes a dominant one as its consequences are worked out. Placing these events within the narrative setting where "there was no king in Israel and everyone did as they saw fit" (Judg 21:24) makes clear that this was a period in Israel's life where they were indistinguishable from the Canaanites, and Achan provides a key pattern around which to shape the presentation of this story. At the same time, the use of the Achan material in Judges is distinct from that in Joshua as it extends it to explore examples of sexual misconduct and what ensues, something not present in the source material in Joshua.

SAMUEL

By far the most extensive use of the Achan material is found in Samuel, where an Achan typology is evident in both the Saul stories and the account of the rape of Tamar. There may be an echo in the story of Nabal (1 Sam 25), but this is dependent upon the word נבלה on its own, so if the typology is present it is only there very faintly. What is notable here is that the use of the typology in Samuel depends in part on material in both Joshua and Judges, whilst also introducing its own elements.

---

26. Hamley, *Unspeakable Things*, 136, notes variances between the narrator's account and his own, suggesting that this makes him "untrustworthy."

Matthew Michael has previously studied the use of the Achan material in 1 Sam 14:24—15:35, and as such we will comment on these texts fairly briefly since Michael's work has outlined some of the key elements of the typology, including highlighting certain narrative parallels between Saul and Achan such as the casting of lots after a defeat.[27] For our purposes, it is probably sufficient to note that Achan and Saul are the only two characters in the Old Testament who are said to have taken things that were חרם (Josh 7:1; 1 Sam 15:9), but we can add to this the fact that Jonathan also accuses his father of 'troubling' (עכר) the land, itself a clear allusion back to Joshua 7:25, and so part of a larger structure which builds allusion to Achan throughout.[28] But as is true with occurrences of the typology in Joshua and Judges, so also here the Achan typology is mixed with other elements. In 1 Sam 14, there is an integration of the Achan material with elements of the Jephthah story, most obviously in Saul's vow (1 Sam 14:24). Here, Saul attempts to manipulate Yahweh to act in his favor, just as Jephthah had done with his vow (Judg 11:30–32). But where Jephthah's vow had resulted in the death of his daughter,[29] Jonathan will be spared even though Saul was apparently willing to execute him (1 Sam 14:39). Moreover, in 1 Sam 14:36–42, it is Jonathan who was taken by the lot even though Saul is being patterned on Achan, as was shown by the fact that he had troubled Israel.

The typology developed here is thus a sophisticated one, and perhaps more than the parody that Michael suggests. It is capable of adapting elements through its integration of motifs from other stories which are fed into it. Most notably, the introduction of the Jephthah motif into the typology through the link between the vows just before the introduction of links to the Achan story means that we now read Saul's "troubling" of Israel as an attempt to manipulate Yahweh. This element will work itself out in Saul's final rejection as king in 1 Sam 15 when he defends his decision to spare Agag and the best of the Amalekite livestock (1 Sam 15:9) on the basis that he intended to sacrifice the animals to Yahweh (1 Sam 15:15). In this, Saul inadvertently reveals that he had placed his own wishes above those of

27. Michael, "Achan / Achor Traditions," 747–51.

28. See also David G. Firth, *1, 2 Samuel* (Nottingham: Apollos, 2009), 164–68.

29. For this reading, see David G. Firth, *Including the Stranger: Foreigners in the Former Prophets* (London: Apollos, 2019), 84.

Yahweh. This is precisely what Achan had done when he coveted the items placed under the ban (Josh 7:20–21). But the allusions to Achan (when joined to those concerning Jephthah) in 1 Sam 14 have also shown that attempting to manipulate Yahweh to serve one's own ends is also an example of this. The Achan element highlights the fact that the attempt to manipulate a deity to serve one's own interests is also a "Canaanite" act, showing the extent of Saul's failure, while also placing his decision to take the items that were חרם in the context of a wider Achan typology.

But although Michael has shown the importance of the typology in 1 Sam 14–15, his study does not consider the importance of the typology for earlier elements in the Saul story. The points of contact between Saul and Achan show that both have an extensive lineage which suggests they might be from important families (Josh 7:17–18, 1 Sam 9:1–2),[30] though this feature on its own would not necessarily be sufficient to establish the presence of the typology. But when placed into the larger context of 1 Sam 9–11, it is an element which points to its presence. This is because in addition to this element, there are numerous references to both the Achan story in Joshua and also to its reception in the story of Judg 19–21. As there, the initial reference to Achan is not a dominant element, but rather one which becomes more important as the narrative develops.

A key element to the development of the typology occurs in 1 Sam 10:17–27 when Saul is proclaimed as king at Mizpah. Although this is a relatively common toponym in Israel, there is good reason to think it is the same as the site mentioned in Judg 20:1 since in both instances it was suitable as a place for Israel to assemble. In that this involves seeing the typology through its reception in the account in Judges we might not regard this as a strong indicator until we note that there are only two accounts in the Old Testament of someone being taken by lot where the process is recorded in full, moving from tribe to father's house and then the individual concerned. There is the slight difference that whereas in Joshua the clan level is called a משפחה, here the term אלף is used, though this may be a stylistic difference reflecting the fact that the term can also be used of a military unit, and a key reason for Israel asking for a king was that he should lead them in battle (1 Sam 8:19–20). But more importantly, in both cases a niphal of the verb

---

30. Michael, "Achan / Achor Traditions," 747.

לכד is used to describe the taking of the one selected. When Joshua finally took Ai, it was also this verb that was used, pointing to its more common use of describing the capture of something or someone. These similarities show that there is a significant Achan typology present in 1 Sam 9–10, something initiated in Saul's introduction and then brought to particular focus when Saul is "taken" and then presented as the one Yahweh had chosen to be king. The typology here is present but initially undeveloped—the background it provides casts a shadow over Saul being proclaimed king, but the nature of that shadow is not yet evident. But it does mean that even in what is typically regarded as one of the "pro-monarchic"[31] elements in 1 Samuel, a major critique lurks in the background, a pattern that will be developed in what follows.

But complications to the typology are introduced here by the inclusion of elements from Judg 19–21, a text we have already noted as containing an important Achan typology. Initially, these elements are subtle but there is enough here to suggest that those developing the typology here were not only aware of the individual elements in Joshua 7 and Judg 19–21, but also that the development of the Achan typology in Judges can be explored further in the typology developed here. We can observe this by noting that the place names here are important for Judg 19–21. We have already noted the importance of Mizpah, but the striking thing to note here is the strong clustering of place names. So, Saul returned to his home in Gibeah (1 Sam 10:26), though Gibeah was also the town noted as the place where the concubine had died, and which was subsequently destroyed by the Israelites (Judg 19–21). Association with Gibeah has long been noted as a potentially negative element in the portrayal of Saul given the events in Judges, though it is not necessarily a point of criticism. Nevertheless, there are two towns destroyed in Judges 19–21, Gibeah and Jabesh-gilead (Judg 21:8–12), and it is the destruction of the latter town which is expressly linked to Canaan. In Saul's story, Jabesh-gilead is attacked by Nahash the Ammonite after his return to Gibeah. Recurrence of these place names on their own might be regarded as coincidental, but when Saul delivers Jabesh-gilead there are more explicit links to the Achan typology. Most

---

31. I am skeptical of attempts to divide 1 Samuel 8–12 into supposedly "pro-" and "anti-monarchical" sections—see Firth, *1, 2 Samuel*, 110–11—so my point is that there is no overt criticism of monarchy here. There are, however, hints of an emerging critique of Saul.

importantly, he slaughtered his oxen, sending the pieces through the country, echoing the actions of the Levite in Judg 19:29–30, the only instances in the Old Testament of acts such as this. The account of Saul's rise prior to the renewal of kingship at Gilgal, a site which does not occur in the Achan material and so breaks the typology, is thus woven through with the Achan typology.

But what might be the purpose of the typology at this point given that most of Saul's actions in these chapters are either positive or at least lacking overt points of critique.[32] That is, we might expect that an Achan typology would be deployed to provide direct criticism of someone for leading Israel towards Canaanite-like structures, but that is not particularly evident here. Rather, the typology here serves to cast a shadow over Saul's achievements, situating even them within the typology so that when the more direct connections with Achan are made in 1 Sam 14–15, these "shadows" provide readers with a frame of reference for understanding them as features that were always present in Saul's reign, even if they only became overt in those later chapters.

There is one other, though minor, occurrence of the typology in Samuel within the account of the rape of Tamar. However, as with other instances of the typology it occurs as an element within a range of intertextual links, the most prominent of which are with the rape of Dinah, though there are also numerous links to elements of the Joseph story.[33] We have, however, already noted that Judg 19 has drawn on the Dinah story as an additional element to its own Achan typology,[34] so an integration of these elements here is thus another example of Samuel drawing on the typology through its use in Judges as well as elements in the original account in Joshua. The most obvious connection to the Achan typology is that when Tamar sees that Amnon intends a sexual relationship with her, she pleads with him not to commit this נבלה. This term was, as we have noted, given prominence within the Achan story (Josh 7:15). The narrator thus characterizes

---

32. Though see Firth, *1, 2 Samuel*, 140–41 for ways there may be implicit critique.

33. For a summary of the main elements, see Firth, *1, 2 Samuel*, 434–36.

34. A common euphemism for sexual intercourse is שכב עם, but Genesis 34:7 and 2 Samuel 13:14 are the two instances where שכב is used without the preposition, both times in the context of rape. This creates a strong link between these stories.

Amnon through Tamar's speech,[35] tying Amnon's actions to those of Achan via the sexual abuse within Israel recounted in Judg 19. Throughout this section of Samuel, the background of the rape of Dinah remains prominent, so the Achan typology here is only a minor contributor to a text that is rich with association, but there is no doubt that Amnon is here portrayed as doing something that is unacceptable in Israel, and hence typical of Canaanite practice.

Samuel thus draws on the Achan typology in complex ways, making its own creative use of it by introducing it into its account of Saul as something that is initially a shadow on his seemingly more positive achievements, before using it more explicitly within its overall criticism of Saul. The more subtle element is also drawn on in the rape of Tamar, though it is not a major element there. But what is distinctive of Samuel is that it shows awareness of both the original story and also of the subsequent development of the typology within Judges. That is, it demonstrates that the typology was not fixed at one point, but rather could be drawn on in creative ways as an emerging element that could be fed into an intertextual mix.

KINGS

Of the books of the Former Prophets, Samuel has the most developed example of the Achan typology. There are, however, three instances in Kings which employ the typology. In two of these cases the connection is with the material in Joshua rather than with the developments seen in the typology in Judges and Samuel, whilst the third depends on other examples within Kings itself. The examples here are concerned with the presentation of Ahab in his conflict with Elijah, of Gehazi in the Naaman story, and Manasseh.

The first occurrence of the typology occurs when Ahab and Elijah meet in 1 Kgs 18:17–19 prior to the events on Mount Carmel. The Elijah stories as a whole make use of a significant range of typologies, most obviously in showing that Elijah is authentically a prophet like Moses.[36] As such, the connection with Achan is a small component in

---

35. So, S. Seiler, *Die Geschichte von der Thronfolge Davids (2 Sam 9–20; 1 Kön 1–2): Untersuchungen zur Literarkritik und Tendenz* (Berlin: de Gruyter, 1998), 98.

36. On this, see especially H. Dharamraj, *A Prophet Like Moses? A Narrative-Theological Reading of the Elijah Stories* (Milton Keynes: Paternoster, 2011).

the story, and of course where the typology for Elijah can be positively connected to that of Moses, here the typology is used to characterize Ahab.

The element which suggests the presence of the typology here is the double use of the verb עכר. This verb, which formed a play on Achan's name in Josh 7:25 does occur in 1 Sam 14:29 when describing Saul, but the absence of other connections to Saul's story suggests that the connection is only to the original story in Joshua 7. When Achan had been exposed, Joshua had challenged him by asking why he had troubled Israel. In an inversion of that, here Ahab initially asks Elijah if he is the one who troubled (עכר) Israel. Ahab thus attempts to characterize Elijah as the one who has troubled Israel, most likely because Elijah was the one who had announced the drought that was then afflicting the land (1 Kgs 17:1). Thus, just as Achan's sin had affected the whole nation, Ahab's claim is that Elijah is the one who has sinned and brought suffering to the nation.[37] The larger narrative context has already problematized this, so readers may see a deep irony in Ahab making this accusation. Even if the irony is not immediately noted, Elijah's response makes clear that the real troubler (עכר) of Israel is Ahab. Elijah can thus deny responsibility for the drought and declare instead that the Ahab is the source of the problem. In particular, Ahab's decision to abandon the commandments of Yahweh to serve the בעלים is the cause of Israel's troubles. Like Achan, Ahab has transgressed Yahweh's commandments, but where Achan's transgression referred to the particular application of חרם at Jericho, Ahab's related to the commandments more generally. Nevertheless, in both instances there is reference to the Decalogue, perhaps a further minor link between them, in that Achan confesses to having coveted (חמד) when he saw the prohibited items, thus referencing the tenth word of the Decalogue, whereas Ahab's decision to worship the בעלים would represent a breach of the first two words.[38] It is probably over-subtle to see this as contributing to the typology since these are

---

37. Similarly, Paul J. Kissling, *Reliable Characters in the Primary History: Profiles of Moses, Joshua, Elijah and Elisha* (Sheffield: Sheffield Academic, 1996), 111.

38. There are, of course, different ways in which the Decalogue is divided in order to achieve ten commandments. I here follow the traditional Protestant division. See further, Mark F. Rooker, *The Ten Commandments: Ethics for the Twenty-First Century* (Nashville: B&H Academic, 2010), 13–15.

clearly different commandments even if it is a further element linking these texts. Nevertheless, the clear conclusion is that Ahab is like Achan in that he has sinned, and that in doing so he has brought harm to the whole nation. Moreover, in that he has served other gods he has acted in a way similar to the Canaanites, even if strictly the form of Baal worship he introduced is that of Sidon (1 Kgs 16:31–32), thus following the pattern established by Achan.

A second example can be seen in the presentation of Gehazi in the Naaman story (2 Kgs 5), though again the Achan typology is a minor feature of the story. The most important intertext here is probably provided by Solomon's prayer of dedication for the temple since Naaman represents the type of foreigner mentioned in his petitions there (1 Kgs 8:41–43).[39] Unlike the other instances of the typology which included key linguistic connections, this one depends more upon similarities between Achan and Gehazi. Nevertheless, there are important parallels here which suggest that the typology is present, even though in this case the effect of the sin is restricted to Gehazi. In this instance, we can note that Gehazi decided to ask for both a talent of silver and two changes of clothing from Naaman, even though Elisha had previously rejected these (2 Kgs 5:15–16, 22). In the end, he received two talents of silver along with the clothing (2 Kgs 5:23). Although the parallels are not exact (since the narrator is not free to invent connections), the fact that Achan had previously taken a cloak from Shinar an two hundred shekels of silver (along with a fifty-shekel bar of gold) means that both he and Gehazi took silver and clothing that was not rightly theirs. There are obvious differences here in that the spoil from Jericho was חרם, and thus belonged to Yahweh, whereas the items Gehazi received were earlier refused by Elisha. But this is not enough to remove the typology, especially as the story concludes with Gehazi afflicted by the skin infection that had previously affected Naaman, so that the Israelite, not the foreigner, was now unclean. Gehazi's exclusion is not as severe as Achan's (and 2 Kgs 8:5 suggests his affliction was not permanent), but there is a clear reversal here that mirrors the relationship between Rahab and Achan in which Rahab enjoys the blessing of life within Israel whilst Achan's execution sees him removed from Israel.

---

39. See Firth, *Including the Stranger*, 157–58.

Our final example is seen in the presentation of the reign of Manasseh (2 Kgs 21:1–18; 22:3–4). Again, the Achan typology is present as a minor element within other components, but still contributes to the passage as a whole, not least because, for Kings, Manasseh is the king whose sin placed the whole nation under divine judgment, just as Achan had done in Joshua 7. The presentation of Manasseh contrasts with that of Hezekiah in the preceding chapters, a point made explicit in the comment in 2 Kgs 21:3, which also aligns him with Ahab. As we have noted, the Achan typology is part of Kings' presentation of Ahab, so an alignment of between Ahab and Manasseh could of itself point to the Achan connection, though on its own it would be a slender one. Overall, the presentation of Manasseh is notable for the fact that it offers a series of brief reports on his reign rather than anything that might be called "narrative." But the statement about his actions in the temple does allude to the introduction to Solomon's prayer (1 Kgs 8:22–30) in that they are, in effect, a reversal of what the temple was meant to be. Reference to Solomon's prayer also provides a link to the Naaman story, since the prayer, the Naaman story and the Manasseh account are the only places in Kings to use the verb סלח (2 Kgs 24:4), a word that was particularly important in the prayer. The report is careful instead to show that all that Manasseh had done was worse than that of the Canaanites from before Israel's entry into the land (2 Kgs 21:9), something that was core to Achan's sin. Moreover, the report goes on to show that his cultic failures also pointed to the social injustices that likewise marked his reign (2 Kgs 21:16). The absence of the elements typical of a story in his case mean that the typology is presented primarily through other texts in Kings which have drawn on it, but even though it is not developed it still contributes to the overall presentation.

CONCLUSION

Achan is introduced into the story in Joshua in a way which marks his story as one which has a high degree of eventfulness. This means it is given particular prominence, a prominence which then enables a contrast to be drawn between Achan and Rahab. In the early chapters of Joshua, Rahab is the archetypal Canaanite who becomes a part of Israel, whereas Achan is the archetypal Israelite who becomes indistinguishable from the Canaanites. Although this is a story which is complete in itself, its high level of eventfulness makes it a story which is likely to be important for subsequent stories within the Former Prophets since, irrespective of the particular model of composition followed, these books are clearly linked and to be read in light of one another.

Accordingly, it has been possible to trace various ways in which a typology which is rooted in Achan's story, though often merged with others, is found across the Former Prophets. Indeed, it is notable that the first use of the typology occurs within Joshua in the conflict over the altar in Josh 22. Although the potential sin involved there is clearly different from that of Achan (and in fact did not happen), the perception was that it was a sin which affected the whole nation, making the typology with Achan appropriate. Judges retains this element as it draws on the typology in the account of the outrage at Gibeon, providing clear linguistic links to Josh 7 whilst also integrating this typology into others, especially the Sodom story from Gen 19. Once again, the implication of the sin affects all Israel. Samuel develops the typology differently, though especially in its lesser use of it in the account of Amnon's rape of Tamar in 2 Sam 13, it shows awareness of the integration of elements in Judges. The typology is an important element that runs through the whole of 1 Sam 9–15, providing a mechanism for assessing Saul. A distinctive element here is that the negative elements of the typology only become explicit in the latter chapters of this section of the book, the typology being used to cast a shadow on Saul's earlier achievements before the more explicit criticisms of him are made. Kings also makes use of the typology, but in a more limited way, using it to show characters within Israel who have ceased to live distinctively as Israelites.

These examples all show that Achan is an important figure for the Former Prophets as a whole, but that although each book receives the tradition about him, each uses the typology in slightly different ways. In part, these variances are conditioned by the particular stories each book needs to tell, but the creativity of each in adapting this typology to enlighten these stories means we need to be careful not to flatten down the ways in which the typology can be deployed. Rather, awareness of the typology needs to be explored in each instance while allowing for the possibility of different compositional patterns and processes.

[*JESOT* 7.2 (2021): 37–71]

The Concept of Discipleship in Deuteronomy: Literary and Lexical Insights into Following YHWH

RICHARD FLOYD

floy2992@lbc.edu
Lancaster Bible College, Capital Seminary and Graduate School
Lancaster, PA 17601

ABSTRACT: Contemporary scholarship on the topic of discipleship has largely neglected the Old Testament as having any relevance. Yet, many would argue that Jesus extensively used the Old Testament in his teaching and formation of his disciples. What, then, could we say that the Old Testament contributes toward a more holistic concept of Christian discipleship? This study examines the literary structure and several lexical cues in order to discern a concept of discipleship in the book of Deuteronomy. The literary structure of the book of Deuteronomy reveals the book as a covenant manual for Israel's discipleship to YHWH, and a lexical study of use of למד, "to teach/learn," and הלך אחרי, "to walk after" or "to follow" in Deuteronomy yields a view that discipleship in the book of Deuteronomy entails learning YHWH's word so as to maintain exclusive covenant devotion to him. Several of these concepts find a close parallel with Jesus' method of making disciples. Therefore, the best way forward for formal scholarly inquiries into the topic of discipleship to Jesus would do well to glean first from the teachings of YHWH's discipleship of Israel in the Old Testament.

KEY WORDS: Discipleship, Deuteronomy, Learn, Follow, Torah

INTRODUCTION

Discipleship[1] within the Christian church is typically understood as a distinctly New Testament topic. The vast majority of both popular and scholarly books and articles on discipleship immediately turn to Jesus' method of disciple making before turning to contemporary church programs and teachings on discipleship to Jesus.[2] What is often overlooked in this focus solely on the New Testament for the concept of discipleship is an almost complete neglect of the contributions of the Old Testament toward the concept of Christian discipleship.[3] Part of

---

1. The English "disciple" is derived from the Latin *discipulus*, used in the Vulgate to render the Hebrew למוד (*limmūd*) in Isa 8:16, and more prominently to render the New Testament μαθητής (*mathētēs*, "disciple") as well as the verb form μαθητεύω (*mathēteuō*, "to disciple" or "to make disciples"); Michael Wilkins offers a helpful definition of "disciple": "The English word *disciple* normally designates a 'follower,' 'adherent' or 'student' of a great master, religious leader or teacher" (emphasis original) in Michael J. Wilkins, "Disciples and Discipleship," in *Dictionary of Jesus and the Gospels*, ed. Joel B. Green et al., 2nd ed. (Nottingham, UK: InterVarsity, 2013), 202.

2. Several discipleship studies turn to the wider New Testament context, examining discipleship terms other than the explicit word μαθητής due to this term being absent from the New Testament outside of the Gospels and Acts. Organized alphabetically, these studies include: James Gregory Lawson, "Patterns of Discipleship in the New Testament as Evidenced by Jesus and Peter" (PhD, Southwestern Baptist Theological Seminary, 2013); Richard N. Longenecker, ed., *Patterns of Discipleship in the New Testament* (Grand Rapids, MI: William B. Eerdmans, 1996); Andrew Ryder, *Following Christ: Models of Discipleship in the New Testament* (Franklin, WI: Sheed & Ward, 1999); Fernando F. Segovia, ed., *Discipleship in the New Testament* (Philadelphia: Fortress, 1985); Wilkins, *Following the Master: A Biblical Theology of Discipleship* (Grand Rapids, MI: Zondervan, 1992); N. T. Wright, *Following Jesus: Biblical Reflections on Discipleship* (Grand Rapids, MI: Eerdmans, 2014).

3. Aside from articles on "learn," and "follow" in *TDNT, TDOT, NIDNTT(E), NIDOTTE*, and a few other "disciple" entries in various other theological dictionaries, the following resources represent the most significant scholarly treatments of the topic of discipleship in the Old Testament: David Birger Pedersen, "Torah, Discipleship and Suffering: An Historical Study of the Development of Interrelated Themes in the Old Testament, Post-Biblical Judaism and the Synoptic Gospels" (ThD, Union Theological Seminary in Virginia, 1971); J. W. McKay, "Man's Love for God in Deuteronomy and the Father/Teacher--Son/Pupil Relationship," *VT* 22.4 (October 1, 1972): 426–35; Michael Wilkins, "The Old Testament Background," in *Discipleship in the Ancient World and Matthew's Gospel*, 2nd ed. (Eugene, OR: Wipf & Stock, 2015), 43–91; Michael Wilkins, "The People Called to Follow God: Discipleship in the Old Testament," in *Following the Master*, 51–69; Charles David Isbell, "The *Limmûdîm* in the Book of Isaiah," *JSOT* 34.1 (September 1, 2009): 99–109; Karen Kogler, "Ch. 3: Disciple Narratives and Teachings in Scripture, Old Testament" in "Disciples in the First Century" (Masters in

the reason for this neglect of the Old Testament in formal discipleship studies is an argument that due to the lack of "disciple" words in the Old Testament there is, therefore, no concept of discipleship present in the Old Testament.[4] As a result of this entrenched view, that discipleship is solely a New Testament concept, scholarship on the concept of

---

Theology, Concordia University, 2009), 36–38; Richard Hicks, "Markan Discipleship According to Malachi: The Significance of Mὴ Ἀποστερήσῃς in the Story of the Rich Man (Mark 10:17–22)," *JBL* 132.1 (2013): 179–99; Russell L. Huizing, "The Importance of Ritual for Follower Development: An Intertexture Analysis of Leviticus 23 in the Pauline Corpus" (PhD diss., Regent University, 2013); Frederick Cardoza, "A History of Disciple-Making: The Old Testament and Intertestamental Periods," in *ED 205, Discipleship in History and Practice*, Logos Mobile Education (Bellingham, WA: Lexham, 2016).

4. Cf. Gerhard Kittel, who says that the verb ἀκολουθέω in the LXX has "no religious significance . . . [and is the] following of a respected person . . . [and] little more than a relationship of respect" in Gerhard Kittel, "ἀκολουθέω," *TDNT*, 1:212–13; cf. also Karl Rengstorf, who argues that the absence of the terms תלמיד and μαθητής (LXX) in the OT indicates an absence of the concept of discipleship in the OT: "If the term is missing, so, too, is that which it serves to denote. Apart from the formal relation of teacher and pupil, the OT, unlike the classical Greek world and Hellenism, has no master-disciple relation. Whether among the prophets or the scribes we seek in vain for anything corresponding to it" in "μανθάνω," *TDNT*, 4:427; Following Kittel and Rengstorf, *NIDNTT* (favorable to examining the Hebrew background to NT words) similarly found an absence of the concept of discipleship in the OT based on the lack of "disciple" words there: Christian Blendinger notes, "There are no OT precedents for the more specific New Testament usage of *akoloutheō*" in Christian Blendinger, "ἀκολουθέω," *NIDNTT*, 1:481; further, Dietrich Müller asserts, "The lack of any OT vocabulary for a learner, such as the teacher-pupil relationship describes, is bound up with Israel's consciousness of being an elect people. What the individual Israelite has to learn in respect of God's will does not make him a 'pupil' in relation to his 'master,' God. For even as a learner the individual always remains a part of the whole chosen people, all of whom encounter in the divine Word the authority of the Electing One. This excludes any possibility of a disciple-master relationship between men because even the priest and the prophet do not teach on their own authority," in Dietrich Müller, "μαθητής," *NIDNTT*, 1:485; In her 2009 master's thesis, Karen Kogler echoes the sentiments of Kittel and Rengstorf, in Karen Kogler, "Disciples in the First Century" (Masters in Theology, Concordia University, 2009), 36–38; Finally, in Moisés Silva's update of *NIDNTT* (*NIDNTTE*), he prefers the LXX background to NT words, which causes him to neglect background Hebrew terms. However, Silva does provide a helpful correction to Kittel and Rengstorf when he says, "it is doubtful that so much should be built on the fact that a term for 'learner' is virtually absent in the OT," in Moisés Silva, "μαθητής," *NIDNTTE*, 3:222. Silva's correction seems to be too little, too late, as the vast majority of both popular and scholarly studies on discipleship have either downplayed or entirely neglected or rejected the concept of discipleship as deriving (either at all or in part) from the Old Testament.

discipleship in the Old Testament is sparse. This makes the scholarship of discipleship on individual books within the Old Testament biblical croups almost nonexistent.

What follows is an attempt to discern a concept of discipleship from the Old Testament beginning in the book of Deuteronomy.[5] Instead of a comprehensive survey of first-century CE disciple-making and the oral or literary sources used in the process of disciple-making, this study presupposes that Jesus' form of discipleship is primarily based on the teachings found in the Jewish Scriptures of his day, primarily the Hebrew Bible.[6] Based on this assumption, that Jesus' primary source material and the foundation for his paradigm for disciple-making derives mainly from the Hebrew Bible, it is expected that connections will be found between Jesus' form of disciple-making and that of YHWH[7] in the Hebrew Bible, and particularly in the book of Deuteronomy. The thesis of this study, then, is that a concept of discipleship can be found in the Old Testament, as evidenced by the book of Deuteronomy, and that Jesus' form of disciple-making bears a striking similarity to YHWH's form of disciple-making found in Deuteronomy.

METHOD

This study examines the concept of discipleship in the Old Testament in the book of Deuteronomy by appealing to the literary structure of Deuteronomy and a comparative lexical study between Deuteronomy and the New Testament. This study first examines the literary genre and structure of the book of Deuteronomy in order to discern any possibility

5. An examination of discipleship in both Jewish and non-Jewish groups has been done by Wilkins in *Discipleship in the Ancient World and Matthew's Gospel*, 2nd ed. (Eugene, OR: Wipf & Stock, 2015), 11–125. However, Wilkins' study was largely based on the term μαθητής (though it also looked at sociological relationships). The present study finds no fault in Wilkins' work, only that Wilkins's purpose was limited to a single term. The present author hopes to expand on Wilkins' work from his Ch. 2 "The Old Testament Background" to the NT use of μαθητής. This article, and the ThM thesis that this article derives from, are the beginnings of this author's exploration of the concept of discipleship in the Old Testament; cf. Richard C. Floyd, "Discipleship in Deuteronomy" (ThM, La Mirada, CA, Talbot School of Theology, Biola University, 2016).

6. Throughout this study Hebrew Bible and Old Testament are used interchangeably.

7. The transliteration of YHWH will be used throughout this study to reflect the Hebrew יהוה, the personal name of the God of Israel in the Old Testament.

that the book of Deuteronomy may have functioned within a context of ancient Israelite discipleship. A literary examination of Deuteronomy illuminates a sort of master/pupil relationship or an instructional relationship between master and servant, with the text of Deuteronomy functioning as a sort of manual on discipleship to YHWH. Second, this study examines "disciple" words in the book of Deuteronomy based on a comparative lexical study between Deuteronomy and the New Testament in order to discern the terminological contribution toward a Christian concept of discipleship from the book of Deuteronomy. In other words, if "disciple" terms can be shown to be present in the text of the Deuteronomy, then the concept of discipleship would necessarily seem to be present also. Yet, a comparative study of NT and OT terms relating to a concept of discipleship has the potential to be particularly anachronistic (reading an NT concept back into the OT). In order to avoid an anachronistic view of the theology of Deuteronomy, therefore, this study will attempt first to understand a concept of Israelite discipleship in Deuteronomy on its own terms before drawing contemporary Christian implications for discipleship to Jesus. Concluding this exploration of the book of Deuteronomy, this study will briefly examine Jesus' form of discipleship and draw several Christian implications as well as suggest topics for further study.

DISCIPLESHIP IN DEUTERONOMY

Why begin a study on discipleship in the Old Testament in the book of Deuteronomy? Why not begin this study in Genesis? One answer would be that the book of Deuteronomy represents a biblical and theological hinge for the Old and New Testaments. Daniel Block notes, "This book provides the theological base for virtually the entire First Testament and the paradigm for much of its literary style."[8] Thus, if the goal of the present study is to refute the idea that a concept of discipleship is not present in the Old Testament, the book of Deuteronomy seems to be a prime candidate for beginning such an inquiry. If the concept of discipleship can be discerned as present in the book of Deuteronomy, then the concept would also likely be present in the literary work that

---

8. Daniel I. Block, "'Do You Hear What I Hear?': Reflections on the Genre and Message of Deuteronomy," in *The Triumph of Grace: Literary and Theological Studies in Deuteronomy and Deuteronomic Themes* (Eugene, OR: Cascade, 2017), 47.

both precedes and follows it.[9] In other words, discerning a concept of discipleship in Deuteronomy is the contextual, literary, lexical, and theological key to understanding the concept in the rest of the Old Testament and into the New Testament.

Interpreting Deuteronomy[10]

If there is a concept of discipleship in Deuteronomy, then why does this concept seem to have been overlooked both in scholarship and in the life of the church? This is perhaps because "Christians have never developed an adequate approach to interpreting Torah, so they neglect it."[11] Thus, not only is the concept of discipleship in the Old Testament almost entirely neglected, but so is the study of the book of Deuteronomy itself widely neglected in the teaching of the church today.

9. Gen through Num of the Torah of Moses, and the so-called Deuteronomic History as well as other OT books that draw on Deuteronomic themes and language. More importantly for contemporary Christian discipleship, this Deuteronomic understanding of discipleship is the primary background for understanding Jesus' form of discipleship and that of the wider New Testament; Throughout this study, Mosaic authorship of Deuteronomy is assumed.

10. Cf. the various recent works aimed (primarily) at Christian interpretation and application of Deuteronomy: J. Daniel Hays, "Applying the Old Testament Law Today," *BibSac* 158,.629 (2001): 21–35; Joe M. Sprinkle, *Biblical Law and Its Relevance: A Christian Understanding and Ethical Application for Today of the Mosaic Regulations* (Lanham, MD: University Press of America, 2006); Block, "Preaching Old Testament Law to New Testament Christians," *Hiphil* 3.1 (2006): 1–24; Daniel Joslyn-Siemiatkoski, "'Moses Received the Torah at Sinai and Handed It on' (*Mishnah Avot* 1:1):TheRel evanceof t heWr it t enandOr al Tor ahfor Chr ist ians,"*AnglicanTheological Review* 91.3 (June 1, 2009): 443–66; Christopher J. H. Wright, "Preaching from the Law," in *Reclaiming the Old Testament for Christian Preaching* (Downers Grove, IL: IVP Academic, 2010), 47–63; Terence E. Fretheim, "What Biblical Scholars Wish Pastors Would Start or Stop Doing about Ethical Issues in the Old Testament," *Word & World* 31.3 (2011): 297–306; Block, *The Gospel According to Moses: Theological and Ethical Reflections on the Book of Deuteronomy* (Eugene, OR: Cascade, 2012); Philip S. Johnston and David G. Firth, eds., *Interpreting Deuteronomy: Issues and Approaches* (Downers Grove, IL: InterVarsity, 2012); J. Gordon McConville, "Biblical Law and Human Formation," *Political Theology* 14.5 (October 2013): 628–40; Patrick D. Miller, "'That You May Live': Dimensions of Law in Deuteronomy," in *Concepts of Law in the Sciences, Legal Studies, and Theology* (Tübingen: Mohr Siebeck, 2013), 137–57; Roy E. Gane, *Old Testament Law for Christians: Original Context and Enduring Application* (Grand Rapids, MI: Baker Academic, 2017).

11. Mark E. Biddle, *Deuteronomy* (Macon, GA: Smyth & Helwys, 2003), 11.

The problem is compounded as one attempts to discern how the church is to "follow Jesus" based on seemingly obscure food[12] or boundary laws? Further, does one understand Moses' teaching on warfare as instruction in Israelite discipleship to YHWH or Christian discipleship to Jesus? To answer these questions, one must seek to understand the book of Deuteronomy first in its literary context. According to Peter Craigie, "The basic principle for interpreting the theology of Deuteronomy rests upon its character as a covenant document. It is the covenant, then, that provides the framework within which the details of theology are to be expressed."[13] Thus, covenant is the literary and theological place to begin interpreting[14] the book of Deuteronomy.

Deuteronomy as Covenantal Discipleship

As a conclusion to the Torah[15] overall, Deuteronomy solidifies, one might say "concludes,"[16] the covenant that YHWH began with Abraham in Genesis. In Gen 15:7 YHWH begins his covenant with Abraham saying, "I am YHWH, who brought you out from Ur of the Chaldeans to give you this land to possess."[17] This phrase of YHWH

---

12. Cf. the command not to boil a young goat in its mother's milk (Deut 14:21)

13. Peter C. Craigie, *The Book of Deuteronomy*, NICOT (Grand Rapids, MI: Eerdmans, 1976), 36.

14. Several other interpretive approaches of note have been the "moral instruction" view of Torah represented by G. K. Beale in *A New Testament Biblical Theology: The Unfolding of the Old Testament in the New* (Grand Rapids, MI: Baker Academic, 2011), 872, and the "derived principles" view represented by Walter Kaiser Jr. in *Toward an Exegetical Theology: Biblical Exegesis for Preaching and Teaching* (Grand Rapids, MI: Baker, 1981), 152; Responding to these views, John H. Walton and J. Harvey Walton advocate for interpreting Deuteronomy as "aspective reflections of wisdom," in which "the Torah is not offering binding principles or rules. Consequently, there is no ought of any kind," in *The Lost World of the Torah: Law as Covenant and Wisdom in Ancient Context*, by John H. Walton and J. Harvey Walton (Downers Grove: InterVarsity, 2019), 162.

15. "Torah" will be used throughout this study in reference to the Five Books of Moses, or the Pentateuch (Genesis through Deuteronomy).

16. McConville, "Book of Deuteronomy," in *Dictionary of the Old Testament: Pentateuch* (*DOTP*), edited by T. Desmond Alexander and David W. Baker (Downers Grove, IL: InterVarsity, 2003), 183.

17. Unless otherwise noted, all Scripture references and quotations are translated by

is echoed throughout the rest of Torah,[18] culminating in YHWH's covenantal conclusion in the Deuteronomy version of the Decalogue, "I am YHWH your God, who brought you out of the land of Egypt, out of the house of slavery" (Deut 5:6; cf. also ברית, *bərît*, "covenant" in 5:2–3). Here, the call to discipleship may be considered as the Master (YHWH) calling his disciples (collectively Israel), beginning with Abraham, and culminating in the restatement of that call in the Decalogue, also called "His Covenant" (Deut 5:6–21).[19]

With the call of YHWH in the Decalogue (Deut 5:6), the call to exclusive devotion in Words 1–2 (no other gods, no images), the call to "imitate"[20] YHWH's rescuing Israel from Egypt in Word 4 (giving slaves Sabbath rest), the Decalogue might be considered to be an example of covenantal discipleship: YHWH is the master who calls and commands; Israel is the disciple who responds in obedience, follows YHWH's example, and imitates the Master. Thus, discipleship as covenant is a theme carried through Torah, and discipleship is offered as a culmination of covenant obedience in Torah in the Decalogue.

Further, Deuteronomy is not simply understood as containing the covenant between Israel and YHWH. Deuteronomy *is* a covenant,[21] and is similar to other ancient Near Eastern (ANE) covenant texts and ceremonies. In terms of Near Eastern treaties, Deuteronomy as covenant

---

this author. At times, the English Standard Version (ESV) will be quoted for comparison.

18. Cf. "I am YHWH" in Exod 6:6–7; 20:2; 29:46; Lev 11:44–45; 22:32–33; Num 15:41; Deut 5:6.

19. That is, YHWH's covenant is represented by the Decalogue that YHWH spoke directly from Horeb (and subsequently wrote on the two tablets of stone): "And he declared to you *his covenant*, which he commanded you to do, *that is, the Ten Words*, and he wrote them on two tablets of stone" (Deut 4:13; 9:9, 11; cf. Exod 19:16—20:21; 24:12; 31:18). Note also the suzerain-vassal context below.

20. Although the theme of imitation is not the focus of this study, it is of note that the Decalogue emphasizes imitation of YHWH as covenantal obedience: The Israelites are to give their servants rest on the Sabbath in remembrance of the way that YHWH himself brought Israel out from slavery in Egypt (Deut 5:14–15). In the Exodus version, the Israelites "imitate" YHWH by resting on the seventh day as YHWH himself rested on the seventh day of creation (Exod 20:8–11).

21. McConville, "Book of Deuteronomy," 184; For additional reference, see the extensive analysis in Kenneth A. Kitchen and Paul J. N. Lawrence, *Treaty, Law and Covenant in the Ancient Near East*, 3 vols. (Wiesbaden, Germany: Harrassowitz, 2012); cf. also Walton and Walton, *Lost World of the Torah*, 46–53.

can be seen in the way the structure of the book follows an ancient Near Eastern treaty pattern. Deuteronomy contains:

1. A preamble announcing the treaty and those who are party to it (Deut 1:1–5)
2. An historical prologue rehearsing the previous relations between the parties (Deut 1:6—4:49)
3. General stipulations (Deut 5–11)
4. Specific stipulations (Deut 12–26)
5. A deposition of the document for the purpose of continuity and public reading (Deut 27:1–10; 31:9–29)
6. Witnesses (Deut 32)
7. Blessings and curses (Deut 27:12–26; 28:1–68)[22]

As a structured covenant relationship document, the book of Deuteronomy has a twofold purpose. The book orients Israel to YHWH, and it describes YHWH's orientation toward Israel. Craigie says, "The treaty structure of the covenant was a reminder to the people of their liberty in this world [God's work] and of their total commitment to God [Israel's response]."[23] Thus, as a covenant document, Deuteronomy can and should be considered more formally as a manual for Israelite "discipleship" to YHWH *in* their covenantal relationship to him. In other

22. McConville, "Book of Deuteronomy," 184–85; Note also the "sermon" structure of the book. Block refers to the broad sections of Deuteronomy as "addresses" and calls Moses a "pastor" in Block, *Deuteronomy*, The NIV Application Commentary (NIVAC), (Grand Rapids, MI: Zondervan, 2012), 36–37; cf. also Deuteronomy as "a series of addresses" in Martin J. Selman in "Law," in *DOTP*, 503; As understood from the cursing section of Deuteronomy, the vassal status of Israel as YHWH's disciple means that Israel will be held accountable for transgressing the covenant and subsequently disciplined (cf. Deut 27:9–26; 28:15–68). Thus, for Israel, all activity (including murder and obedience to parents in the "Ten Words" of YHWH's covenant in Deut 5:6–21) is conducted in the realm of relationship to YHWH, and may thus be properly understood as a part of Israel's discipleship to YHWH; The implications of the vassal covenant partner status of Israel as it corresponds to the Christian's relationship to Jesus should seem evident. All of life and every human relationship is lived out in the Christian's covenant relationship to Jesus (cf. Jesus' reference to his disciples entering into covenant with him in the Lord's table in Matt 26:27–28). Jesus will, thus, discipline his disciples for transgressing the terms of the covenant (cf. John 15:2, 6), and the disciples recognize that every aspect of life and every relationship is in some way a part of the Christian's discipleship to Jesus (cf. Col 3:23–24).

23. Craigie, *The Book of Deuteronomy*, 37.

words, Deuteronomy may be understood as a covenantal instruction manual[24] for *how* Israelites are to relate to YHWH as his followers.

DEUTERONOMY AS INSTRUCTION IN WISDOM, A MANUAL FOR DISCIPLESHIP

In addition to a formal covenant document, as theological literature Deuteronomy may also function as biblical "wisdom," John H. Walton and J. Harvey Walton argue against understanding Deuteronomy as an-cient "law code" and instead argue that "Torah" is better understood as Wisdom Literature.[25] According to Walton and Walton, "the issues that Scripture addresses have to do with wisdom and covenant fidelity, not with legislation and its rules that must be obeyed."[26] Thus, as wisdom, the entire book of Deuteronomy may be understood as *instruction in Wisdom.*[27] David Firth further describes the book of Deuteronomy as

---

24. Note the similarity between Deuteronomy as a manual for covenant relationship between Israel and YHWH and the book of Matthew as a "manual" for Christian discipleship to Jesus. Wilkins calls Matthew's Gospel a "manual" in Wilkins, *Matthew*, NIVAC (Grand Rapids, MI: Zondervan, 2004), 200.

25. Cf. Walton and Walton, *Lost World of the Torah*, 39.

26. Walton and Walton, *Lost World of the Torah*, 44; Despite Walton and Walton's view, there does seem to be an imperatival thrust in the book of Deuteronomy in all of the commands to "keep" and to "do" (cf. Deut 4:6; 6:17–18; 7:12; 13:18 [19]; 17:19; 29:9 [8]). In addition to "keeping" and "doing," frequent other "doing" kinds of words involved in the commandments and statutes of YHWH in Deuteronomy include: "love," "fear," "obey," "walk in His ways," "serve," and "turn" to YHWH (cf. Deut 6:2; 8:6; 10:12–13; 13:4 [5], 18 [19]; 17:19; 19:9; 26:17; 27:10; 28:9, 45–47; 30:8, 10, 16). Block refers to these collocated terms as "The Dimensions of Divine Expectation" (cf. Block's diagram of a hand in Fig. 1.1) in Block, *The Triumph of Grace*, 11. These terms are evenly spread throughout the book of Deuteronomy (indicating literary cohesiveness), and are collocated throughout the book indicating widespread overlap of the theological/spiritual connotations of what it means to "follow" YHWH in the book of Deuteronomy. While I would agree with Walton and Walton that the book is not a prescriptive code of rules to follow, I also note that the emphasis of the book is on obedience not to a code but to a person, YHWH; [Brackets] are used throughout to indicate differences between English, Hebrew, and Greek versification.

27. Rather than the well-known English word "law," a better gloss for the Hebrew תורה (*tôrâ*, "Torah") would be "instruction," as derived from III-ירה (*yrh*) meaning "to teach."

"a programme of catechesis."[28] The "Statutes and Judgments" section (Deut 12–26),[29] more narrowly, can be considered as a "manual" for education or instruction in covenant relationship between Israel and YHWH.[30] Moshe Weinfeld says, "On the whole the Deuteronomic code constitutes a manual for the king and the people."[31] Thus, Deuteronomy is an organized, instructional, covenantal, religious program of Israelite discipleship to YHWH. This is vastly different from the view that many have of the book of Deuteronomy (or Torah as a whole) as "law," or as a "law code." The Torah, then, is far more interested in how Israelites relate to YHWH in obedience, than in a formal list of impersonal commands.

STRUCTURE OF THE חקים AND משפטים, THE "STATUTES AND JUDGMENTS"[32] OF DEUT 12–26: EXPANSION OF THE DECALOGUE

The חקים and משפטים (*hū qqîm* and *miš paṭîm*), the so-called "Statutes and Judgments" of Deut 12–26, are considered by some scholars as an expansion of the Decalogue. Martin Selman notes, "a particularly close link exists between the laws in chapters 12–26 and the addresses of chapters 5–11."[33] Additionally, the laws themselves show evidence of an internal structure and organization. According to

28. Firth, "Passing on the Faith in Deuteronomy," in Johnston and Firth, *Interpreting Deuteronomy*, 164.

29. This is the so-called "Deuteronomic Code."

30. This section can also be understood as an expansion of the Decalogue; cf. John H. Walton, "The Decalogue Structure of the Deuteronomic Law," in Johnston and Firth, *Interpreting Deuteronomy*, 93–117.

31. Moshe Weinfeld, *Deuteronomy 1–11: A New Translation with Introduction and Commentary*, vol. 5, AB (1991, Reprint, London: Yale University, 2008), 55.

32. While the phrase חקים and משפטים (*ḥūqqîm* and *mišpaṭîm*) is often rendered "statutes and rules," (cf. Deut 4:1 in ESV), these Hebrew terms will be referred to as "statutes and judgments" here to emphasize the wisdom and instruction nature of the Torah.

33. Selman, "Law," 503; cf. Stephen A. Kaufman, "The Structure of the Deuteronomic Law," *Maarav* 1 (1979): 105–58; Georg Braulik, "The Sequence of the Laws in Deuteronomy 12–26 and in the Decalogue," in *A Song of Power and the Power of Song: Essays on the Book of Deuteronomy*, 313–35; Walton, "The Decalogue Structure of the Deuteronomic Law," 93–117.

Stephen Kaufman, some scholars characterize the Deuteronomic law "as revealing no intelligible principle of arrangement."[34] Kaufman, however, argues that "the order of the individual laws of the Decalogue is followed in precise detail" throughout the Deuteronomic law.[35] Kaufman views the "Deuteronomic Code" as intentionally patterned after the Decalogue.[36] Although Block disagrees that the Decalogue is the pattern after which the "Statutes and Judgments" are expanded, he does affirm the Decalogue as "the fountainhead from which later revelation springs and on which it will expound."[37] Thus, cognizant of Block's caution, it is the argument of this study that the specific laws of Deut 12–26 are expansions or explications of the Decalogue. In other words, the individual laws of Deut 12–26 are *how* a disciple of YHWH "does" the covenantal discipleship principles of the Decalogue.

If the "Statutes and Judgments" (Deut 12–26) follow the ordering of the Decalogue, then specific laws in this section may be related back to each "Word" of the Decalogue, and principles of contemporary application might be better made.[38] In essence, with a better understanding of how certain (seemingly obscure) laws in the core material of Deuteronomy relate to YHWH's covenantal discipleship principles in the Decalogue, disciples of YHWH may better utilize Deuteronomy as a manual for discipleship in their daily lives.[39]

34. Kaufman, "The Structure of the Deuteronomic Law," 108.

35. Kaufman, "The Structure of the Deuteronomic Law," 112.

36. Cf. Braulik, "The Sequence of the Laws in Deuteronomy 12–26 and in the Decalogue," 313–35; Walton, "The Decalogue Structure of the Deuteronomic Law," 93–117; Block disagrees with seeing Deuteronomy 12–26 as an expansion of the Decalogue, saying, "this approach seems forced," in *Deuteronomy*, 301; cf. Jeffrey H. Tigay, *Deuteronomy* דברים (Philadelphia: The Jewish Publication Society, 1996), 451n19.

37. Block, *Deuteronomy*, 159.

38. A specific connection will be made below in examining the theme of exclusive devotion to YHWH in Deuteronomy 13 in the section, "Excursus: 'Utter Destruction,' חרם, in Deuteronomy 13 *as* Discipleship in Deuteronomy."

39. This might also be Jesus' method of interpretation of Deuteronomy 12–26 in the Sermon on the Mount (Matt 5:21–30) where Jesus *expands* the sixth and seventh "Words" of the Decalogue (no murder or adultery); cf. also John H. Walton, "Deuteronomy: An Exposition of the Spirit of the Law," *Grace Theological Journal* 8.2 (September 1, 1987): 225.

Summary of the Literary Context of Deuteronomy

Although Deuteronomy is a difficult book to interpret, careful attention to the literary structure of the book yields an ability to discern instruction in discipleship to YHWH. As a covenant document, Deuteronomy orients disciples to YHWH and reveals to disciples YHWH's requirement of exclusive devotion. YHWH calls his disciples into a covenantal discipleship relationship with him as between a master and a servant. As biblical wisdom, Deuteronomy is intended to be taught as a manual on discipleship to YHWH. The Decalogue of Deuteronomy is the covenantal/theological grounding for the explications of those covenantal discipleship principles in the laws of Deut 12–26, which are traditionally difficult to interpret. Thus, in order to understand discipleship to YHWH in Deuteronomy, one must understand that discipleship is instruction in covenantal obedience to YHWH.[40] In addition to the literary structure of Deuteronomy, certain "disciple" words used throughout this document also show evidence of a distinct "discipleship" context in the book of Deuteronomy.

"TO TEACH/LEARN" AND "FOLLOW": DISCIPLE WORDS IN DEUTERONOMY[41]

The Hebrew terms למד (*lmd*, "to learn" in the *Qal* stem and "to teach" in the *Piel*) and הלך אחרי (*hālak 'aḥărê*, "to follow"[42] or lit. "to walk

40. Cf. Wilkins, who describes Old Testament discipleship broadly as "the covenant relationship between Israel and God" in "Disciple, Discipleship," in *EDBT*, 175.

41. Throughout this section, Scripture references of "to teach," "to learn," and "to follow" in Deuteronomy will be italicized for emphasis.

42. Hebrew does not have a designated verb for the English word/concept of "follow." The closest single "following" verb in the Old Testament is רדף (*rdp*), but this word carries a more intensified connotation of "pursuit," often in a military context (cf. Deut 11:4). In a wartime scenario, one army or group of soldiers pursues another, typically with an intent to destroy the other. Similarly, individuals may pursue other individuals with a goal of the destruction of the one pursued (cf. Deut 19:6). In Judg 3:28, רדף is used to indicate following a leader into battle. Only occasionally is the word used hyperbolically to describe an intense pursuit of a person or idea, an ideological pursuit or "following" (cf. Deut 16:20; Isa 51:1; Ps 23:6). Aside from רדף, however, the more typical phrase for the idea of "following," would be the preposition אחר paired with הלך (and less frequently, other uses of אחר with a different helping verb: נקש אחר, "to ensnare to follow," מלא אחר, lit. "to be full after" or "to follow fully,"

after")[43] are parallel to the Greek "to teach/learn" words of μαθητής (*mathētēs*, "disciple") and μανθάνω (*manthanō* "to learn"), and the "follow" words of ἀκολουθέω (*akoloutheō*, "to follow") and πορεύω ὀπίσω (*poreuō opisō*, "to go after"). What follows is an attempt to discern the possibility that למד and הלך אחרי can be understood in a discipleship context in the Old Testament, and specifically in Deuteronomy.

Deuteronomy is pastoral, catechetical, and pedagogical. The book is intended to teach the "way of YHWH,"[44] and how disciples "follow" that way. The structure of Deuteronomy provides a relational/covenantal context in which discipleship to YHWH happens, but doesn't reveal the explicit "disciple" language noted above in typical discipleship contexts and studies. Thus, an examination of these terms adds to the weight of evidence that suggests the presence of a concept of discipleship in Deuteronomy, and, by implication, throughout the wider Old Testament.

To Learn and Teach, למד in Deuteronomy

The Hebrew למד does not occur in Torah before Deuteronomy. Prior to Deuteronomy, other words are used for "to teach" or "to learn."[45]

סור מאחרי, "to turn from following," and זנה אחר, "to whore after," used typically in contrast to following YHWH). The focus of this paper is the אחר "follow" idiom using the verb הלך. In addition to these "follow" words, one other idiom may provide some illumination of a concept of discipleship in the Old Testament, and particularly in the book of Deuteronomy: The idea of imitation or emulation, which in the New Testament is typically associated with the words μιμητής (*mimētēs*, "imitator") and μιμέομαι (*mimeomai*, "to imitate"), in the Old Testament is a phrase composed of the Hebrew words עשה כ (*'āśāh kə* "to do like"; cf. Deut 18:19; 20:18). Due to the limits of this study (למד and אחר in Deuteronomy) neither רדף or עשה כ will be examined at length here.

43. Throughout this study this idiom is to be referred to as the אחר "follow" idiom.

44. Cf. the consistent emphasis of the דרך יהוה (*drk yhwh*, "way of YHWH") evenly spread throughout Deuteronomy: 5:33; 8:6; 9:12, 16; 10:12; 11:22, 28; 13:5 [6]; 19:9; 26:17; 28:9; 30:16; 31:29; 32:4. This usage is also evidence of the literary and theological coherence of the book of Deuteronomy.

45. The common "knowing" and "seeing" words are also used to denote the concept of teaching or learning, such as ידע (*yd'*, "to know"), and ראה (*r'h*, "to see"); Another word that has a "teaching" or "learning" context includes: III-ירה (*yrh*), from which the participle III-מורה (*môreh*, "the teacher"), and the substantive III-תורה (*tôrâ*, "instruction") are derived. III-ירה occurs twelve times in the Torah of Moses (four

In Deuteronomy, למד occurs seventeen times in sixteen verses, evenly spread throughout the entire book (cf. 4:1, 5; two times in 4:10, 14; 5:1, 31; 6:1; 11:19; 14:23; 17:19; 18:9; 20:18; 31:12, 13, 19, 22). While למד is a common Hebrew term for teaching and learning, Moisés Silva describes this usage as "Theologically relevant."[46] Thus, significantly, the usage of למד in Deuteronomy is centered around YHWH, illustrating the master/pupil relationship between YHWH and his people and how they learn to fear, to "follow" him. Conversely, למד in Deuteronomy also exhorts Israel to remain exclusively devoted to YHWH by not following the ways of pagans and their gods.

Based on the usage of the verb למד in Deuteronomy, discipleship in Deuteronomy may be understood as YHWH's instruction of Moses and the people to learn how to follow him in exclusive devotion and obedience. Part of this process includes teaching children, and subsequent generations, to do likewise. David Pedersen notes,

> It strikes us as provocative indeed that the two most important technical terms for describing discipleship to Jesus in the Synoptic Gospels—ἀκολουθέω and μανθάνω (μαθητής)—should in the Old Testament be associated with the themes of Torah-teaching and obedient Torah-learning which ultimately takes place in relationship with God himself.[47]

Similarly, Eugene Merrill says it this way, "The most important lesson for one to learn in general is to fear God, for this is at the foundation of covenant relationship (Deut 4:10; 14:23; 17:19; 31:12–13)."[48] The verb למד, in Deuteronomy, is explicitly covenantal

times in Deuteronomy in 17:10, 11; 24:8; 33:10). In each instance of the verb III-ירה in Deuteronomy, it simply means, "to instruct," "instruction," or "to teach." תורה occurs fifty-six times in the Torah of Moses. In Deuteronomy, the word occurs twenty-two times and refers almost exclusively to the the book of Deuteronomy itself with the phrase, "this law"; cf. Deut 1:5; 4:8, 44; 17:11, 18, 19; 27:3, 8, 26; 28:58, 61; 29:21 [20], 29 [28]; 30:10; 31:9, 11, 12, 24, 26; 32:46; "What is probably most likely is a connection [of תורה] with III-ירה in the sense of stretching out the finger, or the hand, to point out a route" in "תורה," *HALOT*, 1711; For other teaching and learning terms in the Hebrew Bible as well as "lexical set" as an example of related words contributing toward a single biblical concept, cf. Wendy L. Widder, *"To Teach" in Ancient Israel: A Cognitive Linguistic Study of a Biblical Hebrew Lexical Set* (Berlin: DeGruyter, 2014).

46. Silva, "μανθάνω," *NIDNTTE*, 3:221.

47. Pedersen, "Torah, Discipleship and Suffering," 77.

48. Merrill, "למד," *NIDOTTE*, 2:801.

and religious in nature and is clearly representative of a concept of master-servant or master-disciple, with YHWH being the master and Israel (collectively) being the servant.[49]

What I would call "discipleship in Deuteronomy," Block describes as "The Heart of Theological Education in the First Testament."[50] In Block's description of theological education in Deuteronomy, he has provided thorough insight into the Deuteronomic educational formula (read, hear, learn, fear, obey, live)[51] with a foundation of fearing YHWH, and implemented by various groups in ancient Israel: family (Deut 6:7), Levitical priests (Deut 31:9–13), prophets (Deut 18:15–19),[52] and kings (Deut 17:14–20).[53] While Block's chapter on theological education in Deuteronomy is helpful for understanding the theological and relational aspects of "teaching" and "learning" in the book of Deuteronomy, he does not provide a thorough description of "teaching" and "learning" as represented by the theologically unique usage of the verb למד in Deuteronomy.[54] His study on education is much more broad.[55] Noting Block's omission of a detailed analysis

49. Though there is also a subtle hint at the individual discipleship relationship between a master and servant in the Deuteronomic use of למד.

50. Block, *The Triumph of Grace*, 1.

51. Cf. Deut 4:10; 5:23–29; 6:1–3; 17:13, 19–20; 19:20; 31:11–13; Block calls this the "Deuteronomic Formula for Life" (not every term is used in every Deuteronomic passage cited above; see Table 1.2) in Block, *The Triumph of Grace*, 14.

52. While למד is not used here, the context is Israel's hearing the words of YHWH that he puts in the mouth of his prophet (cf. Deut 18:18).

53. Cf. Block, *The Triumph of Grace*, 11–12.

54. למד is found in Block's article on p. 2, n. 6, and in one paragraph on p. 4 in Block, *The Triumph of Grace*; It is understood here that a specific examination of למד was not Block's specific purpose.

55. Block describes "Moses' Vision of Theological Education for Future Generations" as a series of ways in which Israelites were to transmit faith to future generations: 1) "Adults were to take advantage of every 'teachable moment' to instruct their children in the Torah (Dt. 6:7; 11:19–20)," 2) to memorize Scripture (Decalogue, two-part Shema, Creedal formulas, and Catechetical questions and answers), 3) participation in feasts, 4) elder rule, 5) Levitical teaching of Torah, 6) succession of prophets, 7) a Torah-faithful king, 8) physical reminders of "YHWH's gracious acts," in the form of the stone tablets, Og's bed, and the pillars of Ebal, 9) a future place for YHWH's Name, and 10) Moses' written record, the book of Deuteronomy itself; Block, *The Triumph of Grace*, 10–13.

(not as a fault of Block's), this study now proceeds to Moses' usage of למד in Deuteronomy.

Deut 1:1—4:44[56]—Moses uses למד five times in his first address. As previously noted, למד has an opposite (though complementary) meaning in the *Qal* and *Piel* stems. In the *Qal*, it means "to learn," while in the *Piel* it means "to teach."[57] In Moses' first address (Deut 1:1—4:44) the word למד is used in vv. 4:1, 5, and 14 in the *Piel* stem, meaning "to teach." There, it is used to indicate that Moses is *teaching* Israel the "Statutes and Judgments" of YHWH in order to prolong the peoples' lives in the promised land. In 4:10, the *Qal* form of למד ("to learn") is used as YHWH reveals his desire that his people would "hear my words, so that they may *learn* to fear me."[58] At the end of v. 10 the *Piel* form is used again to indicate YHWH's desire that the Israelites would *teach* the same fear of YHWH to their children. Thus, here in Deut 4:10, what can be seen is the emphasis on learning with the purpose of teaching. In other words, the student (disciple) learns in order to teach others, to reproduce the learning. Reproduction of faith in YHWH, then, is the purpose of this teaching and learning.

Thus, at the close of Moses' first address in Deuteronomy, teaching and learning has the word of YHWH as the content and the fear of YHWH as the goal. In this section, Moses teaches Israel, YHWH teaches Israel, and Israel teaches their children (spiritual reproduction). With this usage of למד, Israelites are understood as disciples of Moses and YHWH, and the children of the Israelites as disciples of their parents, and, by implication also disciples of Moses and YHWH. In essence, Israel and their children follow human masters only as those human

56. The structure of Deuteronomy observed in this study is a modified version of Daniel Block's four sermon model: First Address: Deut 1:1–4:44; Second Address: 4:45—11:32 (Block views Deut 27:1–26 as the conclusion to the Second Address in this model); Third Address: Deut 12:1—29:1 [28:69]; Fourth Address (and the Song of YHWH and Moses' final benediction): Deut 29:2 [1]—34:12 in Block, *The Triumph of Grace*, 40.

57. This difference in meaning based on stem could be attributed to the distributive sense of the *Piel* stem: In other words, the *Qal* form of למד indicates simply what is learned, while the distributive sense of the *Piel* form of למד indicates distribution of learning, i.e. "teaching."

58. Here, the "words" of YHWH referred to are the "Ten Words" uttered from the mouth of YHWH at Horeb.

masters follow YHWH.[59] Thus, even when discipleship is understood as a human-human relationship, following YHWH is always the ultimate goal.

Deut 4:45—11:32—In Moses' second address, he uses למד four times and a synonym (שׁנן) one time. This address contains the well-known Deuteronomic "Ten Words" (Deut 5:6–21), "The Command" (Deut 6–11), and the more specific Shema (Deut 6:4–9).[60] However, the structure of this second address also contains an *inclusio* of "love YHWH" in the Shema (Deut 6:5) and what might be called a counterpart or conclusion to the Shema in Deut 11:1, 13 (cf. specifically Deut 11:18–20). There is further correspondence here between the "teach" command of the Shema and its counterpart (Deut 6:7; 11:19). This entire section (Deut 6–11) is introduced as "The Command" in 6:1. Thus, this address might be considered to be a single unit, as *The Command to love YHWH within a covenantal discipleship relationship.*[61]

In this "love YHWH" address, Moses again commands Israel to *learn* (*Qal* stem) the "Statutes and Judgments" (Deut 5:1). Moses then proceeds to retell the events of Horeb, and to restate the Decalogue. Within this narrative retelling, Moses recounts how YHWH commanded Moses to receive "the whole commandment" (cf. Deut 6–11) and the "Statutes and Judgments" so that he could *teach* (*Piel* stem) them to Israel (Deut 5:31). In Deut 6:1, Moses describes "The Commandment" (Deut 6–11) that YHWH commanded Moses to *teach* (*Piel* stem) Israel. Next, in the Shema (Deut 6:7), Moses commands the Israelites to *teach* their children the words of Moses' command.[62]

---

59. This is similar to Paul's exhortation in 1 Corinthians 11:1 using the term μιμητής (*mimētēs*, "imitator,") when he says, "Be imitators of me, as I am of Christ."

60. Tigay describes the theological theme of the Shema as "the ardent and exclusive loyalty that Israel owes YHWH"; Tigay, xiii.

61. This phrase is original to this author, but placed in italics for emphasis; Cf. J. W. McKay, "Man's Love for God in Deuteronomy and the Father/Teacher☐Son/Pupil Relationship," *VT* 22, no. 4 (October 1, 1972): 426–35.

62. Whether "these words" of Moses in Deut 6:6 refers to "the Commandment" (Deut 6–11), the "Ten Words" (Deut 5:6–21), the "Statutes and Judgments" (Deut 12–26), the immediately preceding creedal Shema statement, to all of these, or to the book of Deuteronomy overall, the emphasis is on Israel *learning* how to *follow* YHWH,

In the Shema, though, instead of the expected word, למד, Moses uses שנן (*šanan*), meaning "to repeat," or "to speak, or to recite again and again."[63] Then, in the conclusion to "The Command," in Deut 11:19, Moses slightly rephrases the earlier command of the Shema (Deut 6:7) for Israel to *teach* (*Piel* stem) their children, this time using למד.[64] Essentially, by their use in chapters 6 and 11, the verbs שנן and למד might be understood to be synonymous, and as part of the same Biblical concept of discipleship in Deuteronomy emphasizing parental instruction by means of the instructive repetition of YHWH's words.

Thus, in Moses' second address, למד is used again to indicate the content of instruction as the word of YHWH, significantly including the "Ten Words" of YHWH from Horeb, "The Command" to love YHWH, and the national and covenantal formula of the Shema in order for Israel to learn to fear YHWH and subsequently to teach their children to similarly fear YHWH. Thus, discipleship again begins within the word of YHWH, has the activities of the family as the context of discipleship, and has the covenantal love of YHWH as the goal.

Deut 12–26—In Moses' third address, in what Moses refers to as the "Statutes and Judgments," למד is used four times. Twice, the word is used to indicate YHWH's desire that Israel would *learn* to fear him. In one instance, in 14:23, Moses' exhorts Israel to give a tenth (a tithe)

---

by *loving* him, and by *doing* the words Moses is commanding (disciple verbs and discipleship context verbs italicized for emphasis).

63. This verb, ושננתם (*wəšinnantam*, "and you will teach them"), is considered by *HALOT* to be II-שנן, a *hapax legomenon*, occurring only here in Deut 6:7; "II-שנן," in *HALOT*, 1606–7.

64. Note the almost verbatim parallel between Deut 6:7 and Deut 11:19. Main differences noted in English in brackets:

ושננתם לבניך ודברת בם בשבתך בביתך ובלכתך בדרך ובשכבך ובקומך (Deut 6:7).

"And you will repeat them [suffixed to main verb] to your [sg.] sons, and you will speak about them when you are sitting in your house, and when you are walking on the way, and when you lay down, and when you rise."

ולמדתם אתם את־בניכם לדבר בם בשבתך בביתך ובלכתך בדרך ובשכבך ובקומך (Deut 11:19).

"And you will teach them [separated from main verb] to your [pl.] sons, speaking about them when you are sitting in your house, and when you are walking on the way, and when you lay down, and when you rise."

of their harvest to YHWH, "that you may *learn* to fear YHWH your God always." Similarly, in 17:19 the purpose of Moses' instruction for the coming king to read regularly from the Torah is "that he may *learn* to fear YHWH his God by keeping all the words of this law and these statutes, and doing them." In both exhortations, the activity of tithing or reading from the law is intended to teach the "disciple" to "fear YHWH." In other words, tithing and studying the word of YHWH, in Deuteronomy, are equivalent to fearing him, to following him, and to being his disciple.

In contrast to the usage of למד in 14:23 and 17:19, but with a goal of encouraging exclusive devotion to YHWH, the next two instances of למד are intended to discourage the following of any other gods (by means of "following" the practices of the nations that Israel would displace in the conquest). In 18:9, Moses instructs Israel not *to learn* to "*imitate*[65] [עשה כ, *ʿāśâ kə*, lit. "to do like"] the abominable practices" of the previous inhabitants of the land. Likewise, in 20:18 Moses exhorts Israel to thoroughly destroy her enemies so that "they may not *teach* [למד] you *to imitate* [עשה כ] all their abominable practices that they have done for their gods, and so you sin against YHWH your God." In this address, Moses uses both "to learn" (*Qal* stem in Deut 18:9) and "to teach" (*Piel* stem in Deut 20:18) as well as the Hebrew "imitate" phrase. This use is for the purpose that Israel would avoid following or imitating the pagan ways of non-Israelites (and by implication following those pagan gods) so that Israel might not turn from following YHWH.

Here, in the "Statutes and Judgments," למד positively indicates how disciples follow YHWH by giving him a tithe, and how the king studies the word of YHWH in order to learn how to fear YHWH. Conversely, Israel is also warned about imitating the ways of their neighbors and so abandoning their exclusive devotion to YHWH. What is emphasized here is following YHWH, and rejecting the ways of other peoples as they follow other gods.

Deut 27–34—The remaining four instances of למד in Deuteronomy are all found in Deuteronomy 31. In Moses' command for the Levites to read the Torah every seven years at the Feast of Booths, the purpose of this corporate hearing of Torah is for sojourners (Deut 31:12) and

---

65. "To follow" in the ESV.

their children (Deut 31:13) to *learn* to fear YHWH. In other words, the purpose of teaching and learning here is the proselytization of non-Israelites and their growth in the knowledge and practice of faith in YHWH. Next, YHWH commands a song to be written and *taught* to the people (Deut 31:19), and then the narrator reports that "Moses wrote this song the same day and *taught* it to the people of Israel" (Deut 31:22).

Thus, based on the usage of למד at the end of Deuteronomy, discipleship to YHWH may be understood again as "directed to God's law and regulations."[66] Learning to follow YHWH is based on the word of YHWH, it is for Israelites and foreign sojourners (non-Israelites) to learn to fear YHWH, to reproduce spiritually by passing on the faith and proselytizing, and learning is assisted by the incorporation of YHWH's story into song form and taught to the people. In addition to the אחר "follow" idiom, למד helps to situate discipleship in Deuteronomy within a context of divine and human teaching and learning. This study now turns to the usage of the אחר "follow" idiom in the book of Deuteronomy.

---

66. Kapelrud, "למד," *TDOT*, 8:6.

To Follow, הלך אחרי, *in Deuteronomy*[67]

The אחר "follow" idiom is used seven times in Deuteronomy, evenly spread throughout Moses' addresses.[68] With this even spread (similar to the distribution of למד throughout Deuteronomy), a cohesiveness of form, structure, and content is, again, clearly discernible in the book

---

67. The Hebrew word אחר in Deuteronomy has three significant meanings and several minor meanings. אחר is primarily used as a preposition with a temporal, spatial, and plenary meaning. Most significant to this study is the use of אחר as an adverb: "to walk after": Temporal: "after," as in "*after* he had defeated Sihon" (1:4; 12:30; 21:13; 24:4, 20, 21; 31:27, 29); Spatial: "west" or "behind" (11:30; 25:18). An outlier, in 23:14 [15], could refer to YHWH following Israel, likely in an overwatch or protection ("behind") sense, used with the helping verb שוב (*šub*), lit. "to turn from after you" or "turn from following you"; Ideological: In Deut 12:30–31, the אחר idiom refers to following the Canaanites and their ways; Plenary: the literal temporal meaning might be most in view here, but the implied relational and spatial "following" might also be intended (perhaps even the ideological meaning as well). This meaning is primarily used of the "offspring" of the Israelites, as in, "to their offspring *after* them" (1:8; cf. also 4:37, 40; 10:15; 12:25, 28; 29:22 [21]); Verbal: Two uses of the verb אחר occur in Deuteronomy in a sense unrelated to a concept of discipleship (cf. 7:10; 23:21); Relational (adverbial; the focus of this study): Using both הלך (*hlk*) and אחר (*'aḥar*), this phrase in Deuteronomy exhorts exclusive devotion to YHWH, and not to "other gods" (cf. 4:3; 6:14; 8:19; 11:28; 13:2 [3]; 13:4 [5]; 28:14); Adverbial with other helping verbs (*besides* הלך): There are two instances of the אחר "follow" idiom paired with the verb רדף, "to pursue" in Deut 11.4 and 19:6. Another instance of the follow idiom uses the helping verb נקש (*nqš*), as in "to ensnare to *follow*" (cf. Deut 12:30 in "Ideological" above). In Deut 1:36, the helping verb מלא (*ml'*) "to be full" is used, as in "he was *full after*," or "he *fully followed*." In Deut 7:4, אחר is used with the helping verb סור (*sûr*), "to turn away" or "to remove," as in "they would turn away your sons *from following* me." In Deut 31:16, אחר is used with the helping verb זנה (*znh*), "to commit adultery," as in "they will whore after"; אחר without a helping verb: Outside of Deuteronomy אחר is also used alone (sometimes with a prefixed מין), without a helping verb to describe "following" either YHWH or "other gods," and sometimes even following a human person (cf. 1 Sam 12:14; for following a man using only אחר, cf Judg 4:14); Finally, Reverse of אחר idiom: The reverse of the typical use of אחר without a helping verb. In Deut 17:3, the word הלך is used without אחר in what appears to be a "follow" context: "If there is found among you, within any of your towns that YHWH your God is giving you, a man or woman who does what is evil in the sight of YHWH your God, in transgressing his covenant, and has gone and served [וילך ויעבד, *wayyēlek wayya'ăbōd*] other gods." In this instance, הלך, "has gone," is to be understood as "has gone [after]," hence, "has followed."

68. The אחר "follow" idiom is used once in the prologue of Deut 1:1–4:44 (Deut 4:3), three times in "The Command" of Deut 6–11 (Deut 6:14; 8:19; 11:28), twice in the "Statutes and Judgments" of Deut 12–26 (Deut 13:2 [3], 4 [5]) and one final time in the blessings of Deut 28:1–14 (Deut 28:14).

of Deuteronomy as a whole. Moses' use of the אחר "follow" idiom demonstrates the significance, throughout the text of Deuteronomy, of consistency in Israel's relationship to YHWH as his disciples. Yet, this understanding of Israel as a disciple of YHWH has seemed to be suppressed, even in current scholarship on the use of "disciple" words in the Old Testament.

In Silva's article on ἀκολουθέω, he describes the Hebrew background of the New Testament use of ἀκολουθέω as the אחר "follow" idiom. Then, however, Silva makes little mention of this phrase as contributing to a concept of Old Testament discipleship. Instead, in reference to the "follow" idiom in the LXX using πορεύομαι and ὀπίσω, Silva says, "even this combination is rarely used with ref. to the true God (only Deut 13:4 [13:5] and 1 Kgs 18:21)."[69] In saying this Silva downplays the Hebrew "follow" idiom in the Old Testament (though only by examining the LXX usage) as a significant contribution toward an Old Testament concept of discipleship to YHWH. Yet, Silva's observation is not borne out by a search of the occurrence of πορεύω and ὀπίσω together in the LXX.[70] Additionally, even if

69. Silva, "ἀκολουθέω," *NIDNTTE*, 1:204; cf. Blenginger's comment: "There are no OT precedents for the more specific New Testament usage of *akouteō*. Even where other words are used for following, such as *poreuō*, they are applied to Yahweh only with great care (cf. Deut. 13:5 (EVV v. 4) and 1 Kgs 14:8). They never mean becoming like God, but only obeying him. God remains above this world and incomparable even as the Covenant God. The negative usage of hālak̲'aḥᵃrê is therefore the dominant one. It is used as a fixed phrase for backsliding into paganism by going after other gods (cf. Jdg. 2:12; Deut. 4:3; Jer. 2:5)" in Bl endinger, "ἀκολουθέω," *NIDNTT*, 1:481; To the contrary, Pedersen notes many instances in the Old Testament that describe "following YHWH": "Num. 32:11f; Deut. 1:36; 13:4f; Josh 14:8,9,14; 1 Kings 11:6; 14:8 (and other similar texts reflecting the Deuteronomic view). Hosea 11:10 seems to pick up this theme while Jer. 2:2 may refer to a more concrete 'following of Yahweh' in the wilderness, although even here the emphasis still falls upon the obedience of the people," in Pedersen, "Torah, Discipleship and Suffering," 70n34; cf. also the opposite of "following YHWH," in Pedersen: "E.g., Deut. 4:3; 13:2; Judg. 2:12; 1 Kings 11:5, 10; Jer. 2:5; Ezek. 20:16. Since the expression [the אחר 'follow' idiom] is used predominantly in *malam partem* ['in an evil sense'] (perhaps originally to describe a 'following of the Gods' in the cultic processions of ancient Near-eastern religions), the Old Testament writers may have been reluctant to apply it in the direction suggested by Jer. 2:2 (cf. Exod. 13:21f.)," in Pedersen, "Torah, Discipleship and Suffering," 70n35.

70. It seems as though Silva's statement here is in reference only to the use of πορεύομαι and ὀπίσω as glosses for הלך אחר. However, in order for Silva's claim, that the usage in relation to the True God is rare, he needs to examine the use of ὀπίσω and ὄπισθεν (*opisthen*, "after") alone as adverbial phrases meaning "to follow after,"

all of the usage of πορεύω and ὀπίσω together in the LXX pointed at the negative side of following, i.e., "Do not go after other gods," this negative command points to or implies the positive side of "following." In contrast, Israel is to "go after" YHWH alone. Thus, the Hebrew (and Greek in the LXX) "follow" idiom is used enough times in the Old Testament as to contribute to an Old Testament concept of discipleship. In other words, contrary to Silva's assertion that the אחר "follow" idiom is used "rarely" of YHWH, the overall context of the usage of the phrase actually supports the idea that the idiom is used quite substantially and frequently of YHWH in the Old Testament. Whether in the Hebrew Old Testament, or whether in the Greek LXX, the phrase/idiom "go after" *does have* the idea of "following YHWH" as its ultimate referent and goal.

The Hebrew "follow" idiom has a specifically religious meaning in Deuteronomy. Based on the "following" language associated with YHWH's war (cf. Judg. 3:28),[71] Franz Helfmeyer concludes that the "follow" idiom using אחר was originally coined in the context of an army and the commander-in-chief.[72] In this way, "following" may be literally understood by Helfmeyer as "to *follow* the ark as a symbol of leadership, palladium of war, Yahweh's throne, and processional shrine."[73] Even though following a cultic object into battle, such as the Ark of the Covenant, may be the origination of the אחר "follow"

---

as well as the adverbial use of ὀπίσω and ὄπισθεν with the modifying verbs πορεύω, πορεύομαι, and ἀκολουθέω (not to mention the compound prepositional forms of these verbs in conjunction with ὀπίσω and ὄπισθεν). When widening the search, plenty more instances of the OT "follow" idiom appear (cf. 1 Sam. 12:14; 1 Kgs. 11:6 [LXX, 11:8]; 18:21; 2 Kgs. 23:3; Hos. 11:10). When synonyms for "walk/go" and "after/behind" are considered, Silva's point becomes reversed: the אחר "follow" idiom, even glossed in Greek, is used quite frequently in the Old Testament to refer to the ideal disciple: Israel as disciple to YHWH.

71. Though, here in Judges the idiom is the "pursue after" phrase with a military context, formed with the verb רדף.

72. Helfmeyer, "אחרי," *TDOT*, 1:206; The אחר, "follow," idiom in Judg. 3:28 does not use the verb הלך, but rather the verb רדף (*rdp*, "to pursue"); While the implications of a military "discipleship" to YHWH would be interesting, if not incredibly difficult to appropriate and apply to a Christian context, the most common use of the אחר "follow" idiom is not in a military context, but is rather in a religious devotion context.

73. Helfmeyer, "אחרי," *TDOT*, 1:206.

idiom used of YHWH in Deuteronomy,[74] nevertheless, *in* the book of Deuteronomy, the אחר "follow" idiom is never used of a cultic object,[75] like the Ark of the Covenant,[76] and never in relation to warfare.[77] The phrase is used exclusively to encourage Israel's religious devotion to YHWH rather than false gods. The אחר "follow" idiom is used seven times in Deuteronomy,[78] and primarily indicates the devotion and obedience of a servant towards his master.

Deut 4:3—Negative examples of "following" abound in the Old Testament, and specifically in Deuteronomy. That is clear in Deuteronomy with a text such as, "Your eyes have seen what YHWH did at Baal-Peor, for YHWH your God destroyed from among you all the men who *followed* [כל־האיש אשר הלך אחרי, *kol ha'îš 'ăšer halak 'aḥărê*; lit. "any man who walked after"] the Baal of Peor" (Deut 4:3).[79] Here, with the corporate punishment of 24,000 Israelites (cf. Num 25:9), the singular "any man" is used in the narrated report of Deut 4:3. From this might be understood that discipleship is both corporate and individual. And, if following Baal Peor is the negative side of

74. For the possibility that the "follow after" phrase may be intentionally avoided by the authors of the Old Testament so as to reject this idea of the idolatrous "following" of pagan cultic objects, see Gerhard Kittel, "ἀκολουθέω," *TDNT*, 1:211.

75. Unless turning from YHWH to follow "other gods" includes the idea of a processional following of the cultic objects representing those deities.

76. Unlike in Joshua 3:3, the אחר "follow" idiom does not occur in relation to the Ark of the Covenant in Deuteronomy.

77. The exception to this is the use of אחר with the helping verb רדף, with the meaning "to pursue," and typically used in reference to one's enemies, i.e. "to pursue them." Unlike the use of this idiom in Judges 3:2, there is no connection between the use of "pursue after" in Deuteronomy with a religious or personal/ideological (non-military) "follow after" connotation.

78. Like למד, the idiom is evenly spread across the book, and is used in some of the key "exclusive devotion" passages in Moses' first and second addresses (Dt. 1–11) in close proximity to the usage of למד (Both למד and הלך אחר are used in Dt. 4, 6, and 11) giving those sections of Deuteronomy a significant "discipleship" tone.

79. Of note here is the dual nature of discipleship. The Judgment of YHWH referred to here is clearly with a view to national holiness, and thus a corporate context (cf. Num. 25:1–18). Yet, the phrasing of the "follow" idiom here is masculine singular, with an implied plural object. Thus, in this one retelling of the historical Baal Peor incident there is evidence of both individual and corporate discipleship to YHWH.

discipleship in this text, then turning from Baal Peor to follow YHWH is the positive side of discipleship in Deuteronomy. This indicates that repentance is an important part of the concept of discipleship in Deuteronomy. Thus, from this historical retelling of the Baal Peor incident, discipleship in Deuteronomy can be understood as corporate and individual, and as exclusive devotion, to follow YHWH alone rather than other gods, and to repent when one stumbles into idolatry.

Deut 6:14—In Deut 6:14, the Israelites are commanded not to *"follow* other gods" after they enter the promised land (לא תלכון אחרי אלהים אחרים, *lō ' tēləkûn 'aḥărê 'ĕlōhî 'ăḥērîm*) because "A Jealous God is YHWH your God in your midst" (Deut 6:15). Thus, if the Israelites abandon YHWH, they cease to be holy, and YHWH's holy anger would consume them and "destroy" them "from off the face of the earth" (Deut 6:15). Here, discipleship to YHWH is exclusive devotion, and is contrary to following the gods of Israel's neighbors. Additionally, discipleship to YHWH carries a warning, that when YHWH's disciples turn from following him toward following other gods, the result will be the destruction of YHWH's former disciples (by YHWH's hand, no less!).

Deut 8:19; 11:28—Moses warns Israel not to forget YHWH after they enter the promised land (Deut 8:11).[80] If Israel forgets all that YHWH has done for them, they would be tempted "to *follow* [והלכת אחרי, *wəhalaḵta 'aḥărê*, lit. "to go after"] other gods and serve [עבד, *'bd*] them and worship them" (Deut 8:19). The results of such abandoning of their exclusive devotion to YHWH would result in the people perishing. Similarly, in Deut 11:28 the people are warned that they will be under a curse if they "do not obey the commandments of YHWH but turn aside from the way . . . *to follow* [lit. *"to go after"*] other gods" (ללכת אחרי, *laleḵet 'aḥărê*). Of note here is the collocation of

---

80. Significantly, just before this is a description of the relationship between Israel and YHWH as a "father and son" relationship in which the father disciplines the son (Deut 8:5). This relationship, described in the Hebrew with "father" and "son" terms (אב and בן), could also be considered to contribute toward a concept of discipleship in Deut (and throughout the OT).

service, worship, obedience, walking in the way of YHWH/Moses, and the אחר "follow" idiom.

Deut 13:2 [3], 4 [5]—The contrast to "following" other gods is clearly evident in Moses' third address in "the Statutes and Judgments" (Deut 12–26) in a passage describing false prophecy in Israel.[81] In order to better grasp the overall concept of "following YHWH" despite the existence of false prophecy in Israel, it is instructive to look at the usage of this phrase in the slightly larger context of Deut 13:1–4 [2–5]:

> 1 [2] If a prophet or dreamer of dreams arises in your midst, and he gives to you a sign or a wonder, 2 [3] and if the sign or the wonder that he speaks to you comes to pass, saying, "Let us follow [נלכה אחרי, *nēlkâ 'aharê*] other gods," which you have not known, "and let us serve them," 3 [4] you must not *obey* [שמע, *šm'*] the words of that prophet, or that dreamer of dreams. For, YHWH your God is *testing* [נסה, *nsh*] you, to know whether you *love* [אהב, *'hb*] YHWH your God with all your heart and with all your soul [cf. Deut 6:5]. 4 [5] You must follow YHWH your God [אחרי יהוה אלהיכם תלכו, *'aharê . . . tēlēkû*, lit. "*After* YHWH your God you must *walk*"], and Him you must *fear* [ירא, *yr'*], and His commandments you must *keep* [שמר, *šmr*], and His voice you must *obey* [שמע], and Him you must *serve* [עבד, *'bd*], and to Him you must *cling* [דבק, *dbq*].[82]

What is striking about this passage is the connection of "follow" language with idolatry, the contrast of idolatry with "following YHWH, your God," and the other Deuteronomic language associated with following YHWH.[83] Similar to this list in Deut 13, Moses' writing of his

---

81. Deut 13 could be described as teaching "total devotion to YHWH."

82. Explicit "disciple" words using the אחר "follow" idiom are bold and italicized here for emphasis; Other verbs in this pericope that might contribute to a concept of discipleship in the Old Testament are *italicized* here for emphasis.

83. Other verbs associated with the Israelite disciple's "following" YHWH (his life of devotion to YHWH) in this passage show that a disciple: obeys YHWH (used two times), is tested by him, demonstrates complete love to him (cf. the heart, soul and מאדך, *mə'odeka*, "all your strength," or "all your being" of the Shema in Deut 6:5), fears him, keeps him commandments, serves him, and clings to him. The constraints of this study do not permit a more thorough examination of the Deuteronomic context as they contribute toward a concept of discipleship in Deuteronomy; Block refers to these collocated terms as "The Dimensions of Divine Expectation" (see Block's diagram of a

Torah and instructing the tribe of Levi to teach Torah in Deuteronomy 31:9–13 points to what Block calls "The Deuteronomic Formula for Life."[84] Thus, to be a disciple of YHWH is to refuse to listen to false prophecy/teaching, but instead to follow YHWH exclusively.

There is evidence to suggest that this "false prophecy" section of the "Statutes and Judgments" is an expansion of the third Word of the Decalogue (Deut 5:11), "you shall not take the name of YHWH your God in vain" (Deut 5:11).[85] If this is so, and understanding the word נשא (*nś'*, "to take") in its common sense of "to lift" or "to carry," then Israel's idolatry, following other gods in Deut 13:1–4 [2–5], would be an instance of "carrying" the name of YHWH in vain. In other words, if Israel were to follow other gods, they could not rightly be said to "carry" his name (or perhaps be called by his name?). This "carrying" of YHWH's name in vain by following other gods would put Israel in breach of their covenant relationship with him, and thus in danger of discipline.

Two of the primary opponents of viewing discipleship as an Old Testament concept are Karl Rengstorf and Gerhard Kittle in their work in *TDNT*.[86] Contrary to the negative views of both Karl Rengstorf[87]

---

hand in Figure 1.1) in Block, *The Triumph of Grace*, 11.

84. Cf. Block's "teach Torah" list of verbs in Deuteronomy, in Block, *The Triumph of Grace*, 14.

85. Cf. Kaufman, 122–29; cf. also Walton, "The Decalogue Structure of the Deuteronomic Law," 93–117; Block calls this section "Celebrating Covenant Relationship with Yahweh: Part I (Dt. 12:2–14:21)," and "Responding to Yahweh's Call for Exclusive Relationship (12:29–13:18 [19])" in *Deuteronomy*, 45.

86. It seems as though the later English theological dictionaries (*NIDNTT* and *NIDNTTE*) have largely followed in Rengstorf and Kittel's footsteps. What seems to be the distinguishing characteristic of the scholars favorable to viewing discipleship as an OT concept or not is the scholar's particular expertise: NT scholars seem to be largely unfavorable to the view of discipleship as an OT concept, while OT scholars largely seem to affirm the presence of the concept of discipleship in the OT.

87. Rengstorf describes Elijah's call of Elisha story not formally as discipleship or formal following (probably based on the *apriori* understanding that discipleship is inherently "Rabbinic"). Rengstorf says, "It is thus correct to take the וילך אחרי אליהו of 1 K. 19:21 simply as a ref. to the entry of Elisha into the *service* of Elijah, and not, acc. to later [Rabbinic] usage, as the beginning of the discipleship of Elisha" (emphasis added; Hebrew vowel points removed) in Rengstorf, "μανθάνω," *TDNT* 4:428.

and Gerhard Kittel,[88] who view discipleship as a distinctly New Testament concept, Heinrich Seesemann is favorable to this interpretation of "to walk after YHWH" in Deut 13:4 [5] as "following" (disciple) language.[89] Further, Seesemann also adds the additional option for אחרי as "to be obedient to."[90] In this way, Deut 13:1–4 [2–5] can be understood as a strong, and clear instance of instruction in discipleship to YHWH.

Deut 28:14—The final instance of the אחר "follow" idiom in Deuteronomy occurs within the blessing section of Deut 28:1–14, another place where similar "disciple" terms occur: שמע, "to obey," and עשה, "to do" (Deut 28:1–2), שמר, "to keep," and הלך . . . דרך, "walk in His ways" (Deut 28:9), and לא סור, "do not turn aside" or "to go after [אחרי ללכת, *laleket 'aḥărê*] other gods and serve them" (Deut 28:14).

Thus, discipleship to YHWH in Deuteronomy, based on the אחר "follow" idiom, is to follow YHWH exclusively, rather than to follow other gods, and to repent when the disciple stumbles into idolatry. Discipleship is both individual and corporate. Disciples would be in danger of punishment/discipline for failure to keep YHWH's covenant stipulations. Discipleship is associated with obedience, service, worship, being tested by YHWH, loving him, fearing him, keeping his commands, and clinging to him. Finally, disciples rightly carry the name of YHWH, perhaps as a personal identity as his people. If YHWH's disciples follow him exclusively in these ways, they will experience his blessing, rather than the curse (cf. Deut 11:26).

88. Kittel says, "The idea of following Yahweh is much less prominent [than the אחר 'follow' phrase used 'as a technical term for apostasy into heathenism']. It occurs occasionally in a Deuteronomic context, Dt. 1:36; 13:5; 1 K. 14:8; 2 K. 23:3; 2 Ch. 34:31. The main Deuteronomic call, however, is not that Israel should go after Yahweh but that it should walk in His ways (Dt. 5:30 etc.)" in Kittel, "ἀκολουθέω," *TDNT*, 1:211. While Kittel's sentiment here is understandable, the *actual* difference between "following" a person and "walking in his or her ways" is really one of semantics. This study understands the ideological following of one's ways to be synonymous with following the person, i.e., being a disciple of the person (even if the person is long dead and no longer "itinerant"; cf. "disciples of John" long after his death in Acts 19:1–3 or the Pharisees' claim to be "disciples of Moses" long after Moses was dead in John 9:28).

89. Heinrich Seesemann, "ὀπίσω, ὄπισθεν," *TDNT*, 5:291.

90. Seesemann, "ὀπίσω, ὄπισθεν," *TDNT*, 5:291.

EXCURSUS: "UTTER DESTRUCTION," חרם, IN DEUT 13 *AS* DISCIPLESHIP IN DEUTERONOMY

The difficulty in seeing Deut 13:4 [5] as a "discipleship" text is the חרם (ḥrm, "total destruction") context.[91] In Deut 13, as well as in several other places in Deuteronomy, YHWH commands his people to commit idolaters to "the Ban," to "utter destruction." In Deut 7:2, Israel must commit Canaanites to חרם, "the Ban." The reason given is to preserve the Israelites' exclusive devotion to YHWH, described by the אחר idiom as "following": "For they would turn away [סור] your sons *from following me* [מאחרי, mē 'aḥăray, lit. "from after me"], to serve other gods" (Deut 7:4). That חרם was not "genocide" in Deuteronomy is evidenced by Moses' teaching in Deut 7:26, where תועבה (thô'ēbâ, "an abominable thing")[92] must not be taken into Israelite tents. Otherwise, Israelites themselves would, like their Canaanite neighbors, become חרם, "devoted to destruction." The reason given for not bringing תועבה "an abominable thing" into one's tent is so as not to be יקש (yqš), "ensnared by it" (Deut 7:25).

Similarly, regarding false prophets as another way the people can be led astray, the destruction of false prophets and those who go after false gods is the result. Throughout Deuteronomy 13, the Israelites are commanded not to listen to false prophets, and not to follow other gods. The punishment for following false gods is death, whether individuals (Deut 13:5 [6]), including, or especially, family members (Deut 13:9 [10]), or even entire cities (Deut 13:15 [16]).

In Deut 20:17–18, Moses commands Israel to commit the Canaanites to חרם, "the Ban," with a purpose that the Canaanites "may not teach [למד] you to do according to all their abominable practices that they have done for their gods, and so you sin against YHWH your God." With this use of חרם collocated with the emphasis that they not teach Israel to "do like" (כ עשה, "to imitate") their practices, it becomes clear that the concept of חרם has to do with Israel's national holiness, total devotion, to "follow" YHWH alone. In other words, the concept of discipleship in Deuteronomy is closely associated with the concept of total devotion (contrasted with idolatry) as well as the

---

91. חרם is sometimes understood simply as "the Ban."

92. Cf. פסילי אלהיהם "idols of their gods" in v. 25.

concept of utter destruction (the result of failure to exclusively follow
YHWH).

SUMMARY OF DISCIPLESHIP IN DEUTERONOMY

From the literary context of Deuteronomy, discipleship is understood as
covenantal, with YHWH calling Israel to discipleship. The relationship
between Israel and YHWH is understood as a suzerain-vassal/master-
servant relationship. The book of Deuteronomy, as Biblical wisdom, is
understood as a manual for the disciple's (Israel's) instruction in how
to follow YHWH. Finally, the individual laws of Deut 12–26 are understood as explanations of the covenantal "Ten Words," and thus as a
coherent whole.

From Moses' use of למד discipleship can be understood as based
on the word of YHWH to encourage the (religious) fear of him. Discipleship comprehensively covers all segments of Israelite society:
family, priests, prophets, and kings. Learning is emphasized with
a goal of teaching (including repetition of creedal statements and
songs) and reproduction of one's faith in both foreigners (proselytization) and future generations (familial discipleship). Discipleship
is manifest in obedience to YHWH, imitation of him, and exclusive
devotion to him.

Finally, discipleship to YHWH is most closely associated with
the אחר "follow" idiom and the verb למד. The usage of the אחר
"follow" idiom shows evidence that discipleship can legitimately be
understood as an Old Testament concept. Discipleship is repenting
from stumbling into idolatry, following other gods. Discipleship is
individual and corporate and is exclusive devotion to YHWH rather
than other gods. Discipleship in Deuteronomy is to serve and worship
YHWH, to obey His commands, and to walk in His ways. Discipleship
is to know YHWH, to be tested by him, to love him with all of one's
being, to fear him, and to hold fast to him (Deut 13:1–4 [2–5]). Finally,
based on the חרם emphasis, discipleship in Deuteronomy is to guard
the community from the pollution of unholiness by destroying threats
to individual and corporate holiness. Discipleship to YHWH comes
with a warning of destruction (divine discipline) if/when the disciple
transgresses the terms of the covenant relationship.

From the various scholarly views of the אחר "follow" idiom in the Old Testament, the main point of discipleship in Deuteronomy (and the wider Old Testament) might be understood as exclusive devotion and obedience to YHWH, commitment of life and purpose, an intimately close master-disciple relationship between YHWH and his people, to "walk in His ways," and "to imitate Him." From these interpretive options, it seems clear that the idiom (with or without the helping verb הלך) is clearly representative of a concept of discipleship to YHWH in Deuteronomy.

To be sure, the concept of teaching and learning, or discipleship, in Deuteronomy is not filled out by the examination of the literary structure of Deuteronomy and usage of these "disciple" words alone. Instead, the structure of Deuteronomy and these "disciple" words have been examined as some of the best thematic and lexical evidence in the book of Deuteronomy of a concept of discipleship. In Deuteronomy, discipleship to YHWH is in opposition to following any other god, and it is a close, personal, and intimate kind of relationship. The literary structure of Deuteronomy reveals that the book is intended for pastoral use, for teaching and training Israel, the disciples of YHWH, how to "follow" or obey him. The primary exhortation of the book of Deuteronomy is for YHWH's people, Israel, his disciples, to learn Torah, to learn his "Statutes and Judgments" and do them, and in so doing to learn to "fear YHWH." To learn YHWH's law, and to learn to fear YHWH, in Deuteronomy, is the essence of discipleship in the book, and parents are instructed to make more disciples of YHWH by teaching their children to repeat YHWH's words, and thus become His followers as well.

Jesus' Form of Discipleship

Based primarily on the known fact of Jesus' use of the Old Testament, some connections between Old Testament discipleship and Jesus' form of discipleship might be made more clearly here. Like YHWH of the Old Testament, Jesus demands exclusive devotion of His followers. Jesus commands a prospective follower to "leave the dead to bury their own dead" (cf. Matt 8:22).[93] Concerning holiness, Jesus

---

93. Cf. Martin Hengel's treatment of discipleship to Jesus vs. Rabbinic discipleship in Martin Hengel, *The Charismatic Leader and His Followers*, ed. John Riches, trans.

commands his followers to cut off the hand, or pluck out the eye that causes one to sin (cf. Mt. 18:7–9). This can be seen as theologically or conceptually linked to YHWH's command of חרם in Deuteronomy. One significant teaching of Jesus is the "hate your parents" command (Lk. 14:26; Cf. Mt. 10:34–37). In order to make this teaching of Jesus more palatable for a contemporary audience, this command has often been taught with the emphasis on "more than" (i.e., "Do not love your parents *more than* you love Jesus!").[94] However, the textual allusion may be to the חרם command of Deuteronomy 13:6–11 [7–12]. As has been argued here, this command is one of exclusive devotion. In this way, Jesus can be understood, in the New Testament, to demand exclusive devotion, which is a kind of devotion that only YHWH demands of Israel (corporately, or even Israelites individually) in the Old Testament. Thus, Jesus' command of exclusive devotion in the Gospels might be best understood as deriving from the pattern of YHWH demanding the same of Israel in the Old Testament.

The result of this study on discipleship in the Old Testament illuminates the need for further investigations of Jesus' form of discipleship, and that these studies would necessarily begin with the corresponding activities of YHWH and His people and prophets in the Old Testament. While the Old Testament *seems* to use "disciple" terminology sparingly, this study has, hopefully, illuminated a treasure trove of lexical terms and literary devices that yield much fruit in the discernment of a concept of Christian discipleship derived from the Old Testament.

Christian Implications

Interpreting Deuteronomy remains elusive for much of the Christian church. John Walton cautions, "The Bible was written *for* us, but not *to* us."[95] Yet, connections between Old Testament discipleship and New Testament discipleship can legitimately be made. The book of Deuteronomy is theologically rich, and should rightly be a sourcebook for

---

James Grieg (1968; Eugene, OR: Wipf & Stock, 2005).

94. Cf. Matt 10:37 in comparison to Luke 14:26.

95. Emphasis original, in John H. Walton, "Interpreting the Bible as an Ancient Near Eastern Document," in *Israel: Ancient Kingdom or Late Invention*, ed. Daniel Block (Nashville: Broadman & Holman, 2008), 327.

Christian discipleship today.[96] Christians should certainly view some commands of the Old Testament as fulfilled (i.e., holiness/food laws), yet as still relevant: NT Christians are still called to pursue holiness and have New Testament instructions on diet.[97]

When "doing" discipleship in our churches today, Christians should not solely study the New Testament concept of discipleship. Instead, the church should first seek to discern YHWH's form of discipleship in the Old Testament.[98] Then, the church should study Jesus' form of discipleship in order to discern the continuity or discontinuity between YHWH's Old Testament form of discipleship and Jesus' New Testament form. Ultimately, this OT and NT approach to disciple-making helps the church to view God's relationship with mankind as holistic, and to view the instructional and transformational process as a cohesive unity between Testaments.

Conclusion

Scholarship on discipleship has generally tended to ignore or downplay the Old Testament. Scholarship that has explicitly focused on Old Testament discipleship has often been helpful, though not comprehensive,

96. Just as Deuteronomy was a "manual" of Israelite discipleship to YHWH, so now Matthew (heavily OT dependent) can be understood as a "manual" for Christian discipleship today; cf. Wilkins, *Matthew*, 200; Yet, that does not mean that the church should abandon the Old manual (OT) for the New one (NT). Rather, the church ought to read both Testaments together in order to discern the heart of YHWH for his people, and how he expects his people to respond to him in worship and in discipleship, and to transfer the Old Testament understanding of discipleship to YHWH to the person of Jesus in the New Testament; Block closes his article on education with a call to return to Deuteronomy by quoting Paul (2 Tim 3:16) in order to find "a sure and effective instrument for teaching, reproof, correction, and training in righteousness, and equipping for every good work to the glory of God" in Block, *The Triumph of Grace*, 18.

97. Jesus' command to "be perfect" (Matt 5:48) seems to be an echo of Moses' command to "be holy" in Lev 19:2; cf. also Paul's exhortation, "God has not called us for impurity, but in holiness" (1 Thess 4:7); cf. the apostolic teaching of dietary restrictions for Gentile Christians in Acts 15:20.

98. Additional research is needed in order to provide a comprehensive picture of YHWH's form of discipleship in the Old Testament. Also, comparative research could be done in this area in order to determine the similarities and differences between YHWH's form of discipleship in the Old Testament and the ways of theological instruction/ relationship to the deities in other ANE cultures.

and those studies are sparse at best. In response to the trend of neglecting the Old Testament when considering the topic of Christian discipleship, this study sought to discern a concept of discipleship in the book of Deuteronomy as the most likely background and foundation to Jesus' form of discipleship in the New Testament.

From the book of Deuteronomy, this study examined the literary contribution of Deuteronomy in order to discern a concept of discipleship there. From the literary structure of Deuteronomy, discipleship is predominantly understood as covenantal, and the book of Deuteronomy understood as a manual for Israelite discipleship to YHWH. Turning to disciple terms in Deuteronomy, discipleship is understood as a relationship of exclusive devotion. Importantly, though, when disciples stray from exclusive devotion to YHWH, repentance is necessary to restore the discipleship relationship. Thus, discipleship in Deuteronomy is clearly distinguished from following any other gods. The word of YHWH is always the content or source material for discipleship to YHWH in Deuteronomy, and the goal is to increase the learning of fear and obedience of YHWH. As Christians reflect on the structure, language, and teachings of Deuteronomy, may they ever avail themselves of the richness of these words of Moses as they relate to the concept of discipleship to YHWH, and in so doing may the church better understand Jesus' form of discipleship so as to follow him better the way he intended.

[*JESOT* 7.2 (2021): 72–89]

Priestly Instruction in Leviticus and Ezekiel and a Unified Reading of Psalms 15–18

Joel Hamme

SUM Bible College and Theological Seminary
drhamme@sum.edu

Abstract: This article argues that Pss 15–18 can be fruitfully read together in view of the חוקות "statutes" and משפטים "judgments" in the Holiness Code (Lev 17–26) and Ezekiel 18 and 22, with which elements in Pss 15–17 have strong resonance. Contrary to scholars that see Ps 18:21–25 as a Deuteronomistic redaction inserted into Ps 18, this paper considers these "statutes" and "judgments" as related to those found in sources connected to priestly circles; namely, the Holiness Code and Ezekiel 18 and 22. After the article discusses the scholarship that considers Pss 15–24 to be a unified collection in Book 1 of the Psalter, it situates Pss 15–18, 20–21 within that larger collection. It then reads Pss 15–17 in light of Leviticus' Holiness Code (Lev 17–26), and the book of Ezekiel. Psalms 15–17 provide a picture of the perfect person who is delivered by God due to his scrupulous observance of priestly "statutes" and "judgments." Ps 18 is a royal thanksgiving in which the king declares that he is that perfect person that God has delivered. The paper draws on the work of Israel Knohl and argues that Pss 15–17 reflect the same impulse that led to the formation of the Holiness Code, a prophetic critique of the priests, and can be dated to the reign of Hezekiah.

Key Words: Canonical Interpretations; Psalms; Priestly Literature

Psalms 15–18 are fruitfully read together as priestly instruction concerning ethical conduct and proper worship in the temple precincts, which leads to blessing and protection. This argument rests on the statutes and judgments of Ps 18:23 stemming from priestly rather than Deuteronomistic circles. The paper will indicate this by conducting a canonical reading of Pss 15–18 through the lens of Leviticus' Holiness Code (esp. Lev 19 and 25) and Ezekiel (Ezek 18 and 22).[1] The article's approach is "canonical," in that it reads Pss 15–18 together, as articulated by Erich Zenger, "When interpreting the psalms canonically, the relationships that connect one psalm to its neighboring psalms are to be observed."[2]

SCHOLARSHIP THAT READS PSS 15–24 AS A UNIFIED COLLECTION IN BOOK 1 OF THE PSALTER

The reader should take this article's argument in the context of the last few decades' work on Pss 15–24 as a unified subset of psalms in Book 1 of the Psalter (Pss 3–41). Many scholars have considered Pss 15–24 to be a subcollection within book 1 to the point that it seems to have the status of received knowledge.

Pierre Auffret argued that Pss 15–24 has a concentric composition, based largely on an analysis of catchwords and themes that he sees connecting Pss 15 and 24, Pss 16 and 23, Pss 17 and 22, and Pss 18 and 20–21, with Ps 19 at its center.[3] Since then, scholars have accepted Auffret's conclusion and have treated Pss 15–24 as a carefully crafted collection centered on Ps 19.[4] Most of the scholarly work on Pss

1. Jacob Milgrom indicates Ezekiel's reliance on the Holiness Code (H) in a number of cases, and comments on Ezekiel's close following of H in Ezek 18. See Jacob Milgrom, *Leviticus 23–27: A New Translation with Introduction and Commentary*, AYBC 3B (New Haven, CT: Yale University, 2000), 2352–53. See also Israel Knohl, *The Divine Symphony: The Bible's Many Voices* (Philadelphia: Jewish Publication Society, 2003), 154.

2. Erich Zenger, "Was wird anders bei kanonischer Psalmauslegung," in *Ein Gott, eine Offenbarung. FS N. Füglister*, ed. F. V. Reiterer (Würzburg: Echter Verlag, 1991), 399. Translation from the German original. Zenger's quotation reads, "kanonischer Psalmenauslegung sind die Beziehungen eines Psalms zu seinen Nachbarpsalmen zu beobachten."

3. Pierre Auffret, *La sagesse a bati sa maison*, OBO 49 (Fribourg: Éditions Universitaires, 1982), 407–38.

4. See especially the following studies, Frank Lothar Hossfeld and Erich Zenger, "'Wer darf hinaufziehn zum Berg YHWHs?' Zur Redaktiongeschichte und Theologie der Psalmenengruppe 15–24," in *Biblische Theologie und gesellschaftlicher Wandel*, ed.

15–24 deals exclusively with the collection's final form. An exception to this is the work of Frank-Lothar Hossfeld and Erich Zenger. They couple a final form analysis with a study of the collection's diachronic formation.[5] They are interested in how tradents expand the collection's earlier layers as the community rereads the received text for a new day. Hossfeld and Zenger write that the post-exilic Judaean community reread the growing Psalms collection. They redacted the Psalms to support an *Armenfrömmigkeit* in which the faithful servant is the post-exilic Judean community.[6]

Although this article assigns different psalms to the earliest core of Pss 15–24 than Hossfeld and Zenger, their diachronic approach is most similar to this article's method. Psalms 15–18 is part of an earlier stratum that tradents later add to in their formation of Pss 15–24. Jamie Grant correctly states that the *inclusio* formed by the entrance liturgies of Pss 15 and Pss 24 is not enough to set the collection apart from the rest of Book 1. He writes that the *inclusio*, combined with the chiastic structure and lexical concatenation, sets Pss 15–24 apart. Grant states Pss 15–24 is the only collection so clearly demarcated, contrary to Hossfeld and Zenger, who see a few distinct groupings in Book 1.[7]

Georg Braulik OSB et al. (Freiburg: Herder, 1993), 166–82; Patrick Miller, "Kingship, Torah Obedience, and Prayer. The Theology of Pss 15–24," in *Neue Wege der Psalmenenforschung*, ed. Klaus Seybold and Erich Zenger, HBS 1 (Freiburg: Herder, 1994), 127–42; Matthias Millard, *Die Composition des Psalters*, FAT 9 (Tübingen: Mohr Siebeck, 1994), 24–25; Gianni Barbiero, *Das erste Psalbenbuch als Einheit*, ÖBS 16 (Frankfurt am Main: Peter Lang, 1999), 189–324; William Brown, "'Here Comes the Sun!' The Metaphorical Theology of Pss 15–24," in *The Composition of the Book of Psalms*, ed. Erich Zenger, BETL 238 (Leuven: Peeters, 2010), 259–77; Bernd Janowski, *Konfliktgespräche Mit Gott: Eine Anthropologie der Psalmen* (Göttingen: Vandenhoeck & Ruprecht, 2019), 316–18; Peter C. W. Ho, *The Design of the Psalter: A Macrostructural Analysis* (Eugene, OR; Pickwick, 2019), 18, 20, 39, 83, 86, 88–89, 132, 139, 161, 208, 209, 250, 289, 319, 334. Besides these larger studies dealing with Pss 15–24, a number of works simply assume that Pss 15–24 is a self–contained unity.

5. See Hossfeld and Zenger, "Wer darf hinaufziehn," 166–82; Frank-Lothar Hossfeld and Erich Zenger, *Die Psalmen I. Ps 1–50*, NEB 29 (Würzburg: Echter, 1993), 14–15, 144–45. See J.-M. Auwers, "Le Psautier comme livre biblique," in *Composition*, ed. Erich Zenger, 70–71, for a handy explanation and chart of Hossfeld and Zenger's views concerning the diachronic development of Book 1.

6. See Hossfeld and Zenger, "Wer darf hinaufziehn," 169.

7. Jamie Grant, *The King as Exemplar: The Function of Deuteronomy's Kingship Law in the Shaping of the Book of Psalms*, AcBib 17 (Atlanta: Society of Biblical Literature, 2004), 235–38.

Concatenation is a common feature in Book 1 of the Psalter, however, and practically every psalm has lexical connections with neighboring psalms.[8] Although there are words and thematic elements that separate Pss 15–24 from the rest of Book 1 of the Psalms, this article isolates an earlier stratum within the collection based on the themes of not being shaken and the LORD's right hand. This stratum is Pss 15–18, 20–21. Psalms 15–17 comprise a small subgroup within the larger group.[9]

THE THEMES OF NOT BEING SHAKEN AND THE LORD'S RIGHT HAND IN PSS 15–18, 20–21.

Psalms 15–18, 20–21 have thematic and vocabulary connections. One of these themes is the immoveability of the person who trusts in the LORD and does righteousness. The relevant verses are as follows.

עשה־אלה לא ימוט לעולם (15:5)

15:5) The one who does these things will not be shaken forever.

שויתי יהוה לנגדי תמיד כי מימיני בל־אמוט(16:8)

16:8) I have set the LORD ever before me. Because he is at my right hand, I will not be shaken.

תמך אשרי במעגלותיך בל־נמוטו פעמי (17:5)

17:5) My steps have held to your paths; my feet have not slipped.

כי־המלך בטח ביהוה ובחסד עליון בל־ימוט (21:8)

21:8) For the king trusts in the LORD, and with the commitment of the LORD, he will not be shaken.

The texts communicate the faithfuls' unshakeable stability due to their righteousness and trust in the LORD through the particles לא or בל and the verb מוט in a prefix conjugation. Psalms 18 and 20 express the same thought, although differently. Psalm 18:37 reads,

---

8. The concatenation is well-documented in Christoph Barth, "Concatenatio im ersten Buch des Psalter," in *Wort und Wirklichkeit: Studien zur Afrikanistik und Orientalistik*, ed. Brigitta Benzig et al. (Meisenheim am Glan: Anton Hain, 1976), 30–40.

9. Peter C. H. Ho, *The Design of the Psalter: A Macrostructural Analysis* (Eugene, OR; Pickwick, 2019), 86. My difference from Dr. Ho as far as breaking Pss 15–24 into smaller groupings is that whereas he sees the groupings as 15–17, 18–22, and 23–24, I see them as 15–17, 18–21, 22–24.

תרחיב צעדי תחתי ולא מעדו קרסלי, "You widened my steps underneath me, and my feet did not slip." Psalm 20:9 is as follows, המה כרעו ונפלו ואנחנו קמנו ונתעודד, "They bow down and fall, but we arise and stand upright." The word picture in Pss 18 and 20 complements the idea communicated by Pss 15, 16, 17, and 21, but not identical.[10] The image that Pss 15, 16, and 17 expresses through the negative particle with the verb מוט in Pss 15, 16, and 17 concerns the faithful's stability in the LORD's presence on Zion. It is unlikely that Aubrey Johnson is correct in saying that Ps 15 has to do with dwelling in the land as a whole as the LORD's welcome guest and sojourner.[11] Although Psalm 15 is indeed talking about sojourning in the central sanctuary on Zion, his comments on the role that מוט plays here are helpful. Not being shaken is the opposite of being abandoned to *Sheol* and being securely established on Zion.[12] The faithfuls' unshakeability on Zion results in victory over their enemies in Pss 18, 20, and 21:9–13.

The righteous' stability and their victory is due to the LORD's right hand's support. The verses that communicate that theme are as follows.

שויתי יהוה לנגדי תמיד כי מימיני בל־אמוט (16:8)

16:8) I have set the LORD ever before me. Because he is at my right hand, I will not be shaken.

תודיעני ארח חיים שבע שמחות את־פניך נעמות בימינך נצח (16:11)

16:11) You have taught me the path of life. Fullness of joy is in your presence; fortunes in your right hand forever.

הפלה חסדיך מושיע חוסים ממתקוממים בימינך (17:7)

17:7) Show your commitments, savior of those who take refuge in your right hand from those who rise (against them).

---

10. VanGemeren writes that compositionally, images of purity, stability, and people living in God's presence give unity to Pss 15–21. See Willem VanGemeren, *Expositor's Bible Commentary: Psalms*, EBC, rev. ed. 5 (Grand Rapids, MI: Zondervan, 2008), 180.

11. Aubrey Johnson, *The Cultic Prophet and Israel's Psalmody* (Cardiff: University of Wales Press, 1979), 95–101. It seems incredible that Johnson considers the hill mentioned in Ps 15:1 to not refer to the central sanctuary, but the hill country of Canaan.

12. Kevin Madigan and Jon Levenson, *Resurrection: The Power of God for Christians and Jews* (New Haven, CT: Yale University, 2008), 92–93; Johnson, *Cultic Prophet*, 98–99.

ותתן־לי מגן ישעך וימינך תסעדני וענותך תרבני (18:36)

18:36) And you gave me the shield of your salvation, and your right hand strengthened me, and your humility made me great.

עתה ידעתי כי הושיע יהוה משיחו יענהו משמי קדשו בגברות ישע ימינו (20:7

20:7) Now I know that the LORD will save his anointed one, and he will answer him from his holy heaven by the strong salvation of his right hand.

תמצא ידך לכל־איביך ימינך תמצא שנאיך (21:9

21:9) Your hand will find all of your enemies, your right hand the ones who hate you.

In Book 1 of the Psalter, the image of the right hand (ימין) is unique to Pss 15–18, 20–21. In Ps 16, the LORD is at the psalmist's right hand, and thus he will not be shaken (v. 8), and that pleasant things are in the LORD's right hand forever (v. 11). In Ps 17, the LORD saves by his right hand (v. 7) from foes, and God's hand (יד) delivers the faithful from those whose reward is merely in this life. In Ps 18, the LORD's right hand sustains the psalmist (v. 36) in battle. In Ps 20, the LORD saves his anointed by answering from heaven with the power of his right hand. In Ps 21, the LORD's right hand will find his foes (v. 9). A common theme in Pss 15–18, 20–21 is the right hand of the LORD that saves and supports the worshiper. This support and salvation is often, but not exclusively, in contexts that indicate military victory.

Basson argues that the right hand (ימין)[13] serves as an instrument for delivering his people from their enemies. He writes, "The victory of the enemy is assured when his right hand fights on behalf of the psalmist or the people of Israel."[14] In Ps 21:9, the LORD's hand and right hand find all of his enemies and destroy them. The LORD's right hand also expresses the psalmist's dependence and the LORD's support of the faithful. The hand is also a figure of speech for the

---

13. And hand (יד).

14. Alec Basson, *Divine Metaphors in Selected Hebrew Psalms of Lamentation*, FAT 2, Reihe 15 (Tübingen: Mohr Siebeck, 2006), 96–97. See also Peter Brown, *Seeing the Psalms, A Theology of Metaphor*. (Louisville: Westminster John Knox, 2002), 175.

assistance given to keep one from stumbling, and represents the affirmation given in making a covenant.[15]

The description of the righteous in Ps 15 and the protestations of righteousness in Pss 16–17 give unity to the three psalms.[16] Psalms 15–16 depict t he fa it hful per son unmoved and unhar med due t o God's blessing, and Ps 17 shows trust in God's deliverance from enemies due to that righteousness. This righteousness has characteristics similar to those depicted in Ezek 18 and 22 and Lev 19 and 25. These connections with Ezekiel and Leviticus, the חקות and משפטים that the righteous follow that allow them to live, also connect Pss 15–17 with Ps 18:23, כי כל־משפטיו לנגדי וחקתיו לא־אסיר מני, "For all of his judgments were before me, and I did not put his statutes away from me."

STATUTES AND JUDGMENTS IN PS 18:21–25

In Psalm 18:23–24, Gert Kwakkel finds connections with texts from priestly circles such as Ezekiel and the Holiness Code (Lev 17–26). Although Deuteronomy and Deuteronomistic literature frequently use משפטים and חקות they generally use the terms with a third term, such as עדות or מצות; they do not use the pair משפטים and חקות.[17] This pairing is frequent in the Holiness Code and Ezekiel.[18] The word תמים, found in v. 24, is not commonly used in Deuteronomy and Deuteronomistic literature but is quite common in the priestly literature, such as Leviticus and Ezekiel.[19]

---

15. Zeev W. Falk, "Gestures Expressing Affirmation," *JSS* 4.3 (1959): 268–69.

16. L. Delekat considered Ps 16–17 to be from the same author, and Frank-Lothar Hossfeld and Erich Zenger consider the two to be very intertwined to the point that Ps 17 was in view when Ps 16 was composed. See L. Del ekat , *Asylie und Schutzorakel am Zionheiligtum* (Leiden: Brill, 1967), 222–29, and Frank-Lothar Hossfeld and Erich Zenger, *Die Psalmen. Psalm 1–50*, NEB 29 (Würzburg: Echter Verlag, 1993), 109.

17. These triads of terms occur numerous times throughout Deuteronomy and 1–2 Kings. See Deut 6:1; 7:11; 11:1; 1 Kgs 2:3; 6:12; 2 Kgs 17:37; 23:3. There are many other passages where the triads are used.

18. See Lev 18:4, 5; 18:26; 19:37; 20:22; 25:18; 26:15, 43; Ezek 5:6, 7; 11:12, 20; 18:9, 17; 20:11.

19. Gert Kwakkel. *According to My Righteousness : Upright Behaviour as Grounds for Deliverance in Psalms 7, 17, 18, 26, and 44*, OtSt 46 (Leiden: Brill, 2002) 268.

PSALM 15

Psalm 15 draws upon a common cultic tradition exemplified in Leviticus and Ezekiel. It lays out the ethical dimension of what is necessary to be a resident in God's holy hill.

The priestly instruction contained in Ps 15 has links with Lev 19 and Lev 25, Ezek 18, and Ezek 22:1–16.[20] These close parallels are significant because they indicate that Ps 15 draws upon a priestly theology centered in Jerusalem's central sanctuary. An examination of Ezek 18:5–9 is instructive. Ezekiel's law is similar to Ps 15 and belongs to the Jerusalem sanctuary's priestly tradition.[21] Ezekiel 18:5–9 descr ibes t he vir t ues of a r ight eous per son who shal l l ive due to his righteousness (the opposite is also true, see Ezek 18:13).[22] This declaration that the faithful person shall live because of his righteousness, (צדיק הוא חיה יחיה, "He is righteous; he will surely live") corresponds to Ps 15:5c (עשה־אלה לא ימוט לעולם, "the one who does these things will never be shaken"). Both are priestly declarations of judgment.[23] See, for example, Ezek 18:8–9.

בנשך לא־יתן ותרבית לא יקח מעול ישיב ידו משפט אמת יעשה בין איש
לאיש (8
בחקותי יהלך ומשפטי שמר לעשות אמת צדיק הוא חיה יחיה נאם אדני
יהוה (9

8) He does not charge interest and does not take advance interest; he turns his hand from injustice; he does true justice between people.

9) In my statutes, he walks, and he indeed keeps my judgments. He is righteous; He will surely live. Oracle of the Lord Yahweh.

---

20. Walter Beyerlin, *Weisheitlich-kultische Heilsordnung*, BthS 9 (Neukirchen–Vluyn: Neukirchener, 1985), 47–51; L. Delekat, *Asylie und Schutzorakel am Zionheiligtum* (Leiden: Brill, 1967), 169–72.

21. Beyerlin, *Weisheitlich-kultische Heilsordnung*, 49; Glenn Miller, "Between Text and Sermon: Psalm 15," *Int* 65.2 (April 2011): 187; Klaus Koch, "Tempeleinlassliturgien und Dekaloge," in *Studien zur Theologie der alttestamentlichen Überlieferungen*, ed. Rolf Rendtorff and Klaus Koch (Neukirchen: Neukirchener Verlag, 1961), 56–59.

22. In Ezek 22:12, "the bloody city" is brought under judgment for doing these, and a number of other things.

23. Hossfeld and Zenger, *Psalmen I*, 104.

The instruction contained in Ps 15 and Ezek 18:5–9 echoes material in Leviticus. Consider, for example, the material dealing with exacting interest, which receives its classic formulation in Lev 25:36–37,[24]

36) אל־תקח מאתו נשך ותרבית ויראת מאלהיך וחי אחיך עמך

37) את־כספך לא־תתן לו בנשך ובמרבית לא־תתן אכלך

36) Do not take from him interest or usury, but fear your God, so that your brother may live with you.
37) Do not give him your money with interest, and for profit, do not share your food.

Another connection that Ps 15 has with the priestly instruction reflected in Leviticus and Ezekiel deals with the speech life of the one who can sojourn on the LORD's holy mountain. Psalm 15:3 reads,

3) לא־רגל על־לשנו לא־עשה לרעהו רעה וחרפה לא־נשא על־קרבו

3) He does not slander with his tongue. He does not do evil to his companion and does not raise a taunt against his neighbor.

Compare this with Ezek 22:9 and Lev 19:16,

9)
אנשי רכיל היו בך למען שפך־דם ואל־ההרים אכלו בך זמה עשו בתוכך

9) Men who slander to shed blood are in you, and they eat on the mountains in you. They practice depravity in the midst of you.

16) לא־תלך רכיל בעמיך לא תעמד על־דם רעך אני יהוה

16) Do not go as a slanderer in your peoples. Do not stand against the blood of your neighbor. I am the LORD.

Psalm 15:3, Lev 19:16, and Ezek 22:9 are similar in content and vocabulary.[25] The passages concentrate on the destructive use of words that undermine community and destroy lives. It is plausible that "he does not do evil to his companion" is more specifically defined with "and does not raise a taunt against his neighbor." The three cola of Ps 15:3 stand in parallel with each other. Craigie intimates that the phrase "he does not do evil to his companion" refers to the dubious intent

---

24. Miller, "Psalm 15," 187.

25. Jacob Milgrom writes that רכיל in Lev 19:16 may be related to רגל in Ps 15:3. Jacob Milgrom, *Leviticus: A Book of Ritual and Ethics* (Minneapolis: Fortress, 2004), 230.

of the slanderer's speech.[26] Leviticus 19:16 and Ezek 22:9 explain the slanderer's suspect purpose, the spilling of the neighbor's blood.

Ezekiel 18:8 has strong thematic parallels with Ps 15:5a, as both verses describe the righteous person as one who does not give money at interest (בנשך לא־נתן כספו, Ps 15:5a; בנשך לא־יתן, Ezek 18:8a). The idea that the righteous person does not take a bribe against the innocent (ושחד על־נקי לא לקח; Ps 15:5b) comports nicely with Ezek 18:8b, מעול ישיב ידו משפט אמת יעשה בין איש לאיש, "He turns his hand from injustice. He does true justice between people."[27] The righteous person will keep from injustice and perform justly in dealings with legal decisions over which they have authority.

Psalm 15 lifts up the ethical dimension of what is necessary to be a resident on God's holy hill. As will be seen, Ps 16 emphasizes the liturgical devotion required to be shown the path of life.

PSALM 16

2) אמרת ליהוה אדני אתה טובתי בל־עליך

3) לקדושים אשר־בארץ המה ואדירי כל־חפצי־בם

ירבו עצבותם אחר מהרו בל־אסיך נסכיהם מדם ובל־אשא את־שמותם

4) על־שפתי

2) I have said[28] to the LORD, you are my lord. I have no good beside you.

3) As for the holy ones in the earth and the mighty ones, my delight is not in them.[29]

---

26. Peter C. Craigie and Marvin E. Tate. *Psalms 1–50*, 2nd ed. (Nashville: Thomas Nelson, 2004), 150–51.

27. Artur Weiser, *The Psalms: A Commentary*, OTL, trans. Herbert Hartwell (Westminster: Philadelphia, 1962), 170; John Goldingay, *Psalms Volume 1: Psalms 1–41* (Grand Rapids, MI: Baker Academic, 2006), 223. Although Goldingay and Weiser do not connect Ps 15 with Ezek 18 in this matter, they do mention Ps 15:5b with perversion of justice.

28. Read as אמרתי based on OG εἶπα and Syriac אמרת, and multiple Hebrew manuscripts.

29. Psalm 16:2–3 are corrupt in the MT, and it is difficult to make sense of them. I follow Mowinckel's suggestion that כל־חפצי־בם should be amended to בל־חפצי־בם. See Sigmund Mowinckel, "Zu Psalm 16, 2–4," *TLZ* 82 (1957), 654; See also Franz D. Hubmann, "Textgraphik und Psalm XVI 2–3," *VT* 33.1 (1985), 105; L. Delekat, *Asylie,*

4) Those who hasten after another (god) will increase their pains. I will not pour out their libations of blood, and I will not raise their names on my lips.

Ps 16:2–4, Affirmation of Righteousness

The meaning of Ps 16:2–4 is controversial due to difficulties in the Hebrew text. Interpreters generally consider the "holy ones that are in the earth" and the "mighty ones" to be either the psalmist's community of faithful in which he delights or the renunciation of gods of the land,[30]

Whether the phrase refers to other righteous persons with whom the supplicant has fellowship or some divinity that they repudiate has a large effect concerning what Ps 16:2–4 contributes to Pss 15–17. At this point in Ps 16, the psalm has resonances with priestly instruction in Leviticus and Ezekiel that give unity to Pss 15–17 and Ps 18.

My reading follows the idea that Ps 16:2–4 involves the repudiation of deities of the land and their worshipers.[31] The supplicant confesses trust in the LORD and repudiates the gods of the land and those who follow after them. This reading also contributes to the contrast of the righteous and the wicked that dominates Book 1 of the Psalter.

If this is the case, Ezek 18:5–9 is helpful in viewing the relationship between Ps 15:4 and Ps 16:3–4. The language in Ps 16:3–4 is not as close to Ezek 18:5–9 as is the case with Ps 15:5a, but there are strong thematic connections between these passages.

5) וְאִישׁ כִּי־יִהְיֶה צַדִּיק וְעָשָׂה מִשְׁפָּט וּצְדָקָה
אֶל־הֶהָרִים לֹא אָכַל וְעֵינָיו לֹא נָשָׂא אֶל־גִּלּוּלֵי בֵּית יִשְׂרָאֵל וְאֶת־אֵשֶׁת רֵעֵהוּ
6) לֹא טִמֵּא וְאֶל־אִשָּׁה נִדָּה
לֹא יִקְרָב
וְאִישׁ לֹא יוֹנֶה חֲבֹלָתוֹ חוֹב יָשִׁיב גְּזֵלָה לֹא יִגְזֹל לַחְמוֹ לְרָעֵב יִתֵּן וְעֵירֹם
7) יְכַסֶּה־בָּגֶד
בַּנֶּשֶׁךְ לֹא־יִתֵּן וְתַרְבִּית לֹא יִקָּח מֵעָוֶל יָשִׁיב יָדוֹ מִשְׁפַּט אֱמֶת יַעֲשֶׂה בֵּין אִישׁ
8) לְאִישׁ

225n5.

30. But see M. Mannati, who sees syncretism in Ps 16:1–3. He considers that the psalmist not only expresses confidence in the LORD, but in the local Canaanite deities, as well. See M. Mannati, "Remarques sur Ps. XVI 1–3," *VT* 22.3 (1972): 359–61.

31. See also Jean-Luc Vesco, *Le psautier de David, traduit et commenté, vol 1* (Paris: du Cerf, 2006), 182–83.

בחקותי יהלך ומשפטי שמר לעשות אמת צדיק הוא חיה יחיה נאם אדני
יהוה (9

5) And if a man is righteous and does justice and righteousness,

6) Upon the mountains he does not eat, and does not raise his eyes to the idols of the house of Israel, and does not defile his neighbor's wife, or does not come near a menstruating woman,

7) does not oppress a man but returns to the debtor his pledge; he does not commit robbery, his food he gives to the hungry, and covers the naked person with a garment.

8) He does not give at interest and does not take profit. He turns his hand from injustice. He does true justice between people.

9) In my statutes, he walks and faithfully observes my judgments to do (them). He is righteous. He will surely live. An oracle of the Lord Yahweh.

Whereas Ps 15:2–5a concentrates on the theme of social ethics prevalent in the priestly statutes and judgments mentioned in Lev 19 and 25 and Ezek 18:5–9 and 22, Ps 16:2–4 concentrates on appropriate and inappropriate worship, a theme it shares with Ezek 18:6 and Ezek 22:9. Whereas Ps 16:3–4 avers that the psalmist's delight is not in the gods of the land and repudiates those who worship idols, Ezek 18:6 attributes righteousness to the one who does not eat upon the mountains or raise his eyes to the images of the house of Israel.

PSALM 17

The LORD should answer the psalmist because the LORD has examined, tested, and tried them during the night and found them righteous. The supplicant did not transgress with his mouth. Speech is a central theme in Pss 15–17 and a possible avenue for transgression. In Ps 15, the one worthy of sojourning in the LORD's tent does not gossip with his tongue (לא־רגל על־לשנו, v. 3a), or raise a reproach against his neighbor (וחרפה לא־נשא על־קרבו, v. 3c). Psalm 16 includes a positive confession of the psalmist, that he has no good apart from the LORD (אמרת ליהוה אדני אתה טובתי בל־עליך, v. 2), and a statement that he will not take the names of other gods on his lips (ובל־אשא את־שמותם על־שפתי, v. 4b). In Ps 17, the supplicant's lips are free from deceit, and thus the LORD should hear his prayer (האזינה תפלתי בלא

שפתי מרמה, v. 1b). He has also not transgressed with his mouth (זמתי בל־יעבר־פי, v. 3c).

The psalmist has kept away from violent paths by the word of the LORD's lips (v. 4),

4) לפעלות אדם בדבר שפתיך אני שמרתי ארחות פריץ
4) Concerning the works of man, by the word of your lips, I have kept (from) violent paths

In contrast, The LORD has found no depravity in him.[32] It is found numerous times in Ezekiel with similar meaning.[33] The psalmist's keeping watch on the paths of the violent (פריץ) and the LORD's not finding depravity (זמה) in him have lexical and thematic connections with Leviticus and Ezekiel. Ezekiel 22:9 reads,

9) אנשי רכיל היו בך למען שפך־דם ואל־ההרים אכלו בך זמה עשו בתוכך
9) Men who slander to shed blood are in you, and they eat on the mountains in you. They practice depravity in the midst of you.

The result of the supplicant's righteousness is that his feet have not slipped (v. 5). The psalmist speaks of this in terms of having held his feet to the LORD's paths. They have avoided the ways of the violent, concerning which he has kept watch. The words of the LORD's lips have kept the psalmist from their paths. This avoidance naturally flows into the psalmist's keeping hold of the LORD's way. Thus, the protestation of righteousness ends with a statement of confidence in the word of the LORD's mouth that kept the supplicant from violent paths and held them on the LORD's. Given the linkages of the language here with the priestly language in Ezekiel and Leviticus, Ps 17 promotes a similar ethos as the judgments (משפטים) and statutes (חקות) outlined in Leviticus and Ezekiel.

CONNECTIONS IN PSS 15–17

The main rhetorical effect of Pss 15–17 is to show that the petitioner is righteous, and thus the LORD should move to deliver him.[34] This

32. The term זמה (v. 3) is a technical term in Leviticus for depravity.

33. See Lev 18:17; 19:29; 20:14. There are also a number of occurrences in Ezek 16, 22, 23, and 24. See Kwakkel, *According to My Righteousness*, 83–84.

34. This is a common theme in Babylonian and Assyrian protective rituals. The

deliverance issues from the blessing of the LORD in which the faithful asks the LORD to keep him. In both Pss 16 and 17, the psalmist calls on God to guard him (Ps 16:1; 17:8). The psalmist is righteous because he has kept the judgments and statutes that allow him to walk on the LORD's path. The LORD's judgments and statutes are similar to those found in Ezekiel and Leviticus.[35] Groenewald has written that Ps 16, in the context of Pss 15 and 17, shares a temple theology influenced by the wisdom tradition. Because of the ethical characteristics of the person who sojourns in the LORD's tent, the LORD shows them the path of life (16:11), and because the psalmist keeps the LORD ever before him, he will not be shaken (16:8). This wisdom tradition in Pss 15–16 lifts up "honesty, justice, a sense of responsibility, to refrain from syncretism and to adhere to Yahweh."[36]

Psalms 15–17, together with Ps 18, have been characterized by Vesco as concentrating on "l'homme parfait."[37] Not only are they thematically similar, but they have lexical connections. Psalms 15–17 include a statement concerning the psalmist not being shaken. Psalm 15:5c is a promise that the one who fulfills the moral requirements for entrance into Jerusalem's sacred precincts will not be shaken. The root מוט is in Pss 15:5c, 16:8, and 17:5.[38] Weiser writes that the phrase in Ps 15:5c,

---

supplicant is righteous, and the wicked are evil and slanderous. Their attacks are unjust against the righteous supplicant, and so the deity should intervene. For a discussion of this, see Tzvi Abusch and David Schwemer, *Corpus of Mesopotamian Anti–Witchcraft Rituals, vol.* 1, AMD 8.1 (Leiden/Boston: Brill, 2011), 20–21.

35. See discussions under the individual psalms for their connections to Leviticus and Ezekiel.

36. Alphonso Groenewald, "The Ethical "Way" of Psalm 16," in *The Composition of the Book of Psalms*, ed. Erich Zenger, BETL 238 (Leuven: Peeters, 2010), 507.

37. Vesco, *Le psautier*, 176.

38. Psalm 15:5c

עשה־אלה לא ימוט לעולם

The one who does these things will not be shaken forever.

Psalm 16:8

שויתי יהוה לנגדי תמיד כי מימיני בל־אמוט

I put the LORD in front of me always. Because he is at my right hand, I will not be shaken.

Psalm 17:5

"The one who does these things will not be shaken forever," refers to the firm divine support that the upright person has through their lasting communion with God.[39] Kraus relates לא ימוט לעולם to standing on the eternal rock of the Jerusalem temple mount and the stability that that represents, which centers on the LORD in the cultic tradition of Zion.[40] Ross writes that the psalmist's stability is the devouts' spiritual security, and that they will not be moved from the dwelling place of the LORD.[41] The devout person's immoveability in the presence of the LORD translates into their stability in the face of adversity.[42]

Groenwald considers there to be thematic links between the conditions for admission to the sanctuary outlined in Ps 15, and Ps 16:3–4. In Ps 16:3, the supplicant confesses that he is one of the "community of the faithful," a fulfillment of Ps 15:4. He delights in the faithful, and those who do not engage in syncretism (Ps 16:4). As such, he is the LORD's חסיד.[43] Psalm 15:1 מי־ישכן בהר קדשך, "who may dwell on your holy hill," has a connection with אף־בשרי ישכן לבטח, "Indeed, my flesh dwells securely (Ps 16:9)."[44] Groenwald's interpretation draws upon the traditional view that the holy ones in the land and the mighty ones refer to the community of the faithful with which the psalmist aligns

---

תמך אשרי במעגלותיך בל־נמוטו פעמי

Hold fast my steps in your paths (so that) my feet are not shaken.

39. Weiser, *Psalms*, 170–71. See a similar position in Samuel Terrien, *The Psalms: Strophic Structure and Theological Commentary* (Grand Rapids, MI: Eerdmans, 2003), 172–73; Craigie, *Psalms 1–50*, 152–53; Vesco, *Le psautier*, 179–80.

40. Hans-Joachim Kraus, *Psalms 1–59*, trans. Hilton C. Oswald (Minneapolis: Fortress, 1993), 231.

41. Allen P. Ross, *A Commentary on the Psalms, Volume 1 (1–41)* (Grand Rapids, MI: Kregel, 2011), 394.

42. See, for example, Ps 18:37, תרחיב צעדי תחתי ולא מעדו קרסלי, "You enlarge my steps under me, and my ankles do not wobble." Dahood and Anderson consider "he will not be shaken forever" to mean that the devout person will not suffer misfortune (Dahood, *Psalms 1:1–50*, AB 16 (Garden City, NY: Doubleday, 1966), 85; A. A. Anderson, *Psalms (1–72)*, NCBC (Grand Rapids, MI: Eerdmans, 1972), 139–40. In Ps 18, it is in the king's day of adversity that the LORD gives him the stability depicted in Ps 18:37.

43. Alphonso Groenwald, "The Ethical "Way" of Psalm 16," in *The Composition of the Book of Psalms*, ed. Erich Zenger, BETL 238 (Leuven: Peeters, 2010), 507.

44. Groenwald, "The Ethical Way," 507.

himself. He then repudiates the ones who worship the gods of the land. His interpretation is a decent way of linking Ps 16:3–4 with Ps 15:4.

Another way of linking Ps 15:4 with Ps 16:3–4 is to view their relationship through Ezek 18:5–9. This chapter has already indicated the linkage of Ps 15:5a with Ezek 18:5–9 and Lev 25:36–37. The language in Ps 16:3–4 is not as close to Ezek 18:5–9 as is the case with Ps 15:5a, but there are strong thematic connections between these passages.

ואיש כי־יהיה צדיק ועשה משפט וצדקה (5
אל־ההרים לא אכל ועיניו לא נשא אל־גלולי בית ישראל ואת־אשת רעהו
לא טמא ואל־אשה נדה (6
לא יקרב
ואיש לא יונה חבלתו חוב ישיב גזלה לא יגזל לחמו לרעב יתן ועירם
יכסה־בגד (7
בנשך לא־יתן ותרבית לא יקח מעול ישיב ידו משפט אמת יעשה בין איש
לאיש (8
בחקותי יהלך ומשפטי שמר לעשות אמת צדיק הוא חיה יחיה נאם אדני
יהוה (9

5) And if a man is righteous and does justice and righteousness,
6) Upon the mountains, he does not eat, and does not raise his eyes to the idols of the house of Israel, and does not defile his neighbor's wife, or come near a menstruating woman,
7) and he does not oppress a man but returns to the debtor his pledge, he does not commit robbery, his food he gives to the hungry, and covers the naked person with a garment.
8) He does not give at interest and does not take profit. He turns his hand from injustice. He does true justice between people.
9) In my statutes, he walks, and my judgments he observes to do (them) faithfully. He is righteous. He will surely live. An oracle of the Lord Yahweh.

Whereas Ps 15:2–5a concentrates on the theme of social ethics prevalent in the priestly statutes and judgments mentioned in Lev 19 and 25 and Ezek 18:5–9 and 22, Ps 16:2–4 concentrates on appropriate and inappropriate worship, a theme it shares with Ezek 18:6 and Ezek 22:9. Whereas Ps 16:3–4 avers that the psalmist's delight is not in the gods of the lan and repudiates those who worship idols, Ezek 18:6 attributes righteousness to the one who does not eat upon the mountains or raise his eyes to the idols of the house of Israel.

Groenwald helpfully draws a connection between "the one who walks blamelessly (הולך תמים [Ps 15:2])," and the "path of life (ארח

חיים [Ps 16:11])."[45] Psalms 15–17 share the theme of a "way" or a "path" on which the righteous walk. Psalm 17:4 depicts the petitioner keeping from violent paths, and he has held to the LORD's ways (v. 5).

The paths of the violent and the LORD's ways deal extensively with speech, a dominant theme in Pss 15–17. The one who walks the LORD's paths, the path of life, does not slander or raise a taunt against his neighbor (Ps 15:3). Rather than taking the names of other gods on his lips (Ps 16:4), he confesses that the LORD is his lord and that he has no good besides the LORD (Ps. 16:2). The theme of speech is prevalent in Ps 17. The petitioner prays to the LORD with a tongue without deceit (v. 1), and his mouth has not transgressed (v. 3). By the words of the LORD's lips, he has kept away from the paths of the violent (v. 4). The text characterizes the supplicant's enemies by their speech. Their mouths speak arrogant words (v. 10). The concentration on speech and accusation is reminiscent of sorcery's characterization in the ancient Near East.[46]

CONNECTIONS WITH PSALM 18

Both Ezek 18 and Lev 25 categorize instruction concerning not charging interest as חקות and משפטים in terms similar to Ps 15:2–5a. Psalm 18:23 reads, כי כל־משפטיו לנגדי וחקתיו לא־אסיר מני, "Because all of his judgments were in front of me, and I did not put his statutes away from me." Given the connection between what we find in Ps 15 with the חקות and משפטים in Lev 25 and Ezek 18, it is plausible that the judgments and statutes referred to in Ps 18:23 are in part in Ps 15:2–5a. In Lev 25, the judgments and statutes are more ethical in focus and focus on the year of Jubilee and laws concerning slavery and the redemption of the poor. The laws in Ezekiel 18:5–9 are more comprehensive in scope. Psalms 16–17 reflect other elements of the priestly torah (חקות and משפטים) in Leviticus and Ezekiel, as

---

45. Groenwald, "The Ethical Way," 507.

46. Please see the following incantation against slander and parallels in anti–witchcraft literature. O. R. Gurney, "A Tablet of Incantations against Slander," *Iraq* 22 (1960): 221–27; Tzvi Abusch, *The Anti–Witchcraft Series Maqlû,* WAW 37 (Atlanta, GA: SBL, 2015), 79. Numerous rituals in *Maqlû* disempower the tongue and slanderous speech of the witch. For example, see Abusch, *Maqlû,* 47–49.

indicated in the discussion concerning the connections between Pss 15, 16 and 17.

Besides the connection of חקות and משפטים with Pss 15:5a and 18:23, Ps 15:2, הולך תמים, "the one who walks in integrity" has links with Ps 18, as well. Psalm 18:24 reads, ואהי תמים עמו ואשתמר מעוני, "And then I had integrity with him, and I kept myself from guilt." Psalm 18:26 reads, עם־חסיד תתחסד עם־גבר תמים תתמם, "with the committed you show yourself committed, and with the man of integrity, you act with integrity." Not only does the king have integrity, and thus the LORD is committed to him, the LORD's path has integrity, and he gives that path to the king (Ps 18:31, 33). Like the word pair חקות and משפטים, the word תמים frequently occurs in the priesthood-influenced books Ezekiel and Leviticus (mostly the Priestly Torah in Lev 1–16, but also in the Holiness Code [Lev 17–27]). Thus, the connections between Ps 15 and Ps 18 reinforce a sacerdotal tradition that concentrates on the sort of moral integrity that qualifies one who would approach the LORD in his sanctuary.[47]

Psalm 18:23 references חקות and משפטים that the faithful observe, which motivates the LORD to deliver them. As Pss 15–17 have resonances with priestly instruction, they provide unity to Pss 15–18. The themes of God's right hand and the faithful's stability strengthen this unity. The interpreter, then, can read Pss 15–18 as a unity through the lens of the statutes and judgments of the Holiness Code in Leviticus and Ezekiel.

---

47. Miller, "Kingship, Torah Obedience, and Prayer: The Theology of Pss 15–24," 128. Although Miller seems to be talking of the Torah, the חקות and משפטים and the integrity (תמים) that following them gives is related to priestly instruction connected with the sacerdotal traditions in the sanctuary that are applied to all Israel in what lies behind Leviticus' holiness code. The reason for Miller's slightly different reading is that he sees Ps 19 as the center of Pss 15–24, rather than a footnote to Ps 18, rearticulating it to a full-blown Torah piety.

[*JESOT* 7.2 (2021): 90–112]

Exegetical Difficulty and the Question of Theodicy in the Book of Job

ERIC ORTLUND

Oak Hill College
erico@oakhill.ac.uk

ABSTRACT: Somewhat in distinction from other OT books, Job generates not just diverse but flatly contradictory interpretations which can be summarized as "pro-theodicy" and "anti-theodicy:" the same text is read either to demonstrate God's justice and goodness in the face of terrible suffering or to demonstrate God's immorality and malice. Four important passages are examined according to both of these perspectives (the interaction of the satan and YHWH in 1:6–12; 2:1–7; YHWH's being "enticed to destroy Job for no reason" in 2:3; the comparison between Leviathan and YHWH in 41:10–12, and Job's last response in 42:6). It is argued that although these passages contain difficulties which make it possible to carry an anti-theodicy reading very far, such a reading is ultimately untenable. Enough data is present in the text to support a reading of Job as a successful theodicy. However, the text has been written with calculated difficulties which have the tendency to force the reader to draw on the assumptions they bring to the text as well as exegetical decisions made elsewhere in the book of Job and the OT as a whole. This has the effect of reinforcing the reader's assumptions and producing contradictory readings.

KEYWORDS: the book of Job, theodicy, satan, Leviathan, suffering, exegesis

[T]he book of Job incontrovertible proof that a text functions as a mirror, revealing the minds of interpreters in addition to its own contours.[1]

---

1. James Crenshaw, *Defending God: Biblical Responses to the Problem of Evil* (Oxford: Oxford University, 2005), 186.

In formulating Job's answer in this matter, the author must have intended to leave open the question as to whether Job was really convinced by God's inconclusive speech, and throws the ball back to each one of us: if I was convinced . . . I cannot assume any differently with regard to Job.[2]

[T]he poet himself . . . created a situation that can be interpreted in several ways according to the theological inclinations of the reader.[3]

For a variety of reasons, the book of Job is arguably the most challenging book in the OT.[4] The tangled Hebrew poetry presents the reader with many textual and philological problems.[5] Even when one arrives at a defensible translation of a passage, it can be difficult to understand what the speaker means by what they say.[6] Furthermore, beyond these smaller and more local questions loom the larger moral and theological problems surrounding Job's suffering and the nature and justice of God's rule. Philological, exegetical, and theological problems turn up in every OT book, of course, but they recur with a frequency and urgency in Job which is unusual.

Compounding these difficulties is the kind of scholarship which Job has received in the modern era: when one turns to commentaries for help, one discovers that Job is read not just in different, but starkly contradictory, ways. At one level, this is hardly surprising; biblical texts generate diverse and even mutually incompatible interpretations.

2. Yair Hoffman, *A Blemished Perfection: The Book of Job in Context*, JSOTSupp 213 (Sheffield: Sheffield Academic, 1996), 297.

3. William Morrow, "Consolation, Rejection, and Repentance in Job 42:6," *JBL* 105 (1986): 225.

4. This essay was first presented as a postgraduate colloquium at Oak Hill college on January 21, 2020. I am deeply grateful for the following discussion in helping me develop the argument, and especially to my friends and colleagues Christopher Ansberry, Timothy Ward, and Paul Sutton for their comments.

5. See the recent discussion of C. L. Seow, "Orthography, Textual Criticism, and the Poetry of Job," *JBL* 130 (2011): 63–85.

6. For example, in 17:8–9, it is not clear why would Job speak of the upright being appalled at "this" (whatever "this" is), but the righteous holding to his way. Is he imagining how others ought to react to his shameful treatment at the hand of his friends? Even after one settles on the translation of the lines, it is difficult to be sure. See further discussion in Norman Habel, *The Book of Job*, OTL (Philadelphia: Westminster, 1985), 277–78.

Ecclesiastes, for example, has been read as an entirely pessimistic text[7] or as a consistently optimistic one.[8] Regardless of what one concludes about these interpretations, they cannot both be right.[9] The same difficulty faces the student of the book of Job in a more extreme form. One finds not just mutually exclusive but diametrically opposite claims about God's trustworthiness and the justice of his reign. Thus, on the one hand, Christopher Ash speaks for many evangelicals when he concludes his commentary by writing:

> The assurance that [God] can do all things and that no purposes of his can be thwarted is the comfort I need in suffering and the encouragement I crave when terrified by evil. He does not merely permit evil but commands it, controls it, and uses it for his good purposes. . . . This God who knows how to use supernatural evil to serve his purposes of ultimate good can and will use the darkest invasion of my own life for his definite and invincible plans for my good in Christ.[10]

7. E.g., James Crenshaw, *Ecclesiastes: A Commentary*, OTL (Philadelphia: Westminster, 1987), who summarizes the message of the book as: "Life is pointless, totally absurd. This oppressive message lies at the heart of the Bible's strangest book. . . . [T]he world is meaningless. Virtue does not bring reward. The deity stands distant, abandoning humanity to chance and death" (23).

8. E.g., Daniel Fredericks, "Ecclesiastes," 17–263, in Daniel Fredericks and Daniel Estes, *Ecclesiastes and The Song of Songs*, AOTC 16 (Downers Grove: InterVarsity, 2010).

9. I find neither convincing. One the one hand, it is difficult to square Crenshaw's reading with Qohelet's unbounded enthusiasm for enjoying life as God's gift (e.g., 9:7–10). On the other hand, more traditional interpretations can be too quick to dismiss some of Qohelet's harder sayings: Fredericks, for example, understanding הבל to refer to what is temporary, makes a forced interpretation of Qohelet's distress over the lack of judgement on wicked lives in 8:10, 14 as a positive statement, taking it to mean that this injustice is only temporary and will eventually be rectified (*Ecclesiastes*, 188, 194, 197). It is significant that, in his brief review of some recent commentaries, Fox faults both negative and uncomplicatedly positive readings of Ecclesiastes as underplaying one important aspect of Qohelet's thought—either his frustration or his joy (Michael Fox, *A Time to Tear Down and a Time to Build Up: A Rereading of Ecclesiastes* [Grand Rapids: Eerdmans, 1999], xii). Fox further notes that Qohelet himself does not prompt the reader to promote one of the themes of his text at the expense of the other (Fox, *A Time to Tear Down*, xii). I will argue below that the situation is somewhat different in the book of Job.

10. Christopher Ash, *Job: The Wisdom of the Cross* (Wheaton: Crossway, 2014), 424. John Hartley lands in a similar place (see *The Book of Job*, NICOT [Grand Rapids: Eerdmans, 1988], 534, 37).

On the other hand, some scholars read Job not merely an ambiguous or failed attempt to defend divine justice, but actually to demonstrate that God is unjust, immoral, and monstrous. For example, James Crenshaw writes:

> [T]he opening and closing references in the zoological section [i.e., 38:39–39:30] to the violent preying on weaker victims amount to bold admission that in the animal world the strong survive at the expense of the weak. . . .. In this world, "might makes right," if one may justifiably introduce the subject of justice at all. . . .. [B]ut does that principle operate in the human realm too? It would seem so, on the basis of the entire divine speech.[11]

Crenshaw later says that God's main attributes in the book of Job are "malevolence and absence," a "troubling" presentation which YHWH's speeches at the end do nothing to ameliorate.[12] Edward Greenstein agrees, writing of how the predators of Job 39 reflect something predatory in God himself[13] and that the "terrifying power" of Behemoth and Leviathan witness not to God's justice, but to brute (and brutal) strength.[14] The divine speeches "ought to convince any skeptic that the God of the whirlwind is not the God of justice,"[15] but rather "a sadistic and self-centered deity" and "an abusive victimizer"[16] who is "not significantly different"[17] from Job's description of him in his protest

11. James Crenshaw, "When Form and Content Clash," in *Urgent Advice and Probing Questions: Collected Writings on Old Testament Wisdom* (Macon, GA: Mercer University, 1995), 456.

12. Crenshaw, "When Form and Content Clash," 467.

13. Edward Greenstein, "In Job's Face/Facing Job," in *The Labour of Reading: Desire, Alienation, and Biblical Interpretation*, ed. Fiona Black et al. (Atlanta: Society of Biblical Literature, 1999), 309.

14. Greenstein, "In Job's Face/Facing Job," 309–10. Noting the connection between the flashing fire issuing from Leviathan's mouth in 41:11–13 and the same coming from YHWH's mouth in Ps 18:9, Greenstein sees Leviathan as a symbol for YHWH (Greenstein, "In Job's Face/Facing Job," 311).

15. Edwin M. Good, "The Problem of Evil in the Book of Job," in *Mishneh Todah: Studies in Deuteronomy and Its Cultural Environment in Honor of Jeffrey H. Tigay*, ed. Nili Fox, David Glatt-Gilad, and Michael Williams (Winona Lake, IN: Eisenbrauns, 2009), 355.

16. Edwin M. Good, "The Problem of Evil in the Book of Job," 342.

17. Edwin M. Good, "The Problem of Evil in the Book of Job," 353.

against him (e.g., 16:12–14). Other important scholarship on the book of Job could be added here from Edwin Good[18] and Carol Newsom.[19] Although neither expresses their views as forcefully as Crenshaw and Greenstein, both argue that the book of Job does not merely fail to answer the question of suffering and divine justice, but demonstrates that God is unjust. This means that, out of a variety of readings of Job, two identifiable camps have offered not just incommensurate but diametrically opposite interpretations: a "pro-theodicy" reading and an "anti-theodicy" reading. As stated above, this is unusual in the study of the OT. We have moved beyond an expected diversity of interpretation to the point where one wonders how they could be speaking of the same text.

Several factors deepen the perplexity of this modern impasse in the study of Job. First, these opposite readings cannot be explained with reference to interpretative incompetence in one party, for both the com-mentaries both by Ash and Hartley and the work of Crenshaw, Green-stein, Good, and Newsom all pay meticulous attention to the Hebrew of the book and do not betray obvious flaws in argumentation. Although I will argue below that the anti-theodicy reading is demonstrably wrong, making this argument is not always easy on the basis of the text of Job itself.

A second perplexity is that both the pro- and anti-theodicy read-ings of Job tend to appeal to the same passages. One would expect different parts of Job to be invoked in support of these contradictory readings (as with the frustrated and joyful parts of Ecclesiastes), but this is not the case. Certain passages and verses in chapters 1–2 and 38–42 surface repeatedly and in crucial ways to argue both that God in the book of Job is either completely trustworthy or a moral monster.

A third perplexity is that none of the relevant passages or specific verses is especially difficult to translate. The issues in textual criticism and philology which recur in the book of Job do not tend to show up in some of the most crucial verses for interpreting the book. (This is even the case in 42:6, for although more than one translation is defensible,

---

18. Edwin M. Good, *In Turns of Tempest: A Reading of Job* (Stanford: Stanford University, 1990).

19. Carol Newsom, *The Book of Job: The Contest of Moral Imaginations* (New York: Oxford, 2003).

each one falls clearly within the normal semantics and grammar for the words Job chooses.)

Why is it, then, that the book of Job is read not just in diverse, but opposite ways? And which is the best reading? Four important passages will be examined with regard to the question of theodicy in Job. While not exhaustive,[20] these four passages are (in my opinion) especially crucial in deciding whether the God of the book of Job is just or not:

1. The role and activity of the Accuser in relation to YHWH in 1:6–12 and 2:1–7

2. YHWH's claim that the accuser "incited" him (סות) to destroy Job "for no reason" (חנם) in 2:3

3. YHWH's comparison of himself to Leviathan in 41:2 (Eng. v. 10): "Is he [Leviathan] not fierce when aroused? Who then is he who can take their stand against me?"[21]

4. Job's final response to YHWH in 42:6, in which he uses the verb מאס, "despise," without a direct object (is he despising God or himself?) and says he either changes his mind about dust and ashes, is sorry for them, or is comforted about them (Niphal נחם)

Three conclusions will emerge from this examination. First, it is possible to push an anti-theodicy reading of Job very far; there is little which is explicit in the text of Job which prevents such a reading. At the same time, a more positive reading as a successful defence of divine justice in the face of unimaginable suffering is both possible and even compelling as the best reading of the book, not so much because of the particular wording of key verses, but their larger context. Anti-theodicy readings do not adequately account for the larger context of the passages in question.

---

20. Other passages certainly could be added here, such as Job's hope in his Redeemer in 19:25–27, which is identified with God in a very hopeful way by some Christian commentators, or read only as a forlorn hope which never materializes for Job (e.g., C. L. Seow, *Job 1–21*, Illuminations (Grand Rapids: Eerdmans, 2013], 805–6). Within the boundaries of this article, however, the discussion is limited to these four passages because they are relevant in an especially sharp way for the question of God's justice.

21. Translations of Hebrew in this article are my own. The first half of this verse is usually translated along the lines of, "No-one is fierce enough to arouse it" (NIV), but this would fit better with אֵין than לֹא (see G. C. L. Gibson, "A New Look at Job 41.1–4 (English 41.9–12)," in *Text as Pretext: Essays in Honour of Robert Davidson*, ed. Robert Carroll, JSOTSupp 138 [Sheffield: Sheffield Academic, 1992], 105).

Third, I will suggest that this somewhat paradoxical situation may have been intended by the narrator/poet. The ease with which the author could have reworded verses or given more explicit information in ways which would have precluded the anti-theodicy reading at the outset suggests that he has given us a text which is intentionally difficult. This is certainly not to claim that the book of Job is irredeemably ambiguous and impossible to interpret definitively, as Newsom argues.[22] It is rather to note the especially sharp and prolonged form which exegetical difficult takes in Job and the ease with which it could have been avoided. Furthermore, it will be argued that the particular wording which the narrator chooses, together with the lack of explicit information at crucial points, has the effect of forcing the reader to draw on interpretative decisions made elsewhere in the book of Job and the rest of the OT. (Whether one thinks that the portrayal of God in the book of Job must be consistent with his portrayal elsewhere in the OT or not significantly affects what interpretative options are available to reader as they struggle with this very difficult text.) This means that, for readers willing to search, the clues for a more positive interpretation are present in the text—but those content with an anti-theodicy reading will not find many explicit challenges in the text itself. What hermeneutical and theological implications this difficulty might have will be considered at the end of this article.

We proceed by considering the four passages listed above (1:6–12/2:1–7, 2:3, 41:10, 42:6), first by considering the surprising ease with which each can be read as part of an anti-theodicy interpretation, then working our way backwards to argue that each supports a successful defence of divine justice in the face of Job's suffering.

Who Is the "Accuser"? Does YHWH Admit He Was Tricked?

An Anti-Theodicy Reading of Job 1–2: For Christian readers of Job, it can be easy to read about the "Accuser" at the beginning of the book

---

22. See Newsom, *Contest*, 29–30, 236. Newsom argues that the different parts of Job (the prose ending, the poetic debate, and so on) can each be related to each other in multiple ways, with multiple interpretations following from these; but that the text does not put forward any one reading as the final way to read the text (and nor should the interpreter). Instead of a text with a single message, it is as if the reader is caught in an ongoing quarrel between the different parts of the book (Newsom, *Contest*, 23).

and immediately download what we know about the saint's heavenly adversary from the NT (as well as some late OT texts like Zech 3:2 and 1 Chr 21:1). And certainly nothing explicit in the text prevents us from seeing Job 1–2 as another contest between the Lord and "that prince of darkness grim," in which God's favorite saint comes through a time of testing like gold.

Several important commentators on Job, however, read the "Accuser" figure more neutrally as a party which tests God's policies—something like the leader of the opposition in Parliament. As is well known, the noun הַשָּׂטָן is not a proper name, but a title; the definite article does not normally occur with proper names,[23] and the verb שָׂטַן is used elsewhere for accusation from human beings (Pss 38:21; 71:13; 109:4, 6, 20, 29) or human political opposition (1 Sam 29:4; 2 Sam 19:23; 1 Kgs 5:18, 11:14, 23, 25). It is even used for the angel opposing Balaam (Num 22:22, 32). In light of this, some argue there is no necessary reason for attributing any hostility to the "satan" of Job 1–2.[24] Perhaps he is only doing his job by identifying "procedures that are out of order."[25] On the basis of what the narrator explicitly tells us, the most one can say is that this figure is supernatural (he is among the "sons *of God*") but subservient to God ("*sons* of God") and that his role is to accuse or oppose.[26]

Some go so far as to see the "satan" in Job 1–2 as a reflection of "pluriformity" in the divine nature,[27] such that different divine servants are different "manifestations of the divine personality"[28] and this Ac-

23. According to John Walton, the word "Satan" is not used as a proper name until around the second century BC (*Job*, NIVAC [Grand Rapids: Zondervan, 2012], 66).

24. Habel, *The Book of Job*, 89. Habel notes that the verbs which the Satan uses in v. 7 are also used of divine servants who serve God's people in Zech 1:10 (Hitpael of הָלַךְ) and 4:10 (שׁוּט).

25. John Walton, "Satan," in *Dictionary of the Old Testament: Wisdom, Poetry, and Writings*, ed. Tremper Longman et al. (Grand Rapids: IVP Academic, 2008), 716. Walton goes so far as to say that the Satan's role here is "to serve, not disrupt" (Walton, "Satan," 716).

26. Clines points out that the Hitpael of יצב in Job 1:6 describes royal courtiers in service of the king in Prov 27:29 and Zech. 6:5 (D. J. A. Clines, *Job 1–20*, WBC 17 [Nashville: Thomas Nelson, 1989], 19).

27. Clines, *Job 1–20*, 21.

28. Clines, *Job 1–20*, 22.

cuser is "a verbal expression of the deity's hidden side."[29] An important part of this argument involves the text's dual attribution of Job's tragedy both to the satan (1:12) and YHWH (42:11). In light of this, the accuser might be "a projection of divine doubt about human ingenuity that is held in tension with divine trust."[30] This means that God allows Job's agony in order to prove a point about God to himself.[31]

This way of reading the proceedings of the divine council in Job 1–2 hardly bodes well for interpreting the book of Job as a convincing defense of God's justice and goodness even when he allows suffering. Apparently God is willing to sacrifice innocent children to satisfy divine insecurity! Apparently all of Job's exemplary piety (as listed in ch. 31) is not enough to allay God's doubts that Job does not really love him, and the Almighty is willing to kill children to satisfy these doubts.

What decision should the reader make about this? Should we connect what is known from the rest of the biblical canon with the supernatural agent bearing his name in Job 1–2, or ignore later tradition?

Limiting ourselves only to what is explicitly given in the text of Job 1–2 makes it difficult to decide. I will argue below that some clues have been left to nudge the reader in a certain direction—but they remain clues only. The author does not explicitly give us much to go on. If we come to the text with a traditional theological and canonical framework, understanding the same divine Author to have inspired many texts through different human authors, it will be natural to connect the Satan in Job 1–2 with his appearance later in the canon. On the other hand, if it is assumed that the OT is a collection of only human writings, there is no reason to assume a consistency across the canon. This will make a more neutral reading of the Satan appear natural—and the negative implications for the issue of theodicy become inevitable. The explicit information given to the reader in 1:6–12 and 2:1–7 makes it difficult to decide.

Those inclining toward an anti-theodicy reading about the Accuser in ch. 1 will certainly not fail to notice God's statement in 2:3, where, after Job has passed the first ordeal, God says that the Accuser incited him (סות) to destroy Job for no reason (חנם, 2:3). On the face of it, this

---

29. Crenshaw, *Defending God*, 186.

30. Seow, *Job 1–21*, 256.

31. Clines, *Job 1–20*, 22.

looks like open admission from the Almighty that he was manipulated into doing something he only later realizes was unwise. The semantic range of סות confirms this impression: the verb is often used for enticing someone to wrongdoing, e.g., enticing the covenant community into idolatry (Deut 13:7, similarly in 1 Sam 26:19), or David being provoked into an unwise census (2 Sam 24:1/1 Chr. 21:1), or Jezebel's enticing of Ahab (1 Kgs 21:25; see also 2 Kgs 18:32). The only possible exceptions to this are Job 36:16 and Josh 15:18/Judg 1:14, which speak of urging or appealing for something good. Perhaps one might mount an argument that the word should be read with these last two parallels in mind—but this is not a common use of this verb. Furthermore, it is difficult not to wonder whether the verse could have been reworded to avoid this problem from the beginning. If יעץ, "counsel," had been used, this would have more clearly disentangled YHWH's permission from the Satan's malicious intention: "You counseled me to destroy him for no reason, but Job still holds on to his integrity!" All cruelty would be limited to the Accuser. The narrator has, however, given us the more troubling סות. When the satan's "enticement" and the suffering it causes happen "for no reason," it becomes, in an anti-theodicy reading of Job, one of the most damning verses in the entire book:

> [T]his story describes God as one who stops at almost nothing, even murder, to prove a point. Furthermore, God admits that the adversary moved the deity to afflict Job without justification. Surprisingly, the deity makes no concession about the deaths of Job's children and servants, who are eradicated and then replaced without a word of apology. . . . The disturbing feature of this depiction of God is that a heavenly courtier wields sufficient power to manipulate God and thus to inflict grievous suffering on earth—with God's explicit consent.[32]

I will argue below that other readings of 2:3 are both possible and also fit better with the book as a whole. But there is no getting around this extremely difficult verse. The narrator is forcing some very difficult exegetical and theological decisions on the reader very early in their journey through the book. If the reader approaches the verse with

---

32. James Crenshaw, "The Concept of God in Old Testament Wisdom," in *In Search of Wisdom: Essays in Memory of John G. Gammie*, ed. Leo G. Perdue (Louisville: Westminster John Knox, 1993), 12. It is in relation to 2:3 that Greenstein refers to God as sadistic and "an abusive victimizer," quoted above ("The Problem of Evil in the Book of Job," 342).

the assumption that the deity portrayed in Job 1–2 is the same described in (for example) Isa 40:12–31, it will be impossible to imagine God admitting to a mistake, and the reader will go on to find other options to interpret the verse. One might, for example, hear an ironic twist when God speaks about being "enticed": where the Satan simply intended Job's destruction, God allowed the ordeal for the very different purpose of Job's painful but blessed worship in 1:21. On the other hand, if the reader approaches the text at a theological minimum (as some biblical scholars do), it will be easy to see divine doubt and vulnerability to error in 2:3. The implications of the reader's decision about 2:3 and the figure of the Accuser significantly impact how one reads the rest of the book and how one articulates the issue of theodicy. But no easy answers are forthcoming in the early chapters of this book.

LEVIATHAN, YHWH, AND JOB'S RESPONSE: AN ANTI-THEODICY READING OF THE ENDING OF JOB[33]

A third significant ambiguity in the book of Job which is especially relevant for the question of theodicy is found in the transition between the two major parts of the Leviathan speech in chapter 41. This chapter begins with a series of repeated rhetorical questions emphasizing Job's

---

33. Chapters 38–39 figure prominently in anti-theodicy readings, of course, but they are not discussed here because I am not aware of significant ambiguities in YHWH's first speech which give an anti-theodicy reading such apparent plausibility. Anti-theodicy readings of chapters 38–39 are, in other words, more immediately easy to argue against. For example, Carol Newsom argues that YHWH's care for unclean and predatory animals in 38:39–39:30 (such as the lion or raven or hawk) associate God "in positive fashion with these creatures in the fearful beyond." In her reading, this care seems "unnervingly to place God in considerable sympathy with the emblems of the chaotic" and implies 'the nonmoral and nonrational aspects' of the divine nature (*The Book of Job*, 245, 247, 252; this builds on an earlier essay by Matitiahu Tsevat, "The Meaning of the Book of the Job," in *The Meaning of the Book of Job and Other Biblical Studies* [New York: Ktav, 1980], 1–39). But God's care for dangerous or chaotic animals does not imply there is anything dangerous or chaotic about God. As Michael Fox points out, if God's pleasure in and care for creatures implies an identification with them, one could say the same about the creation of sea monsters in Gen 1:21; but no one reads Gen 1:21 that way (see "God's Answer and Job's Response," *Bib* 94 [2013]: 10). The repeated emphasis is chapters 38–39 is merely on God's goodness and care for all his creatures, even animals dangerous or strange to Job—the goodness which Job denied in the debate.

utter powerlessness before Leviathan (vv. 1–9[34]). Then, in vv. 10–11, something strange happens: the Almighty includes himself in the utterly unequal comparison between Leviathan and Job. This is strange because, in other texts describing YHWH's warfare against the raging waters or the monsters living there, no comparison is drawn between the Divine Warrior and his antagonist (see, e.g., Job 26:11–14; Isa 27:1; 51:9–11; Nah 1:2–5; Hab 3:3–15; Ps 18, 29, 46, 74, 89, 93, and 146).[35] But Job 41:10–11 breaks with the expected pattern in just this way: if Leviathan is so unapproachably and overwhelmingly cruel when aroused, who, by comparison, could take their stand against God? If there is no way Job could oppose Leviathan, then there is absolutely no way he could oppose the God who easily masters that beast.[36]

Another surprise meets us in v. 12. After comparing himself to the monster, God proceeds to speak in praiseworthy terms about Leviathan (v. 12), refusing to be silent about the monster's limbs, physical prowess, or what is translated as "goodly frame" (ESV) or "graceful form" (NIV). The use of "graceful" or "goodly" (חֵן) is especially surprising when speaking of a chaos monster![37] The rest

34. I follow the English verse ordering here, which sensibly begins a new chapter at Hebrew 40:25.

35. Not all these passages explicitly mention Leviathan, of course, but I am unable to discern any great difference between those texts which mention Leviathan or Rahab or the twisting serpent and those which mention only the raging waters: YHWH's defeat of cosmic chaos is the consistent theme. This is also a good place to point out that not too much can be made of the flames and glowing coals which come out of Leviathan's mouth in Job 41:18–21 and YHWH's in Ps 18:8 (as argued by Greenstein, "In Job's Face," 311, quoted above), because other texts show chaos and the Almighty engaging in conflict in similar ways without drawing any significant theological conclusions from this (e.g., both roar at each other in Ps 46:4, 7). Similarly, Baal and Mot attack each other in identical ways at the end of the Baal Epic without their identities being confused (for text and translation, see G. C. L. Gibson, *Canaanite Myths and Legends* [Edinburgh: T. & T. Clark, 1978], 80).

36. See Henry Rowold, "Leviathan and Job in Job 41.2–3," *JBL* 105 (1986): 104–9. The above discussion assumes the identity of Behemoth and Leviathan as chaos monsters, in contrast to their more common interpretation as an ordinary hippopotamus and crocodile. For reasons too involved to explore here, I think this more common interpretation generates multiple exegetical difficulties which a supernatural interpretation neatly avoids (see further Eric Ortlund, "The Identity of Leviathan and the Meaning of the Book of Job," *Trinity Journal* 34 [2013]: 17–30).

37. The Hebrew word חֵן (spelled differently here than elsewhere) is used elsewhere to describe favour with God and man (e.g., Prov 3:4) or God's grace (Ps 84:12, Zech

of the chapter makes good on the intention announced in v. 12, as YHWH describes at length the creature's physical invincibility.

Why does God draw a comparison between himself and Leviathan and then speak for twenty-one verses about how powerful and impressive his opponent is? No explicit conclusion is drawn from the description beyond God's even greater invincibility—a point which Job hardly contested (9:3–10, 14–19). God does not push Job toward any particular conclusion on the basis of what he has just said. It is worth noting how other comparisons to the animal world in the book of Job usually make the moral explicit; e.g., Bildad paints a picture of quickly-wilting plants (8:16–17), but secures the point of his illustration by unambiguously applying it to the wicked (v. 19). In contrast, YHWH finishes his description of the monster and simply stops talking. There is no parallel to 8:19 in ch. 41. What was Job supposed to think?

Some scholars read the comparison which God makes between himself and Leviathan to imply God's chaotic nature. The argument is straightforward: if Leviathan is the chaos monster, and if YHWH is to be compared to Leviathan, then YHWH has a "monstrous"[38] or a "dark, irrational side."[39] He is a God of "sheer, morally irrelevant power" and is no different from the bully Job feared in chapter 9.[40] As a result, it makes no sense to complain to such a monstrous deity about injustice. I am probably not the only reader of Job who wants to argue against this conclusion—but what the poet gives us on the page does not obviously provide a lot of evidence against it. We are told YHWH is even more unapproachably fierce than Leviathan, and that is all.

At first blush, Job's response 42:1–6 would seem to speak against this reading of YHWH's final speech: why would Job repent of his criticisms and worship a God who has just revealed his monstrous and sadistic side? Job's response can, however, be enlisted in an anti-theodicy reading, especially v. 6. This is the case because Job's final statement

---

12:10). It also can refer to graciousness or some pleasing attribute in more general ways (Prov 5:19; Eccl 10:12).

38. William Brown, *Wisdom's Wonder: Character, Creation, and Crisis in the Bible's Wisdom Literature* (Grand Rapids: Eerdmans, 2014), 118.

39. James Williams, "The Theophany of Job," in *Sitting with Job: Selected Studies in the Book of Job*, ed. Roy Zuck (Grand Rapids: Baker Academic, 1992), 370.

40. Greenstein, "In Job's Face," 311–12; see further Newsom, *Job*, 252, and Crenshaw, "When Form and Content Clash," 456, 59, 67; *Old Testament Wisdom*, 99.

can validly be read (among several other plausible options[41]) not as penitential worship, but disgust and rejection. It is possible to translate 42:6 in the following way:

Therefore I despise (you, God)   על־כן אמאס
and I feel sorry for dust and ashes.[42]   ונחמתי על־עפר ואפר

This verse presents us with three problems: the lack of an explicit object for the first verb, the meaning of Niphal נחם, and the meaning of the phrase "dust and ashes."

With regard to the first issue, while most modern translations have Job despising himself, he does not explicitly say what he despises. As a result, it does not strictly violate the meaning of the Hebrew to understand Job despising God here. Why does the author not give Job another noun to tell us exactly what he is despising? The line is hardly in danger of being too long, and מאס always takes a direct object outside of the book of Job. Within the book of Job, it usually does as well (see 5:17, 7:5, 8:20, 9:21, 10:3, 19:18, 30:1, 31:13. 34:33). There are three other instances of מאס without a direct object (7:16, 34:33, and 36:5), but in each of these cases, it is easy to infer what is being despised.[43] In contrast, I cannot see any obvious clues in 42:6 which nudge the reader either way as to who or what Job is despising. This lack of explicit information, when it would have been easy to add a direct object, is part of the reason I suspect the difficulties of the book are calculated and intentional.

41. For exhaustive discussion of other translations, see Morrow, "Consolation, Rejection, and Repentance," 211–25, as well as Thomas Krüger, "Did Job Repent?," in *Das Buch Hiob und seine Interpretationen: Beiträge zum Hiob-Symposium auf dem Monte Verità vom 14.–19. August 2005*, ed. Thomas Krüger, ATANT 88 (Zürich: Theologischer Verlag Zürich, 2007), 217–29.

42. First proposed by John Curtis, "On Job's Response to Yahweh," *JBL* 98 (1979): 497–511, and followed by Good, *In Turns of Tempest*, 375, 377, and Greenstein, "Problem of Evil," 359–60.

43. In 7:16, Job refers to his "life" and his "days," and in the previous verse, he says he would prefer death to his own life. This makes it easy to guess what he is despising in v. 16, even if he does not say. In 34:33, Elihu asks Job, "Will he [God] restore it to you, when you reject?" It is hardly a leap to see Job rejecting either God or God's terms here (see the discussion of D. J. A. Clines, *Job 21–37*, WBC 18a [Grand Rapids: Zondervan, 2006], 761–62). Finally, in 36:5, Elihu hails God as mighty and one "who does not despise"—but since the next verse speaks of God giving justice to the poor, it is not difficult to infer who it is that God does not reject.

Beyond the lack of direct object for the first verb in 42:6, one must decide on the translation of the second verb. Niphal נחם has three attested meanings: "to regret" or "change one's mind;" "to be sorry"; and "to console oneself" (*HALOT* 688). Any one of these would seem to fit in context: Job might be expressing comfort here, but he might also be "changing his mind" about dust and ashes or "being sorry" about them.

Third, we must decide on the exact nuance of the phrase "dust and ashes." The phrase is found only elsewhere in Job 30:19 and Gen 18:27. In Job 30:19, it stands as a synecdoche for Job's suffering: "God has cast me in the mire, and I have become like dust and ashes." In Gen 18:27, however, it connotes Abraham's humility as a mere mortal as he arbitrates over Sodom's fate. As a result, it would make sense to understand Job expressing comfort over his suffering (symbolically referred to as "dust and ashes"). It is, however, equally possible to read the verse as Job voicing sorrow over humanity as "dust and ashes" under the thumb of a monstrous deity. If the reader takes this latter option, it is natural to take the unstated object of Job's despising as God himself. Domino-like, the rest of the passage falls under the weight of this decision about v. 6: v. 5 becomes a statement of terror as Job sees this Leviathan-like God for who he really is; the irresistible "purpose" of God in v. 2 is only sinister, and so on. The high point of the entire book is Job's protest against God in chapters 9, 16, etc., and the only relief poor Job gets is venting his anger and horror at this horrible deity.

However much readers might want to resist this interpretation of 42:6 and its implications, it does not violate the Hebrew of the verse. By the same token, it is entirely defensible to understand Job to express disgust over his former protest against God or himself for uttering it (or both), and also change his mind about the "dust and ashes" of his suffering and/or to be comforted about them. How are we to decide between these two options? Simply on the basis of the exact wording of v. 6, it is difficult to be certain. We will probably have to rely on other exegetical decisions made elsewhere in the book to guide our reading here.

I stated above my sense that although the anti-theodicy interpretation of Job can be pushed very far and there is not much explicit in the text to stop it, there are contextual clues which weaken and even topple it. The poet has given us a book with a definite meaning, but one expressed in an intentionally difficult way. There is a case to be made in favor of a more positive reading of 42:6 which does not eliminate the ambiguity in the verse but also does not abandon us within it—and which, domino-like, has significant ramifications for how we read the whole.

DISCERNING JOB'S PENITENT WORSHIP, LEVIATHAN'S DEFEAT, AND DIVINE JUSTICE IN JOB 41–42

Two considerations are especially important for making sense of Job 42:6. The first is the use of Niphal נחם with the preposition על. In the dozen or so other occurrences of this verb with this preposition, it always expresses relenting or repenting some decision, or being comforted over some loss—one never finds the meaning of "being sorry for," as the "anti-theodicy" reading requires. We thus read of how God is either asked to relent from some promised disaster or actually does so (Exod 32:12, 14; 1 Chr 21:15; Ps 90:13; Jer 18:8, 10; Joel 2:13; Jon 4:2), or of how a human being repents their sin (Jer 8:6). We also read of how David is comforted over Ammon's death (2 Sam 13:39), Rachel refuses to be comforted over her children (Jer 31:15), the survivors of exile are comforted over their losses (Ezek 14:22), or Pharaoh is imagined to be comforted over his lost armies (Ezek 32:31). This puts the "anti-theodicy" reading of "be sorry for" on slightly weaker ground. By way of contrast, either expected translation of Niphal נחם with על fits perfectly in context: Job is changing his mind about "dust and ashes" (his suffering) in a way which expresses his comfort over his trauma. The scars and losses which Job thought testified against him about God's irrational anger against him (16:8) no longer have that meaning. Although Job has not yet been restored (42:1–17), nor has anything been explained to him, he now knows God is not his enemy. Thus is he comforted.

The second and stronger consideration against the "anti-theodicy" reading of Job 42:6 has to do with Job's vindication and restoration in vv. 7–17. After all, if Job is criticizing God in v. 6 as being even more of a bully than he previously thought, then God's response of restoring Job contradicts Job's supposed characterization of God as cruel and irrational.[44] What kind of amoral and cruel dictator would respond to criticism with kindness? Good himself seems to sense these problems

---

44. Michael Fox, "Job the Pious," *ZAW* 117 (2005): 366.

as he struggles to explain Job's restoration, since this restoration is evidence of a fair world in which God restores faithful saints, but (according to Good) God's speeches reject any idea of a just universe.[45] The cynical reading of 42:6 also contradicts Job's custom elsewhere of openly and unambiguously protesting against God—why would he cloak his putative criticism in ambiguous Hebrew when he was so unambiguous before?[46] And surely a rejection of God here would count as failing the Accuser's test from chapter 1, a point the Accuser would not fail to bring to the Almighty's attention. Understanding Job to express sorrow for "dust and ashes" under the sway of such a terrible ruler makes no sense in the larger context and sweep of chapter 42.

There are thus significant contextual reasons against seeing further criticism of God in 42:6 which act as a guide to the verse without relieving the ambiguity of the verse's exact wording. Those willing to search can find these clues; but some very close readings of the book find in Job's final statement confirmatory evidence of God's injustice. Given the normal use of מאס, it seems such readings could have easily been avoided at the outset by providing a direct object; but the poet has not done so. A great divide opens between interpreters who see criticism in Job 42:6 and those who see self-loathing and worship. One suspects this result is intentional.

Despite this divide, we have firm grounds for understanding Job to reject his former protest against God's supposed injustice and express comfort over his losses (42:6) in new knowledge of God (v. 5), and for God to respond to Job by restoring him to his former blessing (vv. 10–17). This, in turn, effects how we read the Leviathan speech in the previous chapter and especially God's comparison of himself with Leviathan in 41:10. It is difficult to imagine a simple identification between Leviathan and God as both agents of chaos, as required by the anti-theodicy reading, for who could worship such a deity? This does not resolve the question of the significance of the comparison between YHWH and Leviathan in 41:10, but it makes it impossible to follow

---

45. See his comments in *In Turns of Tempest*, 396–97. Greenstein does not say much about Job's restoration except that it is "the proper conclusion of Job's ordeal" and that because the test is over, conditions prior to the test are restored ("The Problem of Evil in the Book of Job," 362). Neither (in my opinion) really grapples with the significance of God's restoration of Job for how we read his response in v. 6.

46. Michael Fox, "The Meanings of the Book of Job," *JBL* 137 (2018): 20.

the anti-theodicy interpretation of it. Without explicit guidance in the text as to the manner in which YHWH is similar to Leviathan, we must look to the larger context of the book of Job as a whole and the rest of the OT. With this larger perspective in mind, three considerations are significant.

First, it is difficult to forget YHWH's unbroken record of defeating Leviathan and/or the raging waters elsewhere in the OT and in the book of Job itself (26:11–13). Although not decisive for interpreting Leviathan's presence in Job 41, it creates certain expectations. Second, chapter 41 is not the first place in which YHWH has asked rhetorical questions of Job. The questions beginning the Leviathan speech in 41:1–9 echo those throughout chapters 38–39. Furthermore, the expected answer to these earlier questions has not to do merely with God's capacity to accomplish the action under review, but with the fact that he actually does (or has done, or will) that particular action: Job cannot command the sunrise, but YHWH both can and does (38:12). In the same way, when God asks Job if he could fill Leviathan's side with spears and lay hands on the monster in battle (41:7–8), the expected answer is, "I could not, Lord—but you both can and do." As a result, we can understand the rhetorical questions in chapter 41 to imply that God actually will defeat a chaos and evil which Job can barely imagine.

Third, it is significant that Job frequently portrays his suffering as a suffering under chaos. He describes himself as dwelling in darkness (Job 10:26) and roaring in his pain (Job 3:26; cf. Ps 18:8; 77:17; Hab 3:7). In Job's mind, either he is the chaos monster (Job 7:12) or God is (9:4–9).[47] This means that when God describes the chaos monster Leviathan, Job is meant to connect this to his own suffering. As Job hears the description of Leviathan, he can infer that God sees clearly the chaos loose in his creation and the chaos under which Job has suffered. Job can also discern in the speech a promise that YHWH can and will defeat a powerful supernatural foe Job could not even approach (41:7–9). Little wonder, then, that Job speaks of comfort in chapter 42.

If this is correct, then the unequal comparison between God and Leviathan in vv. 10–11 has the effect of presenting God as a far more powerful savior and friend than Job previously thought—or, at least,

---

47. Chol-Gu Kang, *Behemot und Leviathan: Studien zur Komposition und Theologie von Hiob 38,1–42,6*, WMANT 149 (Göttingen: Vandenhoeck & Ruprecht, 2017), 232. Kang argues that the *Chaoskampf* motive is a major structuring device in the book as a whole.

that is what is implied. When God says to Job, "Is Leviathan not fierce when aroused? Who then can stand before me?" then as Job thinks of the chaos which has invaded his own life, considers the questions about the only one who can lay hands on Leviathan in battle, and hears the unequal comparison between the monster and God himself, then God appears to Job as incomparably stronger than the chaos which has invaded is life—more able to save Job than Leviathan is able to harm him. The comforting effect of this comparison can be imagined to continue through the chapter and provide a clue as to why the description goes on at such length. Job knows about Leviathan (he mentions the monster in 3:8). But he has never had the close-up tour which God gives him in chapter 41. But as Job hears line after line about Leviathan's terrifying prowess, the more clearly Job sees God as a mighty savior and friend, who will redeem Job from his chaos and defeat a monster Job could not even touch. This is why Job breaks into such ecstatic worship in chapter 42.

God's praise of his cosmic opponent can be read in the same sort of way. Tone in written texts is obviously difficult to determine, but it seems safe to say that YHWH hardly sounds anxious or defensive when describing the chaos monster. God's final speech rather projects a kind of cheerful and untroubled confidence as he surveys the monster's "goodly frame" with Job. This means that as the description of Leviathan goes on at such length, and as the creature becomes increasingly overwhelming to Job, God stands ever taller in calm mastery of it. "Now my eye sees you" (42:5).

All of this sketches a more positive interpretation of the comparison between God and Leviathan in 41:10–12 than concluding that God has chaotic aspects to his character. It has the benefit of explaining Job's response of worship in 42:1–6 and also fits best with the rest of the OT. But it must be emphasized that this is an interpretation of what is implicit and unstated in chapter 41. All that explicit in chapter 41 is that YHWH is more powerful than Leviathan. My sense is that the Joban poet has left us with enough clues to draw out the comforting implications of the unequal comparison between YHWH and Leviathan. Solely with reference to the explicit statements of chapter 41, however, it is not surprising that this chapter is read in opposite ways. Even if an argument can be made to reject these readings, more could have been said by the author in chapter 41 to prevent them from ever occurring to readers in the first place. As with 42:6, it is difficult not to suspect that a deliberate obscurity informs the expression of chapter 41 which leaves different readers in very different places by the time they finish reading.

LOOKING FURTHER BACKWARDS: YHWH AND THE ACCUSER IN JOB 1–2

I argued above that there is little which is explicit in Job 1–2 to guide our interpretation of the figure of the Accuser in the prose prologue and his interactions with YHWH. But if we are on firm grounds to see Job utterly reconciled to a God who effortlessly masters chaos and whatever resists him at the book's end, this surely informs our reading of the beginning. Could a deity who so calmly surveys the roiling chaos which Job cannot even approach be tricked by one of his subordinates? It is difficult to believe so, and with this in mind, certain features of the narrative of chapters 1–2 become easier to notice which support a different conclusion than that argued by the anti-theodicy reading. (This is even more so if the later identification of the Accuser with that Leviathan-like "ancient dragon" in Rev 12:9 is admissible as evidence; but even without it, the interaction between YHWH and the satan reads differently in light of the interpretation of chapters 41–42 argued above.)

First, it is significant that YHWH has to specify that the satan is allowed to harm only Job's property and cannot touch his own person during the first test (1:12). If the satan were concerned only to test the validity of divine policy, and if the charge brought against Job is that Job obeys God only for the sake of external blessings (1:9), why is it not assumed that the ordeal will pertain only to those blessings? This restriction makes it more difficult to believe that the Accuser is only a neutral party. The satan appears less interested in the moral and relational validity of the law of retribution and more interested in destroying Job, such that he must be kept within strict bounds as the ordeal proceeds.

A second clue is found in the Accuser's failure to say anything about the results of the first test in 2:1–3. As the conversation in 2:1–3 repeats from 1:6–12, what might have been a neutral response to God's first question (1:7) becomes more suspicious the second time round (2:2). Job has nobly and in great tragedy proved that he is loyal to God without any ulterior motive, even when his children are dead (1:21). If the satan is testing without malice the validity of divine policy, surely something would have been said about this?

In light of this, YHWH's statement that the Accuser "incited" him to destroy Job "for no reason" can be read not as admission of fault but a statement only about the Accuser's failed intentions: where the Accuser intended Job's spiritual destruction as his deficient loyalty to God was exposed, God's intention was to guide Job's ordeal so that he stands stronger in his integrity than ever.[48] The Accuser's "enticement" has thus failed; the ordeal has produced the opposite result from that predicted: blessing (1:21) and not curse (v. 11). The echo of the adverb חנם in 2:3 to its use in 1:9 supports this. The adverb can mean "without compensation" (e.g., Num. 11:5), "in vain" (Prov. 1:17), or "without cause, undeservedly" (Ps 35:7, 19; see *HALOT* 334). The Accuser uses it in its first meaning in 1:9, but YHWH means it in the third sense in 2:3: Job is innocent of all charges brought against him, despite the satan's malicious intentions.[49] YHWH is, in other words, not admitting fault but defending his servant. But this need not imply that Job's suffering happens for no reason in an absolute sense—Satan's accusation was without value, but there are deeper reasons why God allowed it.[50]

As a result, no suspicion about Job lies in God's heart which provokes some horrific ordeal just to satisfy divine doubt. YHWH's approval of Job remains unambiguous. His ordeal happens only within the boundaries set by his divine friend, and issues in deeper worship of God (1:21), not the destruction of Job's faith. The God who effortlessly masters chaos in chapter 41 shows the same guidance of the accusation against Job here.

CONCLUDING REFLECTIONS

Four passages of special relevance to the question of theodicy in the book of Job have been examined with regard to potentially deliberate

48. See Ash, *Job*, 50–51.

49. H. H. Rowley, *The Book of Job*, New Century Bible (Grand Rapids: Eerdmans, 1983), 31, 34.

50. Martin Shields, "Malevolent or Mysterious? God's Character in the Prologue of Job," *TynBul* 61 (2010): 268–69.

difficulty. This particular kind of exegetical difficult under examination here has to do not merely with obscurity in translation, but where a verse or passage can be interpreted in more than one way, and the narrator/poet does not give much guidance as to which route the reader should take. It has been argued throughout that this difficulty is intentional because the narrator/poet could have written 42:6; 41:10–12; 2:3; and 1:6–12 either with more explicit information or re-worded certain phrases in order to close off certain routes of interpretation from the beginning. This is not to claim that the book of Job is irreducibly ambiguous or that hermeneutical closure is forever delayed. It is to claim that one is forced to draw upon larger theological and hermeneutical presuppositions in order to make sense out of what one reads—or rather, that the Joban poet is skilfully unearthing the assumptions of the reader in his carefully worded text. To make this claim is not to invoke some authoritarian fideism, according to which it is insisted without argument that one must always read the Bible at a theological maximum. It is to assert that everyone reads Job with certain presuppositions, whether orthodox or not. One either sees God as basically consistent and trustworthy or not, and one either reads the book as consistent within a larger canon or not; but only one set of presuppositions allows the reader to avoid the destructive and even nihilistic conclusions of the anti-theodicy reading of Job.

I have been writing throughout this article as if the reader's assumptions (whatever they are) are stable and stationary throughout their reading of Job. This is probably too simple, however. It seems that there is something about the book of Job itself which provokes and deepens the kind of attitude which the reader brings to the book before reading. If the reader begins the book already suspicious about God's manner of ruling over creation, which allows sometimes extreme suffering, he or she will be even more so by the end of the book. On the other hand, if the reader already trusts this God at the beginning, the God of the book of Job will appear even more trustworthy by the end. Whether the reader reacts positively or negatively to the book of Job and the God portrayed in it, no one remains exactly the same. When considering the diametrically opposite interpretations which the book of Job has generated, it is difficult not to think of Isaiah's "hardening" commission (6:9). What Bruce Waltke wrote about OT theology as a whole seems eminently true of the book of Job in particular: "[s]

piritual discernment is a prerequisite for doing Old Testament theology because, like a parable, it is a masterpiece of misdirection, yielding its wealth only to those with eyes to see and ears to hear."[51]

51. Bruce Waltke, *An Old Testament Theology* (Grand Rapids: Zondervan, 2007), 36.

[*JESOT* 7.2 (2021): 113–46]

The D Stem System in Biblical Hebrew: Meaning and Exegetical Implications

ANDREW E. STEINMANN

Concordia University Chicago
andrew.steinmann@cuchicago.edu

THE D STEM SYSTEM (*piel, pual, hithpael,* and allied conjugations) and its meaning appears to many to be the most enigmatic of the systems in Biblical Hebrew.[1] While there have been studies of comparative Semitics that have come to different conclusions about the nature of the basic semantics of the D stem in Biblical Hebrew, this paper seeks to examine them in light of a comprehensive catalog of all D stem verb roots occurring in the Old Testament.[2]

Many have been taught that the D stem's basic significance is to form an intensive meaning from corresponding G stem (*qal*) verbs. The impetus for this view was found partly in the doubling of the middle root letter in *piel* forms (or in the reduplication exhibited in other forms such as *pilpel*). Thus, the duplication was seen as iconic, signaling that the D stem was intensifying the corresponding meaning in the G stem.

Gesenius defined this intensive meaning as "*to busy oneself eagerly* with the action indicated by the stem."[3] This, of course, was difficult to maintain in light of D stem forms that are clearly causative in meaning when compared to the same root in the G stem. Therefore,

---

1. Throughout this paper I will refer to the various stems by letter designations instead of the traditional names. This is especially helpful in that the D stem has various manifestations, many showing some type of reduplication. D: *piel, palel, pealel, pilel, pilpel, polel, poel*; Dp: *pual, polal, polpal, pulal, poal*; HtD: *hithpael, hothpaal, hithpolel, hithpalpel*. In the G stem system the letter designations are G (*qal*), Gp (*qal passive*), and N (*niphal*). In the H stem system the designations are H (*hiphil*) and Hp (*hophal*).

2. The catalog is available online at https://www.academia.edu/35272706/The_D_Stem_System_in_Biblical_Hebrew.

3. E. Kautzsch and A. E. Cowley eds., *Gesenius' Hebrew Grammar,* Second English ed. (Oxford: Clarendon, 1910), 141 (§52f).

Gesenius attempted to explain this phenomenon by stating, "This eager pursuit of an action may also consist in *urging* and *causing* others to do the same. Hence *Pi'ēl* has also—(b) a *causative* sense (like *Hiph'îl*), e.g., לָמַד *to learn*, Pi'ēl *to teach*." However, since the H stem verbs are nearly always causative, this leaves one to wonder why the H stem was never characterized as intensive. Yet, a causative verb does not in itself signal an "eager pursuit," and this explanation appears to be forced and unnatural. Moreover, as Goetze observed, "The causative-factitive force of the form is customarily said to be an outgrowth of the intensive force. But nobody has ever been able to demonstrate in a satisfactory manner how this development should have been possible."[4]

The consequence of the longstanding assertion that the D stem is intensive has led to some in evangelical quarters to assume it as fact and to produce particularly inaccurate and misleading investigations of the uses of the D stem. One example is the brief study by Timothy Smith.[5] While Smith appears to be vaguely aware of the work of Ernst Jenni (see discussion below), his presentation neither knows of Jenni's predecessor Goetze nor of his successors Waltke and O'Connor.[6] Thus, he analyzes most uses of the Biblical Hebrew D stem as extensions or consequences of the D stem as primarily intensive. When he notes some semantic nuances of certain D stem verbal roots that are not easily explained as deriving from the supposed intensive use (e.g., frequentative, causative, resultative), he offers no analysis of how such refinements in the D stem arose.[7] Clearly, the characterization of the D stem as intensive not only continues among evangelicals, but also has led at times to questionable assertions about its semantics.

More recently, Kouwenberg has attempted to defend the concept that the Semitic D stem was originally intensive. He theorized that it

4. Albrecht Goetze, "The So-Called Intensive of the Semitic Languages," *JAOS* 62 (1942): 3. See also the earlier statement of Bauer and Leander: "At present the question as to how the Semitic intensive gained a causative meaning cannot be answered." Hans Bauer and Pontus Leander, *Historische Grammatik Der Hebräischen Sprache Des Alten Testaments* (Halle: Max Niemeyer, 1922), 293 (§38t).

5. Timothy Smith, "The Piel Stem," https://welsmn.org/wp-content/uploads/2019/09/The-Piel-Stem-Smith.pdf.

6. Smith, "The Piel Stem," 3–5.

7. Smith, "The Piel Stem," 18–21.

subsequently developed a variety of meanings, including verbal plurality (i.e., a frequentative sense, see discussion below)[8] and a strong tendency to make verbs that were originally intransitive into transitive verbs.[9] There are two problems with Kouwenberg's approach with respect to Biblical Hebrew. One is that it does not adequately explain the semantic difference between an intransitive verb in the G stem and a transitive verb in the D stem that share the same root. In fact, in Hebrew the difference between verbs that are transitive and intransitive has been recognized for a long time—the difference is in the causative nature of these D stem verbs, as admitted by both Gesenius and Bauer-Leander (see discussion above). The other problem with Kouwenberg's theory is that it is so flexible that it is not falsifiable[10]—a D stem verb's semantic force can be explained in a large variety of ways so that there is no way to pin down when Kouwenberg's theory might be mistaken. If a D stem verb is factitive, then that is a later development.[11] If the verb is frequentative and transitive, then that is also a later development. If it is frequentative and intransitive, then it does not exhibit much semantic development over time. Thus, if a D stem verb is transitive it must have developed semantically over time. If it is intransitive, then it demonstrates little or no semantic development. No matter what the verb's D stem associated semantics are, there is no way to test whether

8. See the definition of *frequentative* in the Oxford dictionary Lexico: "expressing frequent repetition or intensity of action." "Frequentative," https://www.lexico.com/definition/frequentative.

9. N. J. C. Kouwenberg, *Gemination in the Akkadian Verb*, SSN (Assen: Van Gorcum, 1997).

10. For any theory to be tested and shown to be reliable, it must first be falsifiable. That is, it must provide some way to examine test cases to determine its reliability, whether its assertions are true or false. If test cases can be shown to affirm the theory, then it can be accepted as reliable. However, if the test cases demonstrate that the theory is false, it can be discarded. A theory is of little value if it is so flexible in its explanations of the data that there is no possibility of constructing a test to demonstrate whether or not the theory is false. For instance, if a theory states that all cheeses are yellow or white, then one can construct test cases—looking at various cheeses to see whether they are some color other than yellow or white. However, a theory that states that cheeses can be any color or no color at all is not falsifiable, and therefore, of little use in describing cheeses.

11. See the definition of *factitive* in the Oxford University dictionary Lexico: "having a sense of causing a result and taking a complement as well as an object, as in 'he appointed me captain.'" "Factitive," https://www.lexico.com/definition/factitive.

Kouwenberg's theory is correct. That is, the theory fails because it is not falsifiable—it cannot be proven or disproven.[12]

Yet not all analyses based upon and extending Kouwenberg's work are inadequate. For instance, the recent presentation by John Huehnergard describes the D stem this way:

> D, characterized by doubling of the second radical. The D stem increases the transitivity of the verbal root (Kouwenberg 1997, Beckman 2015). It is especially common as a factitive of stative roots: G *ji-slam* (3-whole.pcs) "he became whole," D *ju-sallim* (3-whole.fact.pcs) "he made whole, completed, restored." For transitive roots, the D may be pluralic or indicate increased effect on the object: *ju-θabbir* "he broke (something) up, apart; he broke (many)."[13]

As will be seen in the discussion below, this is remarkably like the theory presented in this paper that the D stem generally exhibits a causative component in comparison to verbal roots that also occur in the G stem. This is not only evident in the glosses used for stative roots ("became whole, made whole, completed, restored"), but also in the glosses for [G stem] transitive roots that also occur in the D stem (i.e., causative-resultative, "broke up, apart").[14] In fact, as argued below, it is the causative component of the D stem that allows these verbs to increase their transitivity: concepts such as *cause* or *make* are inherently transitive: *cause* something *to happen, make* something *happen.*

During the twentieth century the intensive description of the D stem was challenged by developments in studies of Semitic grammar. Before the Second World War, Arno Poebel presented the first major

12. This is admitted in part even by some who are sympathetic to Kouwenberg's theory. See John Charles Beckman, "Toward the Meaning of the Biblical Hebrew Piel Stem." (PhD diss., Harvard University, 2015), 249. Note that with the theory espoused in the present paper—especially in the contention that verb roots that are intransitive in the G stem but transitive in the D stem are causative—is falsifiable. One need only find convincing examples of verb roots that do not meet this criterion. However, I have found none, meaning that though falsifiable, I believe that it is correct, because although examples in theory could be found to prove it false, none have been found.

13. John Huhnergard and Naʿama Pat-el, eds., *The Semitic Languages*, 2nd ed., Routledge Language Family Series (London: Routledge, 2019), §3.5.5.

14. I know of no use of the root שבר in the Old Testament where it unambiguously means "bread (many)," a frequentative meaning. All the uses in Biblical Hebrew can be adequately analyzed as resultative.

challenge to the intensive view of the Piel.[15] Poebel theorized that Semitic D stems express verbal plurality. Plurality indicates repeated verbal action or results of the action or at times the imposition of a state (i.e., factivity, a causative category). Some subsequent studies have supported Poebel's view of the D stem, though they have departed from his methodology. Greenberg, Kaufman, and Fehri have appealed to wider studies of Semitic languages to argue that the D stem is plurative and factitive.[16] Kaufman in particular has argued that due to the dichotomy exhibited by the G stem (*qal*) in Hebrew between stative and fientive (sometimes called *active*) verbs the D stem has two major modalities: factitive for verbs that are stative in the G stem and plurative for verbs that are fientive.

While these studies argue against the intensive characterization of the D stem, there is a curious parallel in the nature of the basic outlines of their approach to the semantics of the Biblical Hebrew D stem:

Table 1: Comparison of D Stem Intensive and Plurative Theories

Characteristic	Intensive D stem theory	Plurative D stem theory
Views doubled letter as semantically iconic	Yes	Qualified yes
Semantics of the D stem	Pursue with great interest or be iterative/repeated	Plurative ≈ Repeated action or multiplicity in result
Recognizes D stem as causative	Yes—but primarily for statives	Yes—but primarily for statives (factitive)

15. Arno Poebel, *Studies in Akkadian Grammar*, AS 9 (Chicago: University of Chicago, 1939), 65–68.

16. Joseph H. Greenberg, "The Semitic 'Intensive' as Verbal Purality: A Study of Grammaticalization," in *Semitic Studies in Honor of Wolf Leslau on the Occasion of His Eighty-Fifth Birthday, November 14, 1991*, ed. Alas S. Laye (Wiesbaden: Harrassowitz, 1991), 1.577–87; Stephen A. Kaufman, "Semitics: Directions and Re-Directions," in *The Study of the Ancient Near East in the Twenty-First Century: The William Foxwell Albright Centennial Conference*, ed. Jerrold S. Cooper and Glenn M. Schwartz (Winona Lake, IN: Eisenbrauns, 1996), 273–82; Abdelkader Fassi Fehri, "Verbal Plurality, Transitivity, and Causativity," in *Research on Afroasiatic Grammar II: Selected Papers from the Fifth Conference on Afroasiatic Languages, Paris 2000*, ed. Jacqueline Lecarme, Amsterdam Studies in the Theory and History of Linguistic Science, Series IV: Current Issues in Linguistic Theory 241 (Amsterdam: Benjamins, 2003), 151–85.

| Maintains a fairly sharp distinction between D stems of statives (causative) and D stems of fientives (generally not causative) | Yes | Yes |

In contrast to these two views of the D Stem, Albrecht Goetze published a thorough study of the Akkadian D stem to demonstrate that the D stem was not intensive.[17] His work was extended to West Semitic languages by Ernst Jenni and Stuart Ryder.[18] Waltke and O'Connor have used the work of Jenni in modified form to explain the meaning of the D stem.[19] They have been followed in various ways by other grammars.[20] In these grammars the D stem system is seen as causative and distinguished from the causative H stem system by the voice of the action caused. In the H stem system, the voice is active, whereas in the D stem system it is passive. That is, in the D stem the emphasis is on bringing about a state rather than causing an action as in the H stem.[21] Or, to quote Waltke and O'Connor, "The *Piel* tends to signify causation with a patiency nuance, and *Hiphil* causation notion with an agency nuance."[22] (*Patiency* refers to the subject being acted upon and is

17. Albrecht Goetze, "The So-Called Intensive," 1–8.

18. Ernst Jenni, *Das Hebräische Pi'el: Syntaktisch-Semasiologische Untersuchung Einer Verbalform Im Alten Testament* (Zürich: EVZ, 1968); Stuart A. Ryder III, *The D-Stem in Western Semitic* Janua Linguarum, Series Practica 131 (The Hague: Mouton, 1974).

19. *IBHS*, 351–61 (§21), 396–417 (§24).

20. Bill T. Arnold and John H. Choi, *A Guide to Biblical Hebrew Syntax* (Cambridge: Cambridge University, 2003), 41–48 (§§3.1.3–5); Duane A. Garret and Jason S. DeRouchie, *A Modern Grammar for Biblical Hebrew* (Nashville: B & H, 2009), 136–37; Paul Overland, *Learning Biblical Hebrew Interactively*, 2 vols. (Sheffield: Sheffield Phoenix, 2016), 2.235; Andrew E. Steinmann, *Intermediate Biblical Hebrew: A Reference Grammar with Charts and Exercises* (St. Louis: Concordia, 2009), 115–22 (§§40–42); Arthur Walker-Jones, *Hebrew for Biblical Interpretation* (Atlanta: Society of Biblical Literature, 2003), 116; Christo H. van der Merwe et al., *A Biblical Hebrew Reference Grammar*, 2nd ed. (London: Bloomsbury T. & T. Clark, 2017), 81–82 (§16.4.2.1); Ronald J. Williams and John C. Beckman, *Williams' Hebrew Syntax*, 3rd ed. (Toronto: University of Toronto, 2007), 59–61.

21. *IBHS*, 399–400 (§24.1h-I).

22. *IBHS*, 355 (§21.2.2c).

roughly equivalent to *passive voice*. *Agency* refers to the subject being the agent of the verbal action and is roughly equivalent to *active voice*.)

PROBLEMS WITH THE CONTINUED CLASSIFICATION OF D STEM SYSTEM VERBS AS INTENSIVE OR PLURATIVE

The Argument that Doubling the Middle Consonant Is Iconic for Intensity or Plurality

The doubling of the middle radical of the root (e.g., Piel formation) or reduplication of more than one consonant in the root (e.g., Pilpel formation) has often been argued to be iconic, signaling an intensive or plurative meaning. For instance, Gesenius states, "This intensifying of the idea of the stem . . . is outwardly expressed by the strengthening of the second radical."[23] However, repetition is not the same thing as intensity. One can repeat an activity without making it more intense, and one can reduplicate consonants or syllables without making one's speech more emphatic. Even if one were to concede that the reduplication in D stem forms is iconic, that does not thereby argue that represents intensity. It may well be iconic and pointing to something else entirely. Thus, those who view the D stem as plurative have a better case if, indeed, the duplication in D stem formations is iconic.

However, not all D stem system forms involve reduplication. For instance, *poel, poal,* and *hithpoel* formations do not reduplicate any consonants, and geminate verbs that are expressed in the D stem system by *polel, polal,* or *hithpolel* formations do not exhibit reduplication beyond the already identical second and third root consonants.

Moreover, there is little hard evidence that repetition of consonants or phonemes is iconic. Consider the English words *mishmash, hodgepodge,* or *wishy-washy,* all of which exhibit some form of reduplication, though none involves more intense pronunciation of the reduplicated sounds. Nor do they signal more intensity of activity or more plurality in meaning than their synonyms *jumble, mélange,* and *indecisive*. This is also true for English words that reduplicate a middle

23. Kautzch, *Gesenius' Hebrew Grammar,* 141 (§52–53). See also Joshua Blau, *Phonology and Morphology of Biblical Hebrew LSAWS* 2 (Winona Lake, IN: Eisenbrauns, 2010), 229 (§4.3.5.4.1); Jan Joosten, "The Functions of the Semitic D Stem: Biblical Hebrew Materials for a Comparative-Historical Approach" *Or* 67 (1998): 203–4; N. J. C. Kouwenberg, *Gemination in the Akkadian Verb,* 33.

consonant. For instance, the verb *muddle* is no more intensive in meaning than its synonym *confuse*.

Factitive D Stem Verbs of Roots that are Stative in the G Stem

Distinguishing Stative and Fientive Verbs

Before examining how G stem stative verbs are manifested in the D stem, it is necessary to distinguish between stative verbs and fientive verbs.[24] Stative verbs describe a state or circumstance that applies to the verb's subject. Thus, stative verbs depict one of the subject's qualities, characteristics, states, or circumstances. Hebrew stative verbs are often best represented in English by a copulative verb with a predicate adjective:

עַל כֵּן גָּדַלְתָּ אֲדֹנָי יהוה

"Therefore, you *are great*, My Lord Yahweh." (2 Sam 7:22)

At other times, it is more appropriate to express such verbs with *become* plus a complementary adjective:

כֹּל הַנֹּגֵעַ בַּמִּזְבֵּחַ יִקְדָּשׁ

"Everything that touches the altar *will become holy.*" (Exod 29:37)

Not all Hebrew stative verbs are obviously stative in the G stem. There are three basic ways to distinguish Hebrew stative verbs from fientive verbs. First, it ought to be noted that the Masoretic pointing for stative verbs often includes a different theme vowel (i.e., the second vowel) in third person masculine singular forms. Whereas many verbs have *patakh* as the theme vowel, some stative verbs have *tsere* or *holem*: מָלֵא ("he is full"), קָטֹן ("he is small"). Second, many stative verbs are intransitive, so almost every Hebrew G stem transitive verb ought to be classified as fientive, not stative. In the rare case of a transitive verb that might appear to be stative, a simple test can be used: Can the verb's English gloss normally be expressed as a progressive form? If so, it is not stative. Waltke and O'Connor explain:

> For example, a fientive verb like "read" freely forms the progressive, as in "I am reading this book." By contrast, one cannot freely

---

24. Fientive verbs are often called *active verbs*. However, the term *fientive* is preferred here, since *active* is also commonly used to denote voice (in contrast to other voices such *passive, reflexive, middle*). See *IBHS*, 363 (§22.2.1a).

say "I am loving this book." Since "love" describes a stative situation (in this case, a psychological state), one freely says "I love this book." This test may be of use in considering difficult cases.[25]

In fact, the verb אהב ("love") is an interesting exception. Not only is it a rare example of a Hebrew stative verb that is transitive, but the Masoretes point it as a stative when it refers to current circumstances (e.g., וְאָבִיו אֲהֵבוֹ, "and his father loves him"; Gen 44:20). They point it as a fientive when it refers to past circumstances (e.g., וְיִשְׂרָאֵל אָהַב אֶת יוֹסֵף, "now Israel loved Joseph"; Gen 37:3).[26] Moreover, this verb is the only example of a transitive stative verb that also occurs in the D stem. All other stative G stem verbs that have corresponding D stem counterparts are intransitive.

In contrast to stative verbs, fientive verbs describe an action or dynamic situation. They describe what the subject does. Fientive verbs can be either transitive or intransitive. For instance, נגע ("touch") is transitive fientive. It describes what the subject does and can take a direct object: "John touched Sally." The verb ישׁן ("sleep") is intransitive fientive.[27] It describes what the subject does but cannot take a direct object. One can say, "I slept." One cannot say "I slept John."

G Stem Stative Roots as D Stem Factitives

Several elementary Hebrew grammars continue to advocate—at least partially—for the concept of D stem as intensive, at least for some fientive verbs.[28] Few beginning grammars argue for verbal plurality

---

25. *IBHS*, 364 (§22.2.1e).

26. Waltke and O'Connor discuss verb roots that are sometimes stative and sometimes fientive. See *IBHS*, 365–7 (§22.2.3).

27. Note that one can use the English verb *sleep* as a progressive: "John is sleeping." Thus, *sleep* is not a stative verb.

28. Andrew H. Bartelt, *Fundamental Biblical Hebrew* (St. Louis: Concordia, 2000), 160; Russell T. Fuller and Kyoungwon Choi, *Invitation to Biblical Hebrew: A Beginning Grammar*, Invitation to Theological Studies (Grand Rapids: Kregel, 2006), 144; Fuller and Choi, *Invitation to Biblical Hebrew Syntax: An Intermediate Grammar*, Invitation to Biblical Studies (Grand Rapids: Kregel, 2017), 43–45; Jo Ann Hackett, *A Basic Introduction to Biblical Hebrew* (Peabody, MA: Hendrickson, 2010), 142; Gary D. Pratico and Miles V. Van Pelt, *Basics of Biblical Hebrew Grammar* (Grand Rapids: Zondervan, 2001), 307; Allen P. Ross, *Introducing Biblical Hebrew* (Grand Rapids: Baker Academic, 2007), 126; C. L. Seow, *A Grammar for Biblical Hebrew* (Nashville:

in the D stem.[29] However, most of these grammars appear to have conceded that the D stem is not intensive but is *factitive* for G stem stative verb roots. That is, the D stem designates an effected state and becomes transitive. Factitive verbs are a subset of causative verbs. In fact, my survey of every D stem verb in the Old Testament (see Appendix) found that *all the 100 G intransitive stative roots that also occur in the D stem system are factitive, and therefore also transitive.*[30] Thus, it is now widely recognized that for many verbs the D stem system is causative, not intensive.[31] Thus, these grammars are conceding that for stative verbs the D stem is not intensive. In addition, it is important to note why these roots are intransitive in the G stem but transitive in the D stem. The addition of a transitive element arises from adding causation. Thus, in the G stem קדשׁ means "be holy." In

---

Abingdon, 1995), 174.

29. The only one of which I am aware is Brian L. Webster, *The Cambridge Introduction to Biblical Hebrew* (Cambridge: Cambridge University, 2009), 247.

30. One might argue that the verb וַתְּקַשׁ (root קשׁה) at Gen 35:16 is a lone exception. However, this word may be mispointed and perhaps ought to be read either as a G stem (Qal) or a H stem (Hiphil) form. See LXX καὶ ἐδυστόκησεν.

31. Joosten, "Functions of the Semitic D Stem" argues that many of these statives are to be understood as middle voice in the G stem. (Joosten prefers the term *diathesis* instead of *voice*.) Joosten believes that statives or fientives that exist in the G stem *qātîl* formation are actually middle voice verbs. The D stem's transitivity for these verbs is then argued to be simply the active voice counterpart of the G stem. However, there is little evidence for a true middle voice in Biblical Hebrew. I can see little evidence that any of the supposed middle voice G stem verb roots adduced by Joosten are actually middle voice, which he defines—following Marcel Cohen—as verbs whose action take place within the subject (e.g., אהב, *love*). If that were the case, however, the English verb *love* would be a middle voice verb, yet I am not aware of anyone who analyzes it that way. Middle voice is defined as "that form of the verb by which its subject is represented as both the agent, or doer, and the object of the action, that is, as performing some act to or upon himself, or for his own advantage." ("Middle Voice," http://www.webster-dictionary.org/definition/Middle%20voice). However the verb root אהב, like the English verb *love* does not depict the subject as performing some act to or upon himself, and in cases of altruistic love it does not love for the advantage of the subject but for the advantage of the direct object (e.g., Jonathan's love for David, 1 Sam 18:1–4). Most of the verbs Joosten adduces for this supposed middle voice are stative, and some are active voice fientive. The problem with Joosten's analysis is that he argues that the *qātîl* formation must denote a single type of verbal semantics. Yet, that is not the case. Not all morphological structures indicate unwavering semantic values. For instance, while the Hebrew dual termination for nouns often indicates duality, in some cases it does not. See שמים ("heavens"); מים, ("water"), or אפרים, ("Ephraim").

the D stem it is transformed by adding a second verbal component: cause. Thus, in the D stem one might approximate the meaning as "cause someone or something to be holy" which is better expressed as "sanctify" or "consecrate" (see Gen 2:3; Exod 13:2). Note that the base semantic value of קדשׁ (that is, "holy") is not transformed to be transitive. The transitivity is produced by the causation.

Factitive D Stem Roots that Are Intransitive Fientive Roots in the G Stem

Grammars that present the D stem as intensive tend to treat G stem fientive verbs as if they are intensive in the D stem. However, this does not match the evidence. Several verb roots that are intransitive fientive in the G stem are causative and transitive in the D stem, also making them factitive:

Table 2: G Stem Intransitive Fientive Verbs in the D Stem

Root	G stem	D stem
אחר	delay	delay something
בער	burn	burn something
דלג	leap	leap over something
חיה	live	cause/allow someone to live
חמר	foam	make something foam (= ferment something)
ישׁן	sleep	put someone to sleep
קשׁשׁ	gather	gather something

None of these D stem verbs demonstrate an intensification of the meaning found in their G stem counterparts. For instance, ישׁן does not carry the intransitive sense *sleep deeply* in the D stem. Moreover, these roots are clearly not plurative. In the D stem ישׁן does not carry the sense *sleep repeatedly or continuously* in the D stem. Instead, these and all the other examples above are D stem causative counterparts of the G stem and, therefore, they are transitive. In the D stem they denote bringing the direct object into a state or to a result. By my reckoning there are seventy-seven roots that are intransitive fientive in the G stem and factitive in the D, Dp, or HtD stem (see Appendix). Only thirteen roots that are intransitive fientives in the G stem are also intransitive in the D stem. From the examples above it is not only clear that intensification or plurativity are not the modes of action signaled by the D stem, but also that there is little evidence to point one in that direction.

Verb Roots that are Frequentative in the D Stem

So, what gave rise to the intensive or plurative description of the D stem? Fifteen roots are intransitive in both the G stem and D stem. These roots exhibit a *frequentative* meaning in the D stem. That is, they denote a continuing or repeated action in the D stem as opposed to a single action in the G stem. This *frequentative* meaning may take on several nuances: regular/periodic repetition, habitual repetition, customary action, continuity of action (i.e., durative). It is this frequentative meaning exhibited by a distinct minority of D stem verbs that was adduced as support for the assertion that the D stem conveys an intensive or plurative meaning.[32] Consider the following examples:

Table 3: Verbs That Are Intransitive in Both the G Stem and the D Stem

Root	*G stem*	*D stem*
חכה	wait	wait (durative)
מלל	wither	be in the process of withering (durative)
נאף	commit adultery	be prone to commit adultery (habitual)
רוץ	run	run back and forth (regular repetition)
רנן	shout	shout (repeated action)
רקד	leap, dance	leap about (periodic repetition)
שׂיח	complain, meditate	consider fully (durative)
שׁוט	roam	roam about (continuity of action)

In addition, twenty-four roots are transitive fientive in the G stem and are frequentative in the D stem. Examples include:

Table 4: Transitive Fientive Verbs That Are Frequentative in the D Stem

Root	*G stem*	*D stem*

32. See, for example, Fuller and Choi, *Invitation to Biblical Hebrew Syntax*, 44, example c.

חמד	desire something	delight (durative)
ידה	propel something	propel something repeatedly
ירשׁ	possess or inherit something	swarm something (continuity of action)
לקט	gather something	gather things (repeated action)
לקק	lap something	lap something (habitual)
נאץ	despise something	constantly despise something (durative)
נגח	gore someone	gore someone repeatedly (regular)

The frequentative nature of these thirty-nine roots in the D stem lent credence to the concept that the D stem was intensive. However, it ought again to be noted that repetition is not the same as intensity. One can repeat an action without making it intense. A good illustration of this is found in the narrative of Gideon choosing soldiers for his army in Judges 7. Consider Yahweh's instructions to Gideon to separate out the men who "lap the water with their tongue as a dog laps." Here the verb is in the G stem—simple action. However, when the author portrays these men, he says that they were "lappers," using a D stem participle. That is, they lapped out of habit. It does not mean that they lapped intensely (whatever that might signify).

While these roots might lend credence to the concept of verbal plurality for the D stem, they constitute a distinct minority among the 640 D stem roots in the Old Testament. Instead, the origin of these frequentative verbs ought to be sought elsewhere. I would propose that the frequentative aspect is closely related to the causative aspect. That is, it is a kind of pseudo-causative in the sense that these verbs mean *make an action to be repeated or continuous*. This close relationship can be seen in the root עוף, which in the D stem (*polel* formation) means *fly habitually or instinctively as a part of one's created nature* (see Gen 1:20; Isa 14:29; 30:6) or *fly back and forth* (Isa 6:2), both frequentative meanings. But it also can be transitive and mean *make something fly* (i.e., brandish a sword; Ezek 32:10), a factitive meaning.[33]

33. This connection between the causative-factitive mode and the frequentative mode of D stem verbs is apparently missed by Beckman, "Toward the Meaning of the Biblical Hebrew Piel Stem." Instead, he favors Kouwenberg's theory by noting that some of these frequentative D stem verbs are intransitive. However, the fact that only thirty-nine of the 640 roots that occur in the D stem are intransitive and frequentative should give one pause before simply abandoning the clear causative nature of the D

Denominative Roots in the D Stem

The D stem is by far the most used of the stems to form denominative verbs.[34] This phenomenon cannot be explained through the intensive or plurative characterizations of the D stem. For instance, the noun כשׁף means *sorcery*, and this root is used in the D stem to mean *practice sorcery*. That is hardly an intensification of the meaning nor is it inherently making the meaning repeated or durative. Or consider the noun לבבה, *cake* from which D stem verbs meaning *bake a cake* are derived. Certainly, D stem לבב does not have an in tensive or plurative meaning. Denominative verbs tend to be found in the D stem because of its causative nuance. To bring about some state or action associated with the noun most naturally comports with the D stem for many nouns pressed into service as denominative verbs.

Verb roots that are resultative in the D stem

The strongest case for viewing D stem verbs as intensive appears to be for verbs that are transitive fientives in the G stem. Many of these are used in grammars to illustrate the supposed intensive meaning of the D stem. For instance, some grammars note that the root שׁלח means *send* in the G stem but *send away* or *let go* in the D stem, claiming the D stem is thereby intensifying the meaning of the G stem.[35] While the English glosses offered for this root are accurate, they do not communicate any intensification and certainly do not allow plurative connotation. In addition, an intensive concept for the D stem of this root cannot be squared with the evidence. For instance, at Genesis 8:7, 8, 10, 12, Noah sends birds from the ark, and in each case a D stem verb from the root שׁלח is used. Surely for the sending of a bird one does not use intense force! Nor does it denote a continual or repeated sending, since each case of sending a bird is noted separately in the narrative. At Gens 18:16, Abram sends off the

---

stem. It is much more likely that the frequentative mode is derived as a pseudo-causative from the more common causative mode exhibited by most D stem verbs.

34. Denominative verbs are verbs that are formed from nouns or adjectives.

35. Bartelt, *Fundamental Biblical Hebrew*, 158; Hackett, *Biblical Hebrew*, 142; see also Joosten, "Functions of the Semitic D Stem," 222.

strangers who had visited him. The parting is amicable, and there is no idea of forceful ejection nor of continual or repeated farewells.

Instead of being intensive, the root שלח exhibits the D stem's emphasis on the result of an action. When compared to Hebrew, English appears to be rather impoverished with respect to verb formations that indicate causation. However, English can signal the result of a causative action by using an adverbial modifier. In this case *away* signals the result of the sending. That is, when the sending is completed, the direct object is separated by some distance from the subject. Consider the following two sentences:

> Joe sent his son to the store.
> Joe sent his son away to school.

The first sentence simply focuses on the act of sending. In contrast, the second sentence focuses on the result of the sending—that Joe's son is attending school in some location other than where Joe lives. Thus, verb roots that are transitive fientives in the G stem are commonly *resultative* in the D stem. This often can be signaled in English by including an adjectival complement with the gloss. For example,

Table 5: G Stem Transitive Fientive Verbs That Are Resultative in the D Stem

Root	G stem	D stem
אסף	gather something	gather things together
בוס	trample something	trample something down
בלע	swallow something	swallow something up/down[36]
בקע	split something	split something apart
גלל	roll something	roll something up
נשא	lift something	lift something up/high
סתם	seal something	seal something up
צעה	pour something	pour something out
שרף	burn something	burn something up

Another root that is often used to illustrate the so-called intensive force of the D stem is שבר. Grammars advocating the Hebrew D stem as intensive will often claim that this root means *break* in

---

36. It appears as if English has two nearly synonymous idioms for this: *swallow up* and *swallow down*.

the G stem and *shatter* or *smash* in the D stem.[37] In a similar way, those who favor verbal plurativity for the D stem will argue that this root "means 'to break into many pieces, break many times.'"[38] However, this does not comport with the evidence. For instance, during Gideon's nighttime raid on the Midianites, he had his troops hide their torches in clay jars. Then when they were given their orders, they broke their jars (Judg 7:20). The verb is a G stem form of the root שבר, but surely the clay jars were broken into shards—they were shattered into pieces. The same applies at Isa 30:14 where clay jars are described as being broken (G stem), and the remainder of the verse describes a vessel shattered into multiple small shards. The same can be noted at Jer 19:10–11. On the other hand, while the verb שבר is used in the G stem to speak of breaking bones (Exod 12:46; Num 9:12; Prov 25:15), Isa 38:13 describes bones being broken (D stem) and compares them to a lion's breaking bones. Lions generally do not break a bone completely into pieces. They may fracture a bone when killing an animal. They may break a bone when eating meat from it. However, they generally do not break bones completely into bits as the word *shattered* would imply.

So, then, what is the difference between the G stem and the D stem for this root? Koehler, Baumgartner, and Stamm note:

> In the qal only items which can be actually broken, like wood, bones and pottery, are used as objects; but by contrast in the pi. objects made of stone and metal are used, which cannot actually be broken in one action but as a result of some other wasting process can be finally destroyed.[39]

Their observation is good as far as it goes, but it does not get at the difference between the G and D stems. The G stem transitive fientive forms of the root שבר focus on the *action* of breaking. The D stem causative forms focus on the *result* of the action. In fact, when

37. Bartelt, *Fundamental Biblical Hebrew*, 163; Fuller and Choi, *Invitation to Biblical Hebrew*, 144; Fuller and Choi, *Invitation to Biblical Hebrew Syntax*, 43; Overland, *Learning Biblical Hebrew Interactively*, 236n10; Pratico, *Basics of Biblical Hebrew*, 307; Seow, *A Grammar for Biblical Hebrew*, 174; see also Joosten, "Functions of the Semitic D Stem," 222.

38. Benjamin J. Noonan, *Advances in the Study of Biblical Hebrew and Aramaic: New Insights for Reading the Old Testament* (Grand Rapids: Zondervan, 2020), 102.

39. *HALOT* entry 9352, שבר I.

translating D stem forms of שבר it might once again be appropriate to use an adverbial modifier to signal this in English: *break something in two, break something to pieces, break something to bits.*

The resultative force of the D stem forms of שבר also explains the frequent mention of the Israelites breaking Canaanite idols, altars, and standing stones (Exod 23:24; 34:13; Deut 7:5; 12:3; 2 Kgs 11:18; 18:4; 23:14; 2 Chr 14:2; 23:17; 31:1; 34:4; Isa 21:9; Jer 43:13). The point was not to smash them into tiny pieces but to leave them in a broken state so that they would be unusable for pagan worship.

A third root that is used to illustrate the supposed intensive force associated with some D stem verbs is צחק. In the G stem this root clearly means *laugh* and is only used of Sarah (Gen 17:17; 18:12–13, 15; 21:6). Fuller and Choi claim it means *to laugh, to scorn, to mock* in the D stem.[40] However, this meaning is only possible at Gen 21:9, and it is not certain there. It could simply mean something like *joking around.* Genesis 19:14 depicts Lot's prospective sons-in-law as thinking that he was *joking.* Genesis 26:8 uses a D stem verb of this root to depict Abraham *caressing* Sarah, a use with clear sexual overtones. This sexual implication is also most likely present at Gen 39:14, 17 where Potiphar's wife is depicted as holding Jacob's clothing and accusing Potiphar of bringing "a Hebrew man" (איש עברי) into the household "to fool around with us" (לצחק בנו). It would appear that 1 Cor 10:7 also understands the use of a D stem verb from this root at Exod 32:6 as having a sexual connotation. Finally, at Judg 16:25 Samson is brought into the temple of Baal where "he performed in their presence" (ויצחק לפניהם). That is, he entertained them. What do these various senses of D stem verbs from the root צחק have in common? The semantic commonality that explains their meaning in various contexts is causative: *to cause laughing,* whether in the sense of mocking, joking, sexual pleasure, or entertainment. Intensity does not explain these diverse uses of these D stem forms of the root צחק nor does plurality.[41] The root is clearly *factitive* in the D stem.

40. Fuller and Choi, *Invitation to Biblical Hebrew,* 144.

41. Strangely, Fuller and Choi also claim an intensive meaning for D stem verbs from the root קטל. Verbs from this root are used only three times in the OT, always in the G stem (Job 13:15; 24:14; Ps 139:19). How Fuller and Choi know what this root means in the D stem in Biblical Hebrew is a mystery. The cognate root occurs in Biblical Aramaic, three times in the G stem (Dan 2:13, 14; 3:22) and three times in the D stem (Dan 5:19, 30; 7:11). In comparing the six uses, it appears as if the D stem uses in

Perhaps one reason the intensive explanation for the D stem has survived is that English and other Indo-European languages often have few ways to express the difference between simple action and result with transitive verbs.[42] Thus, English readers of the Hebrew text often cannot conceptualize the difference, and to them it appears as if there is none unless it can be explained by intensity or perhaps verbal plurality. For instance, the root קָצַץ, *cut something off; sever something*, is transitive fientive in the G stem (Deut 25:12; Jer 9:25; 25:23; 49:32). It al so occur s in t he D st em (Exod 39:3; Judg 1:6; 2 Sam 4:12; 2 Kgs 16:17; 18:16; 24:13; 2 Chr 28:24; Ps 46:10 [English 46:9]; 129:4). The nuance is difficul t t o r epr esent in Engl ish, and fr om English translations one cannot detect a difference. However, the emphasis is on action in the G stem and result in the D stem. Perhaps the easiest place to see the resultative nuance of the D stem for this root is Psalm 46:10 where Yahweh makes wars cease by rendering spears cut. Result is also in view in passages such as 2 Kgs 16:17; 18:16; 24:13; and 2 Chr 28:24 wher e port ions of pr ecious met al s ar e cut off from various items associated with Jerusalem's temple. Clearly, the result (not intensification or repetition) is in view—a temple less magnificent than the one Solomon intended when it was built.

COMPARING THE G, D, AND H STEM SYSTEMS

To complete our discussion of the meaning of the D stem system, it is helpful to compare it to the other stems in a way that unites the entire Hebrew structure of stems in an overarching representation of the Hebrew verb. The key to this is the notion of causation.[43]

Aramaic are also causative (resultative). It is used in Nebuchadnezzar's order to execute (i.e., make killed) the wise men of Babylon and to note that the heat from the flaming furnace slew (i.e., made killed) the men who threw Shadrach, Meshach, and Abednego into the furnace. The D stem of this root in Aramaic clearly is focusing on the resulting dead bodies.

42. Arnold and Choi seem to acknowledge this when they write, "In some cases, the verb may occur in both Qal and Piel with no discernable difference in meaning" (*A Guide to Biblical Hebrew Syntax*, 42). I assume they mean no discernable difference *for English readers*, not no discernable difference to native speakers of ancient Hebrew.

43. The discussion on this in *IBHS*, 252–61, 396–400 (§§21.2, 24.1) is very good. However, many beginning students will find it difficult, since it relies heavily on linguistic concepts and jargon which will be unfamiliar to them.

Causation in English

Before looking at causation in Hebrew, it is illustrative to examine causation in English, since it can bring to light general principles relating to causative constructions in languages, even though each language treats causality differently. There are several common ways to form English causative constructions. One way is to use a word that denotes the initiating action (i.e., the action that constitutes the cause in the cause and effect). This can be expressed by such as verbs from the roots *cause, make,* or *lead.* Consider the following sentences:

> Three days of heavy rains caused the river to rise.
> The teacher made his students read *The Grapes of Wrath.*
> Atmospheric conditions led the National Weather Service to issue
> a tornado watch.

In each of these sentences the initiating action is required to make the causative construction. Without the initiating action verbs *caused, made,* and *led* we would be left with simple declarative sentences like "The rivers rose" or "The students read *The Grapes of Wrath*" or "The NWS issued a tornado watch." The explicit presence of an initiating action is absolutely required to form a causative construction. Even though the exact actual initiating event is not always explicitly stated, the causative words *caused, made,* and *led* explicitly mention the initiation and point towards a specific causing action that lies behind them. In the case of the first sentence, *caused* may point to any of a number of initiating actions—the reservoirs were overflowing, or the ground was saturated or the like. Similar things could be said about the specific causes referenced by the more general causal verbs in the second and third sentences. In all three sentences *two actions* comprise the causative construction: initiating action: *caused, made,* or *led*; resulting action: *rise, read,* or *issue. Without both an initiating action and a resulting action or state there is no causation.*

Another common way in which causative constructions are formed in English is by use of verbal roots that contain an affix that signals that an initiating action occurred. For instance, the prefix *en-* can signal causation: *enable* (= make someone or something able) or *enfeeble* (= make someone feeble). Or for another example, consider the suffix *–ify*: *magnify* (= make large or great) or *vilify* (= make [declare] someone to be vile). In these cases, the causative affix, and therefore the initiating action, is needed and explicitly indicated by the affix. Otherwise, the verb or associated adjective without the affix would not have a causative meaning. English often uses these affixes in situations where Hebrew expresses the same concept though a verb in the D stem that corresponds to a stative G stem verb: צדק, G stem: *be just*, D stem: *justify someone* or מרר, G stem: *be bitter*; D stem: *embitter someone*.

A third common way to signal causation in English is to use a verb with an inner causative meaning. That is, the verb's semantics include the concepts of both a trigger action and a result as an integral part of its meaning: Some uses of the verb *bring* can be analyzed as an inner causative meaning *cause to go, come, or occur*.[44] For another example consider *kill* which can in some of its uses be analyzed as *cause the death of* as in the sentence:[45]

> John Wilkes Booth killed Abraham Lincoln, shooting him at Ford's Theater.

This could be restated as:

> John Wilkes Booth caused Abraham Lincoln's death by shooting him at Ford's Theater.

Finally, we should note that a causative construction contains a transitive initiating action with a subject (in this case John Wilkes Booth) and a direct object (Abraham Lincoln): "Booth caused Lincoln." The result also contains an action with a subject (Lincoln). The direct object of the initiating action is also the subject of the resulting action. Thus, it can be referenced as the *undersubject*. The subject of the initiating action can be called the *primary subject*.[46]

So, we can conclude the following about causative constructions: Causative constructions *require* the explicit inclusion of both an initiating action (i.e., cause) and a resulting action or state. There are two verbal notions in every causative construction: a verbal action with a primary subject (the subject of the initiating action) and a result with an

---

44. http://www.dictionary.com/browse/bring?s=t. Initiating action stated by *cause*, result stated as *go, come,* or *occur*.

45. http://www.dictionary.com/browse/kill?s=t. Initiating action stated by *cause*, result stated as *death*.

46. For this terminology see *IBHS* 355, 358 (§§21.2.2e, n).

undersubject (the subject of the resulting action that also serves as the direct object of the initiating action). This forms a chain that cannot be missing a single link without losing causation. (However, in Hebrew the undersubject can be present in the verb's semantics but left unstated, especially in the H stem.)[47]

Causation in Hebrew. By far the most commonly occurring causative constructions in Hebrew simply make use of the D or H stem systems. Thus, we could chart the Hebrew verbal system this way:

Table 6: General Characteristics of the Biblical Hebrew System of Stems

	G system	*D system*	*H system*
Focus	Action or state	Effected state	Event caused
Causation	No	Yes	Yes
Voice of "root meaning"	Dictated by stem	passive	active
Voice	Active (G) Passive (Gp) Reflexive/Reciprocal/Passive (N)	Active (D) Passive (Dp) Reflexive/Reciprocal (HtD)	Active (H) Passive (Hp)

The chart, of course, is a simplified version of the more complex character of the verbal system. Nevertheless, it provides a convenient overview of the system and offers a handle to grasp the primary differences among the three major stem systems and among the individual stems. In the G system verbs are either *stative*—denoting a state in which the subject exists—or they are *fientive*—denoting a dynamic action such as motion or change of state. In the D system verbs are *causative* with the undersubject participating passively or participating in a way that brings the undersubject to a state. In the H system verbs are *causative* with the undersubject participating actively. Verbs that occur in several stems illustrate these differences:

Table 7: Root נקם (G stem intransitive)

Stem	*Voice*	*Emphasis*	*Meaning*
G	Active	Action	Take revenge

---

47. See *IBHS*, 442 (§27.3c).

Gp	Passive	Action	Suffer vengeance; be punished
N	Reflexive	Action	Avenge oneself; Avenge on behalf of others
D	Active causation & Passive avenging	Effected state	Avenge someone
HtD	Reflexive causation & Passive avenging	Effected state	Take one's own vengeance (= avenge oneself)
Hp	Passive causation & Active avenging	Event caused	Be made avenged = be avenged; suffer vengeance

Table 8: Root בקע (G stem transitive)

Stem	Voice	Emphasis	Meaning
G	Active	Action	Split something
N	Passive / Reflexive	Action / Action	Be split / Split oneself out (= break forth)
D	Active causation & Passive splitting	Effected state	Make something split (= split in two)
Dp	Passive causation & Passive splitting	Effected state	Be made split (= be split in two)
HtD	Reflexive causation & Passive splitting	Effected state	Split oneself open
H	Active causation & Active splitting	Event caused	Make someone split something

| Hp | Passive causation & Active splitting | Event caused | Be made to split something |

Table 9: Root גאל (G stem stative)

Stem	Voice	Emphasis	Meaning
G	Active	State	Be defiled
D	Active causation & Passive defiling	Effected state	Make something defiled (= defile something)
Dp	Passive causation & Passive defiling	Effected state	Be made defiled (= be defiled)
HtD	Reflexive causation & Passive defiling	Effected state	Defile oneself
H	Active causation & Active defiling	Event caused	Cause something to become defiled

Note that in English some of these could be translated using the same words, though in Hebrew they carry nuances that distinguish them. For instance, both Gp and Hp forms of נקם might be translated *be avenged* in English. The G and D stem forms of בקע could be rightly translated *split* in English. The D and H stem forms of גאל could be translated *defile*. From an English speaker's point of view, it often appears as if there is no difference in meaning. This is why one often reads statements to the effect that "There is often no difference between G and D stem meaning for some verbs," or "The HtD stem is usually reflexive of the D stem but is sometimes reflexive of the G stem." These statements appear to be true to native speakers of Indo-European languages, since they often do not have ways to express the nuances expressed by the various Hebrew verb formations. That is, native speakers of languages such as English, French, Spanish, Italian, or German have difficulty conceptualizing the differences because their view of language and the way it expresses meaning is formed by their native language and not by Hebrew. However, the differences are real and can even be theologically significant.

UNDERSTANDING THE MEANING OF THE D STEM IS IMPORTANT FOR EXEGESIS: A FEW EXAMPLES

By grasping the causative nature of most D stem verbs (or the frequentative nature of a distinct minority of D stem verbs), one can better understand statements in the OT that in English translations would present theological difficulties or logical conundrums or would simply be misleading. But even if a passage does not pose such problems, understanding the force of D stem verbs can help illuminate specific nuances in various contexts. The most difficult cases are often with verbs that are resultative in the D stem (i.e., corresponding verbs from the same root are transitive fientive in the G stem). In addition, not recognizing frequentative D stem verbs can also miss key nuances intended by the Hebrew author. Below I will examine several cases of resultative D stem verbs and one case of a frequentative D stem verb.

1 Kings 8:27: D stem of the root כול *(Resultative)*

Consider the root כול. It is used in the D stem (Pilpal formation) in Solomon's prayer at 1 Kgs 8:27:

הִנֵּה הַשָּׁמַיִם וּשְׁמֵי הַשָּׁמַיִם לֹא יְכַלְכְּלוּךָ

Behold, the heavens, even the highest heavens cannot contain you.

However, what does this mean? Very clearly God is transcendent, and some commentators understand this statement that way.[48] Yet 1 Kings 8:27 cannot simply be a statement about God's transcendence, since an absolute statement of that nature cannot explain other places in the OT where God is clearly depicted as contained—as dwelling—in the temple (2 Chr 29:6; Ezra 7:15; Pss 9:11; 26:8; 43:3; 46:4; 68:16; 74:2; 76:2; 84:1; 132:5, 7). At other times he is said to be contained in

---

48. John Gray, *I & II Kings: A Commentary*, OTL (Philadelphia: Westminster, 1963), 207; Simon J. DeVries, *1 Kings*, WBC 12 (Waco, TX: Word, 1985), 125; Donald J. Wiseman, *1 and 2 Kings: An Introduction and Commentary*, TOTC (Downers Grove, IL: Intervarsity, 1993), 210.

the temple by implication, since he was enthroned above the cherubim on the Ark (1 Sam 4:4; 2 Sam 6:2; 2 Kgs 19:15; 1 Chr 13:6; Pss 80:1; 99:1; Isa 37:16).

Sensing this, some commentators qualify the nature of Solomon's statement by defining God's presence as if only part of the divine nature is being described. For instance, DeVries notes that Solomon says that God's name will dwell in the temple, and therefore seeks to limit God's presence to "a hypostasis or extension of Yahweh's true being, not the Deity in the fullness of his being."[49] The problem with this approach is that there is never any hint in the OT that only a limited part of God is in his temple. In addition, Psalms that place God's glory in the temple would argue that one cannot hold to a limited divine presence in the temple (Pss 26:8; 85:9).

Keil argued, instead, that Solomon was saying that God was not *confined* to the temple and that he was simply stating that God does not "dwell in a house, namely, shut up within it, and not also outside and above it,—a delusion which sometimes forced its way into the unspiritual nation, but which was always attacked by the prophets (cf. Mic. Iii. 11; Jer. vii. 4, etc.)."[50] Keil came to this conclusion from comparing other passages in Scripture and by applying knowledge about God gleaned from the entire Bible. However, there is a more direct way to this conclusion—by understanding the meaning of the verbal root כול in the D stem.

Solomon is not simply stating that God is uncontainable by creation (in which case he should have used a G stem verb). That would have been an incorrect theological statement. One example of how this is incorrect theologically is that God ("the fullness of the deity," τὸ πλήρωμα τῆς θεότητος) was contained in creation in the physical human body of Christ (Col 2:9). Instead, Solomon is stating that creation by its own effort cannot make God to be contained in it (i.e., he cannot be confined in it). For this the D stem is appropriate. Contrast 1 Kgs 8:27 to this sentence at Isa 40:12:

וְכָל בַּשָּׁלִשׁ עֲפַר הָאָרֶץ
. . . and [who has] measured/contained the dust of the earth in a third of an ephah?

49. DeVries, *1 Kings*, 125.

50. C. F. Keil, *The Books of the Kings*, Commentary on the Old Testament 3 (Grand Rapids: Eerdmans, 1976), 127.

Here the measuring (G stem) of the dust of the earth is denoted by a simple action. The question is not "who has confined the dust (i.e., caused it to be contained, D stem—causative)?" but "who has contained the dust (G stem—simple action)." Compare the other rhetorical questions at Isaiah 40:2: "Who has measured the waters . . . or weighed the mountains?"

Thus, for English readers is might be more precise to translate 1 Kings 8:27 as "Behold, the heavens, even the highest heavens cannot confine you." This brings out the force of the D stem and does not create conflicts with other passages that portray God as contained in the Temple or in the physical body of Christ, though in neither case is God confined to those three-dimensional spaces.

Eccl 3:5: G and D stems of חבק *(Resultative)*

The root חבק is used twice in Eccl 3:5, once in the G stem, and once in the D stem:

עֵת לְהַשְׁלִיךְ אֲבָנִים וְעֵת כְּנוֹס אֲבָנִים
עֵת לַחֲבוֹק וְעֵת לִרְחֹק מֵחַבֵּק
a time to throw stones, and a time to gather stones;
a time to embrace, and a time to be distant from an embrace

The second line of this verse is much discussed as to whether or not a sexual meaning is present.[51] However, commentaries generally do not discuss the possible differences in nuance between the G stem infinitive construct ("to embrace" לַחֲבוֹק) and the D stem infinitive construct ("an embrace" or "embracing" מֵחַבֵּק).[52] Yet, the two verbs' distinct nuances heighten the contrast between the two lines. The G stem participle is used again at Ecclesiastes 4:5. There a fool's hands embrace each other (חֹבֵק אֶת־יָדָיו), keeping him from working, and he wastes away. The G stem's emphasis on the action of embracing calls

51. Most often this verbal root *does not* carry a sexual connotation (Gen 29:13; 33:4; 48:10; 2 Kgs 4:16; Job 24:8; Prov 4:8; Eccl 4:5; Lam 4:5). Only in three passages is there a sexual component to the embrace (Prov 5:20; Song 2:6; 8:3).

52. Duane Garrett, *Proverbs, Ecclesiastes, Song of Songs*, NAC 14 (Nashville: Broadman, 1993), 297–98; T. A. Perry, *Dialogues with Kohelet: The Book of Ecclesiastes: Translation and Commentary* (University Park, PA: The Pennsylvania State University, 1993), 85–86; Michael V. Fox, *Ecclesiastes*, JPS Bible Commentary (Philadelphia: Jewish Publication Society, 2004), 21.

attention to what the fool does and invites readers to see the fool's wasting away as his hands are in the motion of clasping each other.

On the other hand, verbs from this root occur in the D stem in two very revealing passages: At Job 24:8 poor people hug rocks (חִבְּקוּ־צוּר) for lack of shelter. The D stem as causative-resultative invites the reader to see the result of their action—to picture them clinging to rocks. In a similar way, Lam 4:5 pictures those who were once royalty picking through a garbage pile for sustenance. They are said to "embrace a garbage heap" (חִבְּקוּ אַשְׁפַּתּוֹת). Again, the picture focuses on the result of their action—the reader is to see these once-regal figures as denizens of the junkyard.

Returning to Eccl 3:5, there is a time to embrace—the G stem picturing for readers the action of forming an embrace. There is also a time to be distant from an embrace—the D stem picturing two people in an embrace. The first image is of the readers themselves participating in the act of embracing. The second image is of the readers staying distant from others' embrace. However, these are not the images given to English readers by most translations in commentaries or English versions. For example:

> a time to throw stones and a time to gather stones;
> a time to embrace and a time to avoid embracing; (CSB)
> a time to cast away stones, and a time to gather stones together;
> a time to embrace, and a time to refrain from embracing; (ESV)
> A time for throwing stones and a time for gathering stones,
> A time for embracing and a time for shunning embraces; (TANAK)
> A time to scatter stones and a time to gather them.
> A time to embrace and a time to shun embraces;[53]

Some of these translations translate the D stem infinitive as an English participle ("embracing")—giving the impression that one's own action, not result, is in view. Others translate the previous infinitive as if one is actively not taking part in forming the embrace ("shunning," "shun," לִרְחֹק). However, the resultative thrust of the second infinitive, מֵחַבֵּק ("an embrace"), pictures the embrace as *already formed*, an image that is not conveyed to the reader in such English translations. The images conveyed by the Hebrew text are difficult to represent in English translation. Murphy's translation is

---

53. R. B. Y. Scott, *Proverbs, Ecclesiastes: Introduction, Translation and Notes*, AB 18 (New York: Doubleday, 1965), 220.

fairly good: "a time to embrace and a time to be far from embraces."[54]
But perhaps Eccl 5:3 could be better translated this way:

> a time to throw stones, and a time to gather stones;
> a time to embrace, and a time to keep one's distance when others
> embrace;

That is, there is a time to initiate a hug and there is a time to allow others to hug and not to intrude in their moment of tenderness and affection.

Gen 9:23 and 37:26: D stem of כסה *(Resultative)*

D stem verbs from the root כסה occur five times in Genesis. In every case the resultative force of this verb is important, but let us examine two cases in particular. At Gen 9:23 we are told:

. . . וַיְכַסּוּ אֵת עֶרְוַת אֲבִיהֶם . . .

. . . they covered up their father's nakedness . . .

This verse contrasts Shem and Japheth's acts on behalf of their father with Ham's looking on Noah's nakedness and failing to conceal it.[55] The focus is not on their act of covering but on the result of their action—that Noah's nudity was concealed when Shem and Japheth finished, whereas previously he remained naked after Ham's act of seeing him. This, however, is difficult to see in most English versions and in translations offered in most commentaries.[56] One version, the NET Bible, however, brings out the nuance of the D stem verb quite well by using the adverbial modifier "up":

> Then they walked in backwards and covered up their father's nakedness.

Later, at Gen 37:26 Judah is quoted:

וַיֹּאמֶר יְהוּדָה אֶל־אֶחָיו מַה־בֶּצַע כִּי נַהֲרֹג אֶת־אָחִינוּ וְכִסִּינוּ אֶת־דָּמוֹ

---

54. Roland E. Murphy, *Ecclesiastes*, WBC 23A (Dallas: Word, 1992), 28.

55. Victor P. Hamilton, *Genesis, Chapters 1–17*, NICOT (Grand Rapids: Eerdmans, 1990), 323.

56. CSB, ESV, NIV, NRSV; Hamilton, *Genesis, Chapters 1–17*, 320; Gordon J. Wenham, *Genesis 1–15* WBC 1 (Waco, TX: Word, 1987), 151.

Judah said to his brothers, "What will we gain if we kill our
brother and cover up his blood?"

For this verse almost every English translation conveys the resultative force of the verb וכסינו, either by translating as "and cover
up" or as "conceal," which focuses the English reader on the result
of the action that Judah is urging his brothers not to take. Note the
following examples:

> Judah said to his brothers, "What do we gain if we kill our brother
> and cover up his blood? (CSB)

> Then Judah said to his brothers, "What profit is it if we kill our
> brother and conceal his blood? (ESV)

> Judah said to his brothers, "What will we gain if we kill our
> brother and cover up his blood? (NIV)

> Then Judah said to his brothers, "What profit is it if we kill our
> brother and conceal his blood? (NRSV)[57]

Comparing these translations of Gen 37:26 to their translations of
Gen 9:23, it would appear that the context of Gen 37:26 more clearly
conveys the resultative force of the D stem there than it does at Gen
9:23. Much of this is cultural—the sense of shame associated with nakedness in ancient Semitic cultures (Gen 9:23) is not nearly the same as
shame for nakedness in modern Western culture, making the contextual
clues that would lead to understanding the verb as resultative in that
case much less obvious to readers today. Yet we are still familiar with
conspiracies to hide crimes, so it strikes contemporary translators much
more reasonable to add an adverbial modifier such as *up* or to find a
verb such as *conceal* that points readers to the resultative force of the
D stem at Gen 37:26.

This, however, demonstrates why it is important to understand
what nuance is conveyed by the D stem: Whether native English speakers will naturally detect the causative force of the D stem may well
depend on contextual factors that resonate with their worldview. Rely-
ing on such intuitive factors to accurately translate or comment on a
particular occurrence of the D stem in the scriptural text can result in

---

57. See also the translations in Gordon J. Wenham, *Genesis 16–50*, WBC 2 (Dallas:
Word, 1994), 347 and Victor P. Hamilton, *The Book of Genesis: Chapters 18–50*, NICOT
(Grand Rapids: Eerdmans, 1995), 420.

overlooking or distorting the original author's careful choice of words. We need, instead, to be aware of the nuance conveyed to the ancient reader or hearer of the text by the author's choice of a D stem verb form.

Prov 11:19: D stem of רדף *(Frequentative)*

The D stem use of the root רדף is relatively rare, occurring only eight times in the Old Testament (as compared to 132 occurrences in the G stem). However, the D stem of רדף appears often—six times—in Proverbs and carries a frequentative meaning (Prov 11:19; 12:11; 13:21; 15:9; 19:7; 28:19). Typical is its first occurrence at Prov 11:19:

> כֵּן־צְדָקָה לְחַיִּים וּמְרַדֵּף רָעָה לְמוֹתוֹ
> Just as righteousness leads to life, so the person who constantly pursues evil leads to his own death.

Most English versions do not recognize the frequentative-durative force of this D stem verb and translate it simply as "pursues."[58] Most commentaries overlook it.[59] However, the point is not that a single pursuit of evil leads to death. After all, who does not sin? The thrust of the sage's observation is that habitual, persistent chasing after evil leads to death. One commentator who notes this is Clifford, who describes this proverb as teaching that "Righteousness leads to a long and happy life whereas *frantic pursuit* of evil brings death closer" (emphasis added).[60]

This frequentative meaning is operative in the other five proverbs that employ the D stem of רדף. In contrast, note one of Proverb's rare uses of the G stem at Proverbs 28:1:

> נָסוּ וְאֵין־רֹדֵף רָשָׁע וְצַדִּיקִים כִּכְפִיר יִבְטָח
> The wicked flee when no one pursues them, but the righteous are bold like a lion. (CSB)

---

58. CSB, ESV, NIV, NRSV.

59. See Scott, *Proverbs*, 86; Garrett, *Proverbs, Ecclesiastes, Song of Songs*, 126. I even failed to note it in my commentary. See Andrew E. Steinmann, *Proverbs*, Concordia Commentary (St. Louis: Concordia, 2009), 285, 294.

60. Richard J. Clifford, *Proverbs*, OTL (Louisville: Westminster John Knox, 1999), 125.

Here the simple act of pursuit is in view. There is no hint of a frantic, repeated, or relentless pursuit that would require the D stem verb. Instead, the point is that the wicked flee even when they suspect that they will be pursued (G stem), not when someone doggedly chases them (D stem).

Moreover, the frequentative nuance of this root in the D stem is important in the two places in the prophets where it occurs, confirming the frequentative nature of the D stem of this root in Proverbs. At Hos 2:9 the prophet characterizes the adulterous wife who is like idolatrous Israel:

. . . וְרִדְּפָה אֶת־מְאַהֲבֶיהָ וְלֹא־תַשִּׂיג אֹתָם

She will continually pursue her lovers but not find them . . .

The characterization of this unfaithful woman is not that she chases her lovers in a single quest for them but that, like Israel, she continues her mission to find lovers over a long duration of time.

Nahum 1:8 also uses this root in the D stem to speak of God's relentless pursuit of Nineveh until he has destroyed it:

וּבְשֶׁטֶף עֹבֵר כָּלָה יַעֲשֶׂה מְקוֹמָהּ וְאֹיְבָיו יְרַדֶּף־חֹשֶׁךְ

But he will destroy Nineveh with an overwhelming flood, and he will relentlessly chase his enemies into darkness.

Nahum's choice of the D stem verb is intentional, and he seeks to convey to his readers that Yahweh will not stop his pursuit until Nineveh's army is destroyed (see Nah 1:9–10).

CLOSING OBSERVATIONS

The causative nature of most D stem verbs in Biblical Hebrew was not recognized by modern grammars until the work of Goetze in the mid-twentieth century. By that time, the notion that the D stem is intensive was fairly thoroughly entrenched. This notion is often taught in introductory Hebrew grammars to this day. However, there always existed evidence that should have called this view into question: Some verbs were known to be causative in the D stem, especially verbs that are stative in the G stem are causative-factitive in the D stem. This has been recognized for at least 179 years.[61] Moreover, it ought to have

---

61. For instance, it was recognized by Wilhelm Gesenius in the twelfth German

been obvious that neither the intensive characterization of the D stem nor the plurative characterization explains how roots that are fientive and intransitive in the G stem become transitive in the D stem. Making an action more intense does not magically transform it into a transitive notion nor does making an intransitive root repeated or durative via verbal plurality produce transitive verb from an intransitive one. Instead, it is clear from the evidence gleaned from Biblical Hebrew that a causative characterization best explains the D stem's mode of action, with a distinct minority of D stem verbs displaying a frequentative mode of action as a kind of pseudo-causative. When this is recognized and placed in the service of exegesis, features of the Old Testament's message that previously have not been appreciated or fully apprehended can be better employed in service of proclaiming the entire counsel of God (Acts 20:27).

APPENDIX

This appendix contains a summary of the result of my analysis of all verb roots occurring in the D stem system in Biblical Hebrew.[62] They also were classified as factitive, resultative, frequentative, or denominative. In cases where biblical Hebrew has no corresponding G or H stem verb, or corresponding noun or adjective, the verb was classified as "undetermined." This classification was used even when later Hebrew may have provided this information. However, I thought it best not to incorporate this later information, since it is difficult to determine whether later texts are using well-established terms from

---

edition of his grammar. See Wilhelm Gesenius, *Hebräisches Elementarbuch* (Leipzig: Reuger'sche Buchhandlung [Friedrich Volkmar], 1839), 98 (§51.2). I have not been able to locate earlier editions, so I cannot state whether the causative mode for some D stem verbs in Biblical Hebrew was recognized by Gesenius earlier than 1839. The first edition was published in 1813.

62. For the complete analysis presented in a Microsoft Excel spreadsheet see https://www.academia.edu/35272706/The_D_Stem_System_in_Biblical_Hebrew. While this spreadsheet offers English glosses for Hebrew terms, it is not a substitute lexicon and does not attempt to portray all possible nuances of every word. This site also contains a link to a document explaining the system of stems in Biblical Hebrew. This document's intended use is to teach beginning students about the modes of action associated with the various stems.

the biblical period or whether those terms arose through subsequent developments in the language.

Table 10: Classification of D Stem System Roots

resultative (G fientive transitive)	185	
factitive	179	
factitive (G stative)		101
factitive (G fientive intransitive)		79
denominative	160	
denominative—action associated with noun		118
denominative—production of noun		38
denominative—removal of noun		4
frequentative	39	
transitive frequentative		24
intransitive frequentative		15
undetermined	78	
total	640	

Note: The root עוף has both a factitive and frequentative D stem

Table 11: D Stem System Roots by Stem

D stem only	296
Dp stem only	72
HtD stem only	75
D and Dp stems	63
D and HtD stems	78
Dp and HtD stems	14
D, Dp, and HtD stems	43
Total	640

Table 12: Total Number of Roots Occurring in Each Stem

D	480
Dp	192
HtD	210

BOOK REVIEWS

Non-Semitic Loanwords in the Hebrew Bible: A Lexicon of Language Contact by Benjamin Noonan. LSAWS 14. University Park, PA: Eisenbrauns, 2019, vii +512 pp., $149.95, hardcover.

Many reference works remain in the realm of mere quick reference guides. The reader only picks the book up to skim one entry or may need a quick bibliographical survey of one such topic. In terms of lexicons, most are used in much the same way, a way for a translator or textual critic to glean some small semblance of lexicographical data in a brief entry with a few glosses. Benjamin Noonan has crafted within the pages of *Non-Semitic Loanwords in the Hebrew Bible: A Lexicon of Language Contact* something much more than the title suggests. The usability and many practical applications of both the content and collected data of the lexicon far outweighs the value of a simple lexical volume.

Noonan separates his work into seven chapters, each focusing on a particular topic, the bulk of which goes into the third chapter which surveys the actual lexical data of Non-Semitic words found in the Hebrew Bible. Given the nature of the book as containing a lexicon, the volume does not just stop there. Noonan seeks to offer several different approaches to his lexical data to help the reader use the lexical entries wisely.

Noonan starts his lexicon with a survey of research on loanwords and borrowings in general linguistics and focuses his parameters for what constitutes a loanword as "a lexical item that has been adopted from one language (the doner language) and made part of the vocabulary of another language (the recipient language)" (p. 8). This distinction is important as it shows that features of a word such as the phonological and morphological qualities are not in view here, rather the lexeme is directly in discussion, not the specific qualities of a language that can be borrowed and used. This distinction allows Noonan to identify loanwords based on the kernels of phonetic transfer exhibited in loanwords. This phonetic element is retained, even though the morphology of the word is partially melded into the morphology of the receiving language. Noonan also clarifies his definitions of a core borrowing in contrast with a cultural borrowing (p. 10) and defines the idea of code-switching in contrast with his definitions of loanwords to demonstrate the difference between the two categories (pp. 11–12).

Noonan moves into a discussion of non-Semitic contact as it occurred in Ancient Palestine, describing the cultures of Egypt, Greece, the Hittites and Luvians, the Hurrians, Indo-Aryans, and the Iranians, the primary groups responsible for the words found in the lexical section of the book. Noonan describes how these various group were historically in contact with the greater Palestinian area and how words may have passed into Semitic language through diplomacy, trade, and conquest. Noonan gives expansive bibliography to each group, as well as historical documentation based on archeological sources and textual sources. This chapter sets the tone for the lexical data as it situates the user of the lexicon in a firm philological and morphological pattern established in chapter 1 and a historical and geographical survey in chapter 2.

Noonan then provides the meat of the work in the form of lexical entries. A helpful list of all words is found on page xxxi in the front matter for those using the work as a quick reference. Each entry begins with the word in question as it appears in the Hebrew Bible. The standard dictionary references are given from *HALOT* and *DCH*, as well as the scriptural citation for occurrences. Noonan also provides the Greek, Latin, and Targumic (where applicable) witnesses' glosses for each word and a suggestion on if the word is a potential cultural loan or not. Noonan also traces some of the other later (or in some cases earlier) uses in other Semitic languages. The actual entries focus on a survey of literature where applicable and a discussion of Noonan's derivation and subsequent decision of parent language and how the lexical entry made its way to the target language. Ample bibliography for each lexeme guides the user to further discussion and the ability to assess Noonan's conclusions.

While most lexicons stop at this point, Noonan is only getting started with the data. Noonan moves to an entire section of analysis in which he hopes to provide a vivid picture of how the data is spread across the corpus of the Hebrew Bible and the implications of the loanwords in their canonical and source critical divisions. Noonan hopes to use this analysis to inform the discussion of how loanwords in Biblical

Hebrew are typically studied and used in diachronic analysis. Noonan utilizes phonological, morphological, and archeological data to provide a snapshot of how, when, and why these words were utilized in the Hebrew Bible. Noonan concludes the work with a call for further study in the area of contact linguistics as well as a helpful appendix where he demonstrates words that he feels have been erroneously labeled as Non-Semitic loans.

While there is not much to critique in Noonan's work, the usability of the volume is limited to a select niche group of researchers. The presentation of the data, as well as the methodology of examination, is a terrific example of how lexicographical work in any field can be accomplished, especially in terms of language contact, a somewhat underrepresented field in most language studies. Other works in the field generally focus on contact in terms of how similar language families interact and how words are transmitted via shared lexical traits as well as some elements of cultural contact. Noonan uses his space to focus specifically on non-related languages and their interaction within the corpus of the Hebrew Bible, providing a tool for the biblical scholar to evaluate the data and reach conclusions of chronology and exegesis.

In *Non-Semitic Loanwords in the Hebrew Bible: A Lexicon of Language Contact*, Benjamin Noonan has sought to present a methodology for determining foreign loanwords in the Hebrew Bible that do not originate from the broader Semitic lexicon. Noonan seeks to establish a firm foothold for future studies in lexicography in ancient Near Eastern studies as well as entrench the lexicographical data in its linguistic, historical, and archeological roots.

Matthew Christian
Southeastern Baptist Theological Seminary

Not Scattered or Confused: Rethinking the Urban World of the Hebrew Bible by Mark McEntire. Louisville, KY: Westminster John Knox Press, 2019, 300 pp., $40.00, paperback.

There is an underlying urban theme that pulses throughout the Bible. Mark McEntire, professor of Biblical Studies at Belmont University, explores the role of urban settlements and urban culture in the Old Testament. Biblical scholarship is beginning to catch up to something urban missiologists have long known—that the city is the context of so much of the Bible and speaks to how we are to dwell rightly in our cities of today. Until recently, most treatments of the urban theme in the Bible have remained superficial and unnuanced. McEntire understands this gap and responds to unveil what the Old Testament says about cities.

McEntire understands that grasping cities requires many disciplines. McEntire brings his discipline to bear on this important topic. While he acknowledges that the cities described in the Old Testament are significantly different from cities today, he also recognizes important themes that have marked urban settlements throughout history. According to the author, even the passages that seem rural betray an urban framework.

This work offers a couple of key contributions to Old Testament studies. He makes a strong case for a pervasive urban influence on biblical writers. The urban context influences the language and themes. This is not necessarily a new thought, but McEntire extends and deepens the case with his broad survey of Old Testament literature and literature beyond the biblical canon.

McEntire challenges a default assumption held by many that the Bible is largely anti-urban. In particular, he addresses the urban pessimism in the writings of Jacques Ellul and Augustine (whose anti-urban posture is up for debate) by offering a more nuanced perspective. There are certainly passages that direct judgment towards city dwellers, but it is not because they live in cities, but rather for other actions that defy God. Overall, McEntire sees a progression from an agrarian context towards a divinely intended urban civilization, which leads scribes to shape the text to address urban dwellers. Contra Ellul, McEntire presents a more nuanced treatment of the city in the Old Testament. The biblical writers were not blind to the negative repercussions of urbanization, but also recognized that cities were part of God's gift to his people. His critique of Augustine's proposal in *City of God* is that it leaves the reader with a negative understanding of the earthly city and only upholds an abstract idea of the city, whereas the Old Testament views urban living in real time and space to be of benefit to God's people even as they look to a future, greater city. He borrows the phrase "big shoulders of the city" from Carl Sandburg to describe the beneficial role of cities throughout the Old Testament.

This work is the product of an Old Testament scholar. His interpretation throughout the work relies heavily on assumptions that we can discern different sources and that each source has its intended meaning. Combined with the author's non-inerrant understanding of the Bible, this approach seems to be a more disjointed and scattered understanding of cities that offers a trajectory toward a clearer biblical view of cities. Which is to say McEntire leaves it a bit muddled.

McEntire does not intend his book to be an urban theology or to have devotional insights for urban dwellers. His treatment is more detached in nature. Although he attempts to end his chapters with correlations with modern urban realities, these connections feel thin and, because of his commitment to remain aloof from theologizing, his observations lack gravity.

McEntire's focus remains primarily limited to the intent of the redactors and the broad historical developments of Judah and Israel. He gives far less emphasis to the exegesis of relevant passages and the message that emerges from these passages. He operates more as a historian making observations with little desire to engage the meaning of texts, which could add much to his treatment. For example, he limited his treatment of Isaiah primarily to narrative passages relating to historical events and does very little to engage with the content of the prophet's message, much of which relates to an urban context.

For the academician or serious student, *Not Scattered or Confused*, has some rewarding nuggets. But readers will need to be ready for a neo-documentary approach to interpretation and should not expect much in the way of direct ministry application. Although the theme of "city" in the Bible is receiving more academic attention in recent years, more work is needed. For the experienced Bible scholar, this volume by McEntire is a worthy contribution to this field.

Michael Crane
Gateway Seminary

The Genesis Creation Account in the Dead Sea Scrolls by Jeremy D. Lyon. Eugene, OR: Pickwick, 2019, ix + 225 pp., $29.00, paperback.

Despite the fact that the manuscripts from Qumran known as the Dead Sea Scrolls were discovered about fifty years ago, the scholarly world's understanding about how those at Qumran understood major biblical themes and events is limited. Now with the full publication of these manuscripts, scholars can turn their attention to this important area of study. Jeremy Lyon's work *The Genesis Creation Account in the Dead Sea Scrolls* contributes toward this aim. After providing a helpful review of the text of Gen 1–2 as found at Qumran, he moves on to discuss in detail how those at Qumran interpreted and understood Gen 1–2. His discussions are characterized by clear organization in an accessible format. Specialists and well-informed non-specialists will welcome this contribution for these reasons despite a few drawbacks.

The work begins with a short introduction (pp. 1–6). Here, Lyon briefly discusses how the scrolls were discovered (1). The main topic of the book is stated next and is followed by a brief survey of the topic's past research (pp. 2–6).

After introducing the topic and locating it within the wider field of Qumran studies, Lyon discusses the text of the creation account in two chapters (chapters 2–3). Chapter 2 surveys the biblical manuscripts that preserve Genesis 1 and/or 2. His discussion of each biblical manuscript follows a simple and consistent format: 1) He provides introductory issues to each manuscript; 2) he discusses physical features of the manuscript such as the manuscript's column height, if margins are present, and the size of the writing block; and 3) he provides a reconstruction of the text along with a brief discussion of textual variants. He offers a few conclusions about the text of Gen 1–2 at Qumran at the end of the chapter.

He, then, discusses how those at Qumran interpreted and understood the creation account (chapters 4–9). Here, he discusses in detail several non-biblical texts (i.e., *Words of the Luminaries* [4Q504] *Paraphrase of Genesis and Exodus* [4Q422], *4QInstruction* [4Q416, 4Q417 and 4Q423], *Meditation on Creation* [4Q303–5], *Miscellaneous Rules* [4Q265], and *Jubilees* [4QJubᵃ]). His typical format for discussing each non-biblical text is as follows: there is an introduction to each text followed by a physical description of the manuscript. A history of research is often found next. Finally, there is a discussion of the content of each manuscript.

In chapter 10, Lyon concludes the work by restating his major conclusions about the text of Gen 1–2 and how these passages were employed at Qumran. His conclusion about the text of Gen 1–2 is twofold: First, every text that preserves portions of Gen 1–2 preserves the Masoretic Text tradition (p. 154). Second, the presence of some readings found in the LXX and not in the MT demonstrate that these readings were based on Hebrew texts that differed from the MT (p. 155). His conclusions about how those at Qumran understood and employed Genesis 1–2 are more extensive. In all, he lists fifteen conclusions in this section. A sampling of these include the belief that the universe was created by the word of God (pp. 157–58), the creation of angels on day one (p. 159), and the belief that God elected Israel on the seventh day (162).

There is much to commend about Lyon's work on Gen 1–2 at Qumran. First, the work is well organized. As already mentioned, Lyon follows a simple and consistent methodology when discussing the biblical and non-biblical texts that helps the reader stay focused on the book's main topic. Furthermore, the introduction follows a logical direction by moving the reader from the broad subject of Qumran to the narrow topic of the text and interpretation of Gen 1–2 at Qumran. Moreover, the work can basically be broken up into four sections: an introduction, a discussion of the text of Gen 1–2 at Qumran, a discussion of how Gen 1–2 is interpreted at Qumran, and a conclusion. Overall, readers will appreciate the author's organization since it focuses the reader on the main topic.

Second, the work is highly accessible. For example, Lyon makes it a habit to define common germane words in the field such as the term lacunae (missing portions [p. 21]) and *Vorlage* (base text [p. 32]). Additionally, whenever further comment is made on a Hebrew or Greek text, a translation is provided. The presence of tables graphically depicts in picture form the topic of paragraphing (e.g., p. 37). Finally, Lyon, from time to time, will include a picture of the actual manuscript under consideration. These characteristics make the work accessible for the well-informed non-specialists.

Despite these strengths, and there are many others, there are a few drawbacks. For example, although Lyon draws three conclusions about the text of Gen 1–2 on pages 32–33, he only lists two of these in his concluding chapter. His third conclusion found on pages 32–33 that the Qumran manuscripts preserving Gen 1–2 attest to a variety of text traditions during the Second Temple period is missing in the final chapter of the book. This conclusion is particularly puzzling since he states elsewhere in his book that "all of the manuscripts . . . reflect the Masoretic Text tradition" (p. 154). The reader is left to wonder which texts preserving Gen 1–2 reflect an alternative tradition. Lyon could be clearer here.

Moreover, the evidence Lyon uses to claim that the translator of the LXX faithfully copied his Hebrew base text should be nuanced since the evidence from 4QGen^k is not as clear as Lyon presents. For instance, Lyon interprets the Hebrew word ותרא "and it appeared/and let it appear" as an indictive, not a jussive, and on this basis, he argues that 4QGen^k agreed with the LXX against the MT. This conclusion though is far from certain since the form of 4QGe^k can be understood as either an indicative or a jussive. 4QGe^k may simply be updating the grammar of the MT here, and thus, it does not follow that the 4QGe^k reads with the LXX against the MT.

Overall, Lyon's work is a well-organized and accessible discussion of the text and interpretation of the Genesis creation account at Qumran. All readers can benefit from this work, and although there are a few drawbacks, some of which are mentioned here, the strengths of the work make it both enjoyable and informative.

Anthony Ferguson
Gateway Seminary

Opening Israel's Scriptures by Ellen F. Davis. New York: Oxford University Press, 2019, xi + 451 pp., $99.00, hardcover.

In this indispensable collection of thirty-six essays on the Old Testament/Hebrew Bible, *Opening Israel's Scriptures* carries on the strange and profound work of biblical interpretation. Ellen F. Davis, Amos Ragan Kearns Distinguished Professor of Bible and Practical Theology at Duke University, draws upon thirty-five years of teaching to compose student-conscious essays, which divulge the theological complexities of the Old Testament while engaging the questions, however basic, of first-year graduate students. Readers of this rich volume, whether veteran academics or novice students, will be enriched by the theological interpretation that Davis accomplishes.

These essays span the literature of the Old Testament, from Genesis to Chronicles, in the order of the Masoretic Text (Torah, Prophets,

Writings) with some exception: the essay on Ruth is relocated after Judges instead of Proverbs, and some essays pair books, such as Ezekiel and Haggai. Most essays are short in length, and only the books of the Torah receive more than one essay. The purpose of the essays, however, is not to merely survey themes and structures of Old Testament books like an introductory textbook, but rather Davis advances and models contemporary theological exegesis with the purpose of illuminating the literary coherence and theological unity of the books. She does not oversimplify the canonical coherence to a "grand narrative," but rather acknowledges the "polyphonic coherence" within individual books (p. 5). Further, her exegesis demonstrates an acute awareness of the economic, social, and political conditions of ancient Israel, often addressing the agrarian influence on the Old Testament. Her theological exegesis shrewdly discerns the literary structures and devices as they relate to and accentuate the theological themes posed by the writers. As a result, this work effectively invites readers to hear the voices of the Old Testament afresh, opening the spacious world of Israel's scriptures.

For the sake of brevity, this review will not cover every essay, but rather make mention of notable contributions while also commenting on her theological exegesis. Of the essays regarding the Torah, Davis's two essays on Leviticus are worthy of note. In particular, these essays present a reading of Leviticus that does not compartmentalize portions of Leviticus as either moral or ceremonial. Rather, Davis engages in a poetic and holistic reading that seeks to fully realize the proposition that YHWH is immediately present in Israel. This fact sparks the religious imagination of Leviticus and transforms one's understanding of the most ordinary aspects of daily life, such as eating or living in the land. Associating the act of sacrifice with eating food, she notes that food, from the economic vantage point of sacrifice, is no longer viewed as an industrial commodity, but as a gift from God. Sacrifice reminds the participant of God's place as the source of life, and reinforces the "manna economy" which opposes excess. Likewise, the land is reenvisioned as a covenant-partner. The land, according to Davis, mirrors human existence: it may be "filled with evil-devices," it may be "uncircumcised," or even "go into prostitution" (p. 78). Like humans, land is capable of relationship and dependence on God, and subject of both blessing and curse. In the examples of sacrifice and land, Davis exposes the rich theological imagination embedded in otherwise banal texts.

Like her section on Leviticus, Davis's essays on lament dive into forms of theological work obscure or uncomfortable to most modern readers. Her essays on Lamentations and the psalms of lament provide practical insight into the theological complexity of expressing one's emotions amidst crisis. Davis compares Lamentations to the rise of poetry and songs among prisoners in Nazi-occupied eastern Europe, noting that in the midst of chaos and crisis, poetry brought structure "through the medium of ordered language" (p. 294). In Lamentations, ordered language is evidenced by the density of acrostic poems in the book. Davis rightly characterizes lament as an "exacting theological work" or "learned skill" as opposed to complaint or whining (p. 325). From this view, lament is a transformative work that frees one from the "tyranny of our own emotions" to be honest with God (p. 325).

Further, Davis's reading of the Song of Songs notably immerses readers in a dreamy agrarian vision of intimacy, both sexual and divine. Her essay considers the interpretations of early Jewish and Christian writers who, like modern readers, have searched for an underlying righteous message deserving of its canonical status. In her estimation, she sees no need to separate or prefer either the religious and sexual interpretations of the Song, but that the Song intentionally evokes imagery of sexual and divine love. However, instead of discerning a theological message through allegory, she notes the echoes of divine love weaved into the poetry. Similarly, she contends for the Song's relationship to the canon on the basis of intertextuality, noticing references to the Torah, Prophets, and the Psalms. Woven throughout the depiction of sexual intimacy between a woman and a man is an intertextual thread of Israel's relationship with God. Further, Davis's interpretation notes the level of intimacy that exists between humans and creation, suggesting that the Song represents an "agrarian dream" or return to the garden. The intimate imagery portrayed through agricultural metaphors brings one back to the garden of Eden, a place of unadulterated intimacy between God and man. This essay effectively conveys why the Song has long captivated the theological imagination of its readers, and moreover, leaves its reader desiring to explore the "indefinite ripple of meanings" evident in this text.

While there are many admirable qualities of Davis's work, there are features which are negative; in particular, the brevity of the essays. Discussions of individual books are selective, normally expanding on three to four theological themes or questions. While the brevity is not necessarily problematic, the selectivity of discussion at times exhibits selectivity of data. Her positions on critical questions, such as dating, authorship, and provenance, are more often assumed than discussed. In some cases, she is not concerned with the historicity of events (i.e., the events of the conquest), yet there are cases where the historicity of economic situations appears essential to her interpretation (i.e., the class exploitation in Micah). Rather than weighing both literary and historical evidence, preference may be given to one over the other. One notable example is her preference for a metaphorical reading of conquest and violent texts in Numbers, Deuteronomy, and Joshua. Her interpretive decision seems to prefer a metaphorical reading on the basis that it is the more ethical or less-dangerous reading, even though she concedes that either a literal or metaphorical reading can remain dangerous (p. 99).

Overall, Davis's theological exegesis exhibits a learned and insightful reading of Old Testament books that accounts for the economic realities, the literary strategies, and the theological themes of each book while also drawing illuminating parallels to modern situations and literature. Despite the length of the essays, Davis's work stimulates the imagination, challenges common assumptions and preconceptions, and provokes needed discussion on the Old Testament's enduring relevance for Christian practice. In *Opening Israel's Scriptures*, Davis offers a compelling invitation to enter into the wealth of theological resource that is the Old Testament.

Joshua Huver
Wheaton College

Judges by David J. H. Beldman. The Two Horizons Old Testament Commentary. Grand Rapids, MI: Eerdmans, 2020, xiv + 316 pp., $34.00, paperback.

David. J. H. Beldman is an associate professor of religion and theology at Redeemer University College in Hamilton, Ontario, Canada. Beldman acquired his doctorate in Old Testament studies from the University of Bristol in 2013, where he wrote his dissertation on the literary structure of the epilogue of Judges (Judg 17–21). This is not his first commentary on the book, writing a more popular introduction for the Lexham Press "Transformative Word" series entitled *Deserting the King: The Book of Judges* (2017).

Judges has a tripartite structure: theological introduction, theological commentary, and theological reflection. This division follows the Two Horizons Old Testament Commentary guidelines and purpose, as the series seeks for volumes to merge rigorous exegetical investigation with greater conversation in the fields of biblical and systematic theology.

In the first section, Beldman lays out his hermeneutic for the commentary. He remarks that Judges is "a prophetic clarion call for the people of God today," in that it details, with seemingly unfiltered narration, the drastic and miserable consequences of when God's covenantal nation engages in divided religious loyalties (p. 2). It is a text that has perennial relevance, a book "for our time" and all of history as well (p. 1). Beldman contends that Judges' relevance derives, not only from content but inspiratory character. The work is *Sacred Scripture* and by reading Judges we are hearing God speak to us. Theological interpretation is "the best position to hear the divine address," as "historical, literary, and ideological approaches [are] not always helpful in hearing and understanding the biblical texts. . . . they may distort or even silence the message of Judges" (pp. 4, 5). Beldman's hermeneutic throughout the commentary is thus highly theological and respectful to the text's divine inspiration, calling the work a "foolproof composition" (p. 16). The author does not engage in speculation about sources (e.g., Deuteronomistic History), supposed contradictions, or apparent doublets. The commentary treats Judges as a singular work by a singular author, interconnected with the whole of redemption history (pp. 12–18). Nonetheless, Beldman does not believe Judges is a straightforward chronicling of events, rather there was a "careful and deliberate shaping of events of the past" (p. 13). Yet, this is an honest portrayal of the function and structure of biblical historical narrative, as scriptural "accounts . . . were not written solely for the sake of historical interest," but are "history *with a purpose*" (p. 13). Beldman's theological reading/hearing in the commentary is always attuned to how the author of Judges is narrating a purposeful and theological history. The remainder of the introductory section touches on the cultural, historical, and geographic context of pre-monarchic Israel, along with a small section on the reception history of Judges in the Christian tradition.

In the next section, theological commentary, Beldman focuses on the cyclical structure of both the book *in totum* and the individual narrative components. In the comment on for 2:6—3:6 (pp. 66–70), Beldman describes the six-part structure that governs the narrative presentation of the succeeding Judges. Yet, he methodically details the divergences from the deliverance cycle with each new judge narrative, indicating a progressive degradation that afflicts Israel with each accompanying liberation from foreign bondage. In chapters 17–21, Beldman argues that these chapters take place at the beginning of the Judge's historical chronology, even when textually situated at the end (primarily on the basis that Jonathan of 18:30 was Moses' grandson). This does not mean that Israel lacks a progressive decay away from God, but that such brazen immorality was a part of Israelite society from their beginning inhabitation of Canaan. Beldman remarks that the author intended to introduce such chronological mismatching to "confuse and disorient" the reader and dispelling one's notion that Judge's has a set progressive narrative. The subsection "A View of Judges from the End" provides an overview of different reading strategies for making sense of chapters 17–21, emphasizing the strategies of completion, circularity, and entrapment.

Beldman's primary exegetical conclusion is that, in any period the text narrates, Israel has had their hearts "[grow] cold to Yahweh—[they have become] a people who had abandoned King Yahweh and his good purposes for them" (p. 221). This is a cyclical rejection, one that has—in the contained book of Judges—no definite beginning or end. What we think is the end is actually the beginning, vice versa. Israel, to Beldman, is lost in a period of "social amnesia" without Yahweh or the Torah to ground them, thus the narrative itself also loses an immediate sense of order and linearity (p. 229). Judges, like the very period of Israel's history in that time, is circular.

The final section has three subsections, considering Judges' potential role in past/present/future biblical and systematic theology, as well as the text's relevance to our own contemporary theological, political, and social issues. In the biblical theology portion, Beldman sees the "themes and motifs" of Judges as shared throughout scripture, both Old and New Testaments, rather than explicit or evident intertextual references. In the systematic theology portion, the author contends that Judges "illuminates five doctrinal areas of systematic theology" (p. 277), which are the doctrine of God, the Holy Spirit, providence, sin, and political theology. Beldman goes no further than these because Judges "has very little to offer" with regards to other doctrinal areas (p.

253). While Beldman concedes that Judges is strictly "narrative" and not a systematic textbook, the biblical material nonetheless "will reinforce the typical teachings of systematic theology, deepening our appreciation of the church's doctrine" (p. 253). In the final portion, "Judges for Today," Beldman examines both the problematic themes in the book (e.g., violence, the depiction and treatment of women, etc.), but also means by which contemporary readers might better hear and apply the message of the text. He strongly asserts that the constant idolatry of Israel in Judges is still present today, yet manifesting as "individualism, consumerism, and secularism" rather than Baalism, et al. (p. 294). Thus, Christian leaders, congregations, and adherents must be committed to proclaiming "a more faithful, undivided witness to the gospel" lest they fall into the same snare as our Israelite ancestors (p. 297).

The primary strength of this commentary is its theological and literary breadth. Beldman expertly analyzes how the author of Judges weaves literary devices and theological themes throughout verses, chapters, and the book as a whole. Nearly every page of this commentary is filled with valuable insights on how to better understand the text for all its worth and practically utilize it in our religious and social lives. The portions on the final chapters of Judges are also strong, innovatively applying literary theory and concepts to shed light on the function of God's word. Additionally, the final section itself is worth the price of the book. I know of no other commentary/treatment of Judges which features a sustained engagement of how this oft-neglected text is itself valuable for biblical and systematic theologians in their discussions of sin, the Holy Spirit, and political theology.

The text's primary weakness is Beldman's discussion on ancient Near Eastern history and Canaanite culture. This commentary lacks critical interaction with contemporary scholars in those fields, even scholarship by conservative and evangelicals (Richard Hess is noticeably absent). The primary text Beldman utilizes in his exposition on the context of Judges is Bernhard Anderson's *Understanding the Old Testament* from 1959. Beldman's commentary frequently mentions the Israelites succumb to "Canaanization," emulating the culturally destructive mores of the Palestinian inhabitants, yet this thesis is not uniformly accepted and has serious critiques across the academic landscape. Thus, Beldman interacting, but not necessarily agreeing, with more recent scholarship would help support his broader comments on Israelite and Canaanite societies.

Nonetheless, Beldman's *Judges* is a helpful, theologically informed evangelical commentary. Pastors will find it an indelible resource when preaching on the text. Beldman is quick to point out how characters and narratives relate to the problems of our own time, as well as eagerly and skillfully situating the text within the broader flow of redemptive history and systematic theology. Theological students will also be benefitted by reading the text, as it lacks any overly technical language, nor does it require knowledge of Hebrew. Beldman's subsection on biblical theology is as much an introduction to the disciple itself as it is in relation to Judges. Academics in biblical theology/theological interpretation of Scripture might also find this resource.

Jackson T. Reinhardt
Vanderbilt Divinity School

Andrea D. Saner, *"Too Much to Grasp": Exodus 3:13–15 and the Reality of God*, Journal of Theological Interpretation Supplement 11 (Winona Lake, IN: Eisenbrauns), 2015, xv + 266 pp., $34,95, paperback.

Few phrases in Scripture have occasioned as much discussion as has the "I am who I am" of Exod 3:14. What does this phrase mean? How does it relate to the divine name, YHWH? Is it an answer to Moses? question (v. 13), or an evasion of an answer? In *"Too Much to Grasp": Exodus 3:13–15 and the Reality of God*, Andrea Saner argues for a way forward for twenty-first-century readings of the passage, using Augustine of Hippo as representative of the misunderstood interpretive tradition. She argues that read within the literary contexts of the received form of the book of Exodus and the Pentateuch as a whole, the literal sense of Exod 3:13–15 addresses both who God is as well as God's action. That the first aspect is quite often denied and seen as betraying the influence of platonic and Hellenistic thought. When Saner is right the Septuagint makes a point when it translated the phrase "I am who I am" with Ἐγώ εἰμι ὁ ὤν.

The approach of Saner is that of theological interpretation of Christian Scripture which includes an openness to learn from premodern interpretation. Her research is firmly rooted in Old Testament studies and at the same time reads the text in dialogue with the Christian tradition. With regard to Exod 3:14, Gerhard von Rad has stated that this verse supplies an etymology of the divine name and is not a statement about the nature of God. The contemporary consensus interpretation is the focus is on God's actions. Saner's problem is that when all statements about God are replaced with statements about God's actions, we may lose the subject matter of the text. I completely agree with her and would it put ever more strongly. Then we do lose the subject matter.

"Too Much to Grasp" consists of two parts. In the first part she gives an overview of the reading of Exod 3:13–15 from Von Rad to Child and beyond and in the second part she rebuilds the theological interpretation of Exod. 3:13–15. In part 1 of *"Too Much to Grasp"* Saner critiques Von Rad's claim that Exod 3:13–15 concerns an etymology of the divine name. She has learned from Breward Childs. In *The Book of Exodus* (1974) Childs sets the text not only within the Old Testament and New Testament context, but also gives the history of exegesis. Saner rightly points to the fact that there is in Childs' commentary on Exodus no overarching context. Although Childs argues for the validity of the ontological interpretation of the divine name, he does not really articulate what are the consequences of this interpretation.

Saner does not follow the multilevel approach of Childs. She finds Hans Frei's account of the literal sense of Scripture more helpful. According to Frey the coherence of the Bible with its two testaments stems from the unifying pressure of the person of Jesus Christ with regard to the content of Scripture. Saner uses the concept of the literal sense to draw together elements from the semantics of the text to historical and contemporary theological understanding of these semantics. Following Frei she is more concerned than Childs about the intertwined nature of text and reality. However, in distinction from Frey she gives more attention to the literal sense of Old Testament texts in their own context.

Contra Von Rad Saner argues that etymology is not a helpful means of understanding Exod 3:13–15. Both on philological and historical grounds she identifies Exod 3:14a following among other Vriezen as paronomasia or wordplay. She concludes that the translation "I am the one who is" does not exhaust the meaning of Exod 3:14a but stands within the semantical potential. She points both the Deut 4:32–40 and 34:10–12.

These passages do not speak only about the relationship of YHWH with Israel but also the uniqueness of YHWH himself. They describe a pattern whereby YHWH has a unique relationship with his people, through an auditory and visual encounter. YHWH is the only God of the universe not comparable to any other god. He really exists and therefore can really save. YHWH can only be compared with himself. It is clear when we want to do justice to this matter, it is a short step to see ontological aspects in the divine name.

In my view Saner really succeeds in pointing to the fact that the Old Testament itself gives leads for the ontological interpretation of Exod 3:14. Her conclusion is that Augustine's ontological language fits with the Pentateuch's comparative statements about the identity of YHWH. YHWH is the only God who can save because he is the only who really exists in the fullest sense of the word. Everything and everybody stays under his authority and depends upon him. We can learn from Saner's study that although the Old Testament is not explicitly metaphysical, underneath the message of the Old Testament is a worldview with metaphysical aspects.

Pieter de Vries
Free University
Amsterdam, the Netherlands